DATE DUE

AP 6 '67	JUN 0 7 1991		
MY 14 '68			
MY 20 '68			
MY 24 '68			
SEP 12 1968 RESERVED			
Engfold			
DEC 9 9 A.M.			
DEC 11 1 P.M.			
DEC 11 9 P.M.			
DEC 12 8 P.M.			
DEC 13 5 P.M.			
MAY 5 1 P.M.			
MY 23 '70 4			
JE 27 '70			
FE 16 '7 JUN 0 7 1991			
DEC 21 1975			
GAYLORD			PRINTED IN U.S.A.

THE DISCIPLINED HEART:
Iris Murdoch and her Novels

THE DISCIPLINED

HEART: Iris Murdoch and her novels

BY PETER WOLFE

COLUMBIA • MISSOURI

UNIVERSITY OF MISSOURI PRESS

*Publication of this book
has been aided by the Ford Foundation program
to support publication,
through university presses, of work in the
humanities and social sciences*

**WITH LOVE AND WONDER
TO
MARIE**

PREFACE

My BOOK is already longer than originally planned. The only prefatory remark I have to make concerning it is that I am glad it is about Iris Murdoch. I hope my book becomes part of an important, yet still inchoate, trend to discourage professors in our universities from side-stepping the contemporary novel. Too many English departments still cleave to the outdated practice of offering a single course in modern fiction that includes English, Irish, and American novels and stops at 1940. Conrad, Lawrence, Joyce, and Faulkner are major writers, but we can no longer consider them as contemporary. To continue neglecting postwar literature is to deprive our students of an inspiration grounded in *their* world. The potential dangers inherent in the established curriculum are too numerous to broach now, but I firmly believe that they are philosophical and political as well as aesthetic.

My first expression of thanks must go to Professor Paul L. Wiley of the University of Wisconsin. He carefully read and reread the entire manuscript and made many detailed, sympathetic comments concerning style, organization, and content. Although he has been widely admired for a number of years as a first-rate scholar, Mr. Wiley deserves equal recognition as a teacher and as an editor.

I am indebted also to J. Denny Fischer, Lee T. Lemon, Keith Opdahl, and Arthur Schwartz for commenting on the manuscript; to my father, Milton B. Wolfe, for his persistent encouragement; to Audria B. Shumard, who typed and retyped the manuscript with loving care; to Betty Hoyenga for her valuable help in proofreading; and to the University of Nebraska Research Council for a grant that covered expenses connected with preparing the manuscript.

The following is a list of people whose indirect help with the book amounts to a major contribution: Milton J. Slocum, Carl F. Strauch, Richard Brown, Zuleika Pickford, Paul Tortoricci, Robert A. Miltenberg, Dietrich Degenhardt, Nina Johnson, and Bonnie Paley Carter.

As my dedication suggests, my greatest debt of gratitude is owing to Marie. My bestowing of a single paragraph to her is but scant recognition of the tremendous help she provided at every stage of the book's preparation.

P.W.

Lincoln, Nebraska
February, 1966

ACKNOWLEDGMENTS

T HE AUTHOR and the publisher join in expressing their thanks for permission to quote copyright passages from the following:

Under the Net, Copyright 1954 by Iris Murdoch; *The Flight from the Enchanter,* Copyright © 1956 by Iris Murdoch; *The Sandcastle,* Copyright © 1957 by Iris Murdoch; *The Bell,* Copyright © 1958 by Iris Murdoch; *A Severed Head,* Copyright © 1961 by Iris Murdoch; *An Unofficial Rose,* Copyright © 1962 by Iris Murdoch; *The Unicorn,* Copyright © 1963 by Iris Murdoch; *The Italian Girl,* Copyright © 1964 by Iris Murdoch; *Fantasia of the Unconscious* by D. H. Lawrence, Copyright © 1922 by Thomas Seltzer, 1950 by Frieda Lawrence; all reprinted by permission of The Viking Press, Inc.

To Barnes and Noble, Inc., for Bertrand Russell, *Mysticism and Logic;* to the Bollingen Foundation for C. G. Jung, *The Structure and Dynamics of the Psyche* and *Two Essays on Analytical Psychology,* Bollingen Series XX, both of which appear in *The Collected Works of C. G. Jung;* to Criterion Books, Inc., for G. S. Fraser, "Iris Murdoch: Solidity of the Normal," in *International Literary Annual,* II, edited by John Wain; to Dodd, Mead & Company for Rupert Brooke, "Grantchester," in *The Collected Poems of Rupert Brooke;* to *Encounter* for Iris Murdoch, "Against Dryness: A Polemical Sketch" (January, 1961); to *English Studies* for Jacques Souvage, "Symbol as Narrative Device: An Interpretation of Iris Murdoch's *The Bell*" (April, 1962); to *Essays in Criticism* for O. M.

Meidner, "Reviewer's Bane: A Study of Iris Murdoch's *The Flight from the Enchanter*" (1961) and for Stephen Wall, "The Bell in *The Bell*" (1963); to *The New Statesman* for Dan Jacobson, "Farce, Totem and Taboo" (16 June 1961); to Oxford University Press, Inc., for R. M. Hare, *The Language of Morals;* to *Time and Tide* for the cartoon accompanying Raymond Queneau, "A World of Fantasy," trans. by David Pryce-Jones (6 July 1961); to John Wiley and Sons, Inc., for Avis M. Dry, *The Psychology of Jung: A Critical Interpretation;* to the Regents of the University of Wisconsin, The University of Wisconsin Press, and *Wisconsin Studies in Contemporary Literature* for Frederick P. W. McDowell, " 'The Devious Involutions of Human Character and Emotions': Reflections on Some Recent British Novels" (Autumn, 1963); to Yale University Press and *The Yale Review* for Iris Murdoch, "The Sublime and the Beautiful Revisited" (December, 1959).

CONTENTS

One

INTRODUCTION

IRIS MURDOCH has earned a place among the important British novelists who began writing after 1950. Articles devoted to her fiction have appeared in journals with such widespread interests and audiences as *Revue des langues vivantes, English Studies in Africa,* and *New Left Review.* Studies of recent fiction (Paul West, *The Modern Novel,* Walter Allen, *The Modern Novel*) have acknowledged her significance by including brief but respectful comments about the novels and their pertinence to England's cultural milieu. William Van O'Connor, in *The New University Wits,* an exploratory study of England's latest literary generation, selects Iris Murdoch as one of four postwar writers deserving of an entire chapter; other full-length studies, both social (Kenneth Allsop, *The Angry Decade*) and literary (James Gindin, *Postwar British Fiction*), have also affirmed her undisputed position among the leading novelists exemplifying Britian's dissentient mood.

Although her critics have acclaimed her originality and technical adroitness, the criticism pertaining to her novels is largely inadequate. Only one, a Yale student named Kevin O'Sullivan, of all her commentators, has discussed the intellectual tradition in which she is working and the long-range polemical interests pervading her work. But O'Sullivan's interest is philosophical rather than literary, and he does not present her thought as a balanced whole. Most of the observations that other critics have made about the novels tend to fall into two groups. The most serious errors in judgment have appeared when critics like G. S. Fraser and Gabriel Pearson advance in a brief essay

1

a single idea by which they try to explain all of her fiction. Iris Murdoch's thought is too manifold and complex to release its meaning in a short analysis. Fraser claims that she posits familiar, everyday reality as a reliable defense against social or psychological disorder; "the solidity of the normal," Fraser insists, refers to an accepted morality by which she judges the actions of her characters.

This interpretation is, unfortunately, far afield. It disregards the thematic substance of *The Flight from the Enchanter* and overlooks some of her major tenets as they are stated and developed in her speculative writing: for example, that our fundamental imperfection prevents our recognizing static goodness, if indeed the quality could exist in the external world. Freedom, for her, is the knowledge that the world consists of independent centers of significance. This realization is the greatest single discovery we can make about ourselves and the world at large. The civilized, liberal response to this discovery is a just, loving apprehension of other people as our equals. The world of people, objects, and events is prereflective; any attempt to explain a person by an arbitrary code falsifies his status as a self-legislating entity and deprives us of an important access to being.

Pearson's description of Iris Murdoch's novels as romantic fails because it ignores her rejection of romantic elements in Jean-Paul Sartre's work. Departing from the Sartrean view of man as a useless passion, her minimal definition of a person is that he is a social being. Eschewing received political values, her emphasis is upon man's understanding of his fellows as immediately perceivable entities. Her investigation of love as a social principle, which Nona Balakian posits as the central theme in her novels, rigorously excludes romantic precepts and the romantic quest for an organic necessity linking the spiritual and material world. Love, in Iris Murdoch's view, is a disciplined mode of perception that affirms the irreducible reality of the other person and grants the perceiver his own moral identity. (Miss Balakian, in her short survey-type article, does not have the space to develop the philosophical groundwork for her judgment.) Taken by himself, man is indeterminate, a thinking substance consisting only of possibilities and potentialities. Through encounters with others like him, namely, active perceiving minds, he creates his personality and affirms his contingent status in the human community. The novel of plot, then, rather than the romance, the panoramic chronicle, or the highly finished novel of patterns, provides the concrete situations in which an author can test his characters' moral principles and at the same time suggest the obscure depths at which human fortunes converge. "Romantic" suggests misleading qualities by which to describe the novels. As do fantasy and religious idealism—to which it is psychologically linked—romanticism tends to ignore personal relations as ends in themselves. Iris Murdoch is more cautious about abandoning the secular for the spiritual realm. Contrary to Pearson, there is nothing abstract or necessitarian in the morality she advances. The concrete interaction of people—or intersubjectivity, to use the term that critics have applied to Gabriel Marcel—furnishes a more dynamic and more workable social ethic than the intuitive act, in spite of intuition's power and immediacy. Freedom is not a legitimate end in itself; man's indeterminacy and contingency ensure that values cannot be authentic unless they arise from social interaction.

The critics who have refrained from generalizing about Iris Murdoch's polemical interests offer more helpful commentary. But aesthetic criticism is limited, since it considers an artist's manner of selection rather than his understanding of the general character of that from which he selects. Each of the critics who have treated Iris Murdoch in some detail in book-length works is guilty of this kind of superficiality. Allsop, for instance, states that she is probably the most talented novelist of the present generation, but does not justify his praise; Gindin traces thematic motifs through imagery but cannot unify his comments on the basis of any driving artistic or moral concern; Frederick R. Karl worries about an alleged imbalance between funny and serious elements in the novels; O'Connor, finally, accomplishes little more than the clarification of narrative elements through plot summary. There is, of course, no complete criticism; a Marxist analysis, a psychological interpretation, or a study of the congruity and correctness of a writer's rhetoric has only partial value. The needs of each age are different. Iris Murdoch tells us more about contemporary society, however, than most of the prevailing criticism can explain. In short, what is lacking is a demonstrable groundwork of thought against which critical analysis can be securely buttressed.

The point of departure in this study will be Iris Murdoch's philosophical essays, especially her remarks about fiction. Although it is

too early to suggest the best critical method of studying her development as a novelist, the thematic dovetailing in her work of
philosophy and social comedy justifies a theoretical-descriptive approach. The first chapter discusses the static elements of her thought:
influences, basic assumptions, and the emergence of a fresh view of
man that explains both a literary style and a set of assumptions informing narrative structure and point of view. The subsequent
novel-by-novel approach allows us to observe, from various perspec-
tives, social interaction and private motives. The distance between
man's inner life and the ways in which his needs and convictions are
externalized creates a variety of social criticism rooted deeply in
both irony and philosophy. Another tension that defines itself
as social criticism rises out of the opposition of the amorphous, nonreflective world and man's responsibility as a creator of values. Her
belief that private standards of conduct cannot be validated until
they are tested in social experience places great narrative and
philosophical emphasis upon particular situations. These situations,
at once so radically particular and so interlaced with irony, are best
understood in their aesthetic contexts. The complex network of
private and public values within each novel demands, furthermore,
a critical technique that can observe degrees of commitment in
thematically interrelated social contexts.

The problem of language in philosophical fiction is discussed in
several places below. The great difference between the language in
Iris Murdoch's novels and in her philosophy, say, resides in method.
Although her fiction may embrace the same values as her philosophical essays and reviews, it requires a much more graphic and
dramatic literary technique. One could write a first-rate philosophical essay using terms like "sensibilia," "*l'être en soi*," and
"verifiability criterion of meaning" in every paragraph. The same
stylistic practice would be intolerable in a sustained novel (in contrast to the shorter intellectual spoof, referred to by Northrop Frye
as an "Anatomy" or Menippean satire). Style and technique depend
upon the rhetorical conventions of the genre that a writer has selected.
In *Nausea* (1938) Sartre develops the same point, using surrealistic
language, that he exploits at greater length in the more systematic
and technical *Being and Nothingness* (1943).

The philosophical similarity between Iris Murdoch and Bertrand Russell reflects another aspect of the problem of style in philosophical literature. In "Mathematics and the Metaphysicians," "On Scientific Method in Philosophy," and *Our Knowledge of the External World,* Russell argues the necessity of studying the material world without the intervening barriers of behavioral theories or psychological biases: the human point of view, Russell insists, is an arbitrary and limited standpoint from which to interpret reality; it is, in addition, only *one* point of view. Akin to this skeptical pluralism is the moral intention governing Iris Murdoch's novels. Like Russell, she aims at an objective appraisal of the world as a phenomenon existing independently of our concepts and desires. The significant difference between the two writers, supplied by the rhetorical media they have chosen, is method. Russell's logic invents formulas and equations to describe our world of facts, propositions, and brute matter. Iris Murdoch has chosen the novel as her vehicle of philosophical expression because of its ability to convey various aspects of social reality by means of description, point of view, and character interplay. As a novelist, the stuff of her discipline is the individual minds of her characters. The influence of British skepticism (especially that of Hume and of Wittgenstein) and her own humanistic temper limit her perceptions to the here-and-now. The method of describing moral and political questions at their origin—the individual operating mind—creates further opportunity for irony and social criticism. Her direct application of private commitment to particular situations, furthermore, rules out the constraints of determinism in the form of heredity, environment, or the will of the author and allows for the free flow of variegated life.

Both writers, then, Murdoch and Russell, resist smuggling human concepts and desires into the empirical reality they investigate. But while Russell's method is analytical, hers must be both analytical and synthetic—synthetic because the social and psychological events she describes gradually cohere as a discernible moral world. Rather than aiming at technical accuracy, the language of her fiction is chosen to convey the spontaneity of sensory and psychic experience. If her moral interests aspire to social criticism, she must create a social and linguistic context acceptable to her readers. Without a solid matrix of language and setting, the writer cannot advance a set of sharable values that the reader will identify as social satire.

When we recall the bracing, dynamic character of Iris Murdoch's philosophy and the emphasis she places upon specific personal encounters, we can further understand her need to sustain immediacy. This challenge, once again, requires a fictional method that is dramatic rather than reflective. The governing idea of man's fragmentary, yet perfectible, nature has discovered, as it were, its own stylistic level for the purpose of describing solidity, change, and incompleteness, three inescapable concomitants of the human condition.

At this point, I feel obliged to clarify further my use of the term *philosophical novelist* as it applies to Iris Murdoch. Unlike L. H. Myers or Thomas Mann in *The Magic Mountain,* she does not openly discuss philosophical ideas in her fiction. When her characters consider problems in ethics and morals, the problems are never presented as abstract doctrine. Her philosophical interest is always social morality rather than a moral code or set of principles that the reader is invited to apply to action and plot. Blending moral action and narrative structure, her novels convey a great urgency. The theme of prose fiction since the eighteenth century has been man's life in society, and the prevailing narrative method has been empirical. By refusing to sacrifice the individual to a principle or a universal, Iris Murdoch has contributed to and possibly enlarged the great tradition. Her philosophical essays make clear that without theory there can be no morality; with Socrates, Buber, and Marcel, she believes that the clarification of thought must precede man's redemption. This theoretical bias gains expression in the novels in the form of closely observed character interaction. The portrayals of Michael Meade in *The Bell,* Emma Sands in *An Unofficial Rose,* and Otto Narraway in *The Italian Girl* reveal that ethical systems matter far less than personal conduct. The final test of any professed morality is direct social experience. Life is not a thought system, and any attempt to reduce it to one involves a falsification. But by dramatizing concrete situations, the novelist shows personal conduct fortifying and even creating moral value.

The priority of distinct, incarnate beings and the attendant belief that man is his own measure also rule out a political reading of the novels: Iris Murdoch's primary emphasis as a moralist is the free discovery of self and of other selves within the living tissue of human imperfection. Although she has stated an academic preference for

Guild Socialism in one of her essays, I do not find the criticism of political institutions a major accent in her novels, with the possible exception of *The Flight from the Enchanter*. Like Amis, Wain, and Sillitoe in this aspect, she never uses such terms as *the proletariat* and *dialectical materialism*. But, unlike these writers, she studies the individual as a conscious entity responsible for making decisions that acknowledge the same degree of consciousness and reality in others. In this respect her awareness of social life may be called philosophical, for she sees the concrete presence of other people as something to be thought as well as perceived through the senses. The emphasis in her work on immediate experience suggests the term *novels of social education* rather than *novels of ideas,* per se. And her philosophical attitude is permeated by her artistic method, which combines objectivity and closely observed social relations; in our contingent world, dynamic interpersonal relations furnish the only escape from materialism and abstraction and the only likely approach to transcendent values.

As has been stated above, there can be no thoroughly exhaustive criticism of an author. But the kind of criticism most essential to a sound appreciation of Iris Murdoch must examine concepts from their source in philosophy proper and determine how they cohere dramatically as social comedy. The depth of her formal knowledge and her intellectual affinities to other thinkers justify, prima facie, an exposition of her philosophical position. Although her standing as a literary artist is the decisive factor prompting this study, any full-length introductory account of her work must first explain how her creative talent borrows from and amplifies upon received ideas to produce a body of novels both exciting as literature and penetrating as moral philosophy.

Two

VALUES AND INVOLVEMENTS

I<small>T IS NOT ACCIDENTAL</small> that Iris Murdoch, as a theoretical moralist, has found the novel a suitable artistic mode; fiction's traditional practice of observing moral conduct, usually in social situations, corresponds extremely well with her leading philosophical principles. Aside from the psychological depths and crosscurrents that it can explore, the novel is able to convey, through symbol, point of view, and closely documented observation, the concreteness of individual persons. There is sufficient evidence in her philosophical writings to demonstrate her belief in the sovereignty of literature in general. Contrasting the study of science with that of literature, she argues the superiority of the latter; the basis of her judgment, we must note, is boldly and outspokenly didactic:

> There is only one culture. . . . But the most essential and fundamental aspect of culture is the study of literature, since this is an education in how to picture and understand human situations. We are men and we are moral agents before we are scientists, and the place of science in human life must be discussed in *words*. This is why it is and always will be more important to know about Shakespeare than to know about any scientist.[1]

This declaration, urgent though it may be, does not express in itself a convergence of philosophical ideals and literary practice in Iris Murdoch's thought. The phrase that does suggest a thematic continuity between her fiction and her philosophy, however, is "an education in how to picture and understand human situations." Earlier in the same essay, she complains that many philosophers have

8

overlooked the truth that "love is a central concept in morals."[3] We have, then, four recurring terms or values by which she interprets the reality of the external world and our responses to it: *love, to picture, to understand,* and *human situations.*[3] One of my aims is to show how she compresses the terms *to picture* and *to understand* into *love.* As has been mentioned, Miss Balakian locates her ruling theme as "a search for the meaning of love and its frequent elusiveness."[4] Love, in both Iris Murdoch's philosophy and her fiction, refers to a highly disciplined mode of moral and sensory perception.[5] Dora Greenfield (*The Bell*) and Effingham Cooper (*The Unicorn*) discover the shimmering density of the material world by chance; it is the decision to reflect and to act on one's observations, however, that affirms man's perfectibility as a moral agent. The road to freedom, knowledge, and happiness requires a selfless absorption in the irreducible reality of other people. Fiction supplies the social contexts (the "human situations" referred to above) in which individuals make themselves known to each other. Perhaps more effectively than any other medium, the novel can exploit various levels of psychological and social behavior without sacrificing dramatic immediacy.

In line with her insistence upon the importance of studying literature (with an implied emphasis upon what Sartre calls the "literature of situations"),[6] Iris Murdoch has acknowledged a unity of attitude and intention in her writing. Let us examine, once more, the terms she employs and their implications. Her philosophy and her fiction converge, she says, "in a general sort of way—in considering, for example, what morality is and what goes into making decisions."[7] Morality is again represented as a quality that can be located, if not grasped. It grows out of social experience as a function of conferring equality upon other people. The centricity of choice or decision making directs her to existential contexts, which, in turn, manifest themselves as social comedy. Both her fiction and philosophy, we shall see, posit a world that is rich, ambivalent, and inherently hostile to rational categories or systems. Her unrest with the two major philosophical schools in the Western world and with the two modes of narrative-dramatic expression that dominate the novel today creates an artistic method admirably suited to her social criticism. After stripping away all social, moral, and political manifestoes, she forces us to see ourselves as underived, self-responsible, and, indeed, the only creators of supersensible values in a contingent world.

She has not, as Wain, relinquished academic concerns for the independent pursuit of literature. She has, in fact, published a major philosophical essay nearly each year for the past decade. In her case, the lucid objectivity of the one discipline and the dense involvement in subjectivity of the other are mutually sustaining. Speaking of this tension, O'Sullivan refers to the opposing elements in her life as well as in her thought:

> In all her novels it has been a tension between the objective and the subjective approaches, between closeness of observation and the wildest fantasy, involvement with content and an interest in form as a thing in itself; in her life a tension between the Oxford philosopher and the existentialist, between the Treasury bureaucrat and the relief worker in a shattered Europe.[8]

The kind of fiction she is trying to introduce demands an absorption in ideas that a university environment, as a community of active minds, can perhaps encourage and perpetuate better than any other. As a moralist, she seems to be seeking a theoretical zone of cross-fertilization nourished by literature and philosophy and buttressed by the best that is known, thought, and discussed in the cultured world today. Her commanding interest is an investigation of moral values. Implicit throughout is an astute awareness of the backdrop of social deracination against which her thought is projected.

The modern world has been able to draw little spiritual leadership from the opportunism of today's administrators, the determinism of Marx and Freud, or the cleavage in Western philosophy. A possible result of this lack of leadership is the drift toward acceptance of an unreflecting empiricism as a guide to personal conduct. In her essay "A House of Theory," Iris Murdoch interprets this drift as a symptom of our bureaucratic society. Her description of the Special European Labor Immigration Board (SELIB) in *The Flight from the Enchanter* contains her most biting remarks on the shortcomings and the excesses of welfare bureaucracy. She recommends "an area of translation" to convert experiences into values. Today's polarized society of highly trained technicians and uninformed masses needs a layer of theory to fill the gap intervening between esoteric operational concepts and the simple moral views that most of us depend on in times of stress or discomfort: "Theory is needed to refresh the tired imagination of practice. Our available techniques seem uninteresting because we lack the vision to grasp their possibilities."[9] Formal religion and its surrogates—communism, pacifism, and internationalism—used to be consolations and guides. In place of these allegedly obsolete shibboleths, Iris Murdoch suggests a more theoretical examination of Guild Socialism, particularly of its sensitivity to public opinion as a guide to political morality. We shall see the same distrust of empiricism's inability to erect values and the same political attitude expressed in her fiction: One explanation for the torments suffered by the characters in *The Flight from the Enchanter* is the ineptitude of welfare bureaucracy and the tyranny that private ownership, personified by Mischa Fox, unconsciously begets.

It is both easy and somewhat instructive to sketch a novelistic continuum linking Jane Austen, George Eliot, and Iris Murdoch. All three sympathize with their characters without condescension or sentimentalizing; each, in spite of a compassionate awareness of humanity, is perhaps less successful in the creation of male characters than in other areas of fictional art; *in* each is an active concern with moral philosophy. And, to correspond to an increasing breadth in social range as we pass from one to the next in time, the works of the three writers reflect a growing distrust of received social values. Jane Austen accepted the social conventions of her time; George Eliot questioned moral standards in print and flouted them in her private life; Iris Murdoch, showing that received rules of conduct have little basis in reality, has been devising a new ethical code as a way of rescuing modern man's social dignity. As a thinker, she is heavily influenced by British skepticism and by nineteenth-century political thought, including the liberalism of Mill and the search for a God-surrogate in writers like Ruskin and Arnold. The critical emphasis upon her existentialist bias has obscured this strong English philosophical strain in her writing. Her distrust of inherited moral standards is, of course, representative of our age. When highborn resolutions either fall short of fruition or become embroiled in a welter of chance, the heroes of today's novels lack secure moral identities. Jake Donaghue of *Under the Net* is a philosophical roughneck who directs his creative impulses to translating second-rate French novels;

William Mor of *The Sandcastle* and Martin Lynch-Gibbon of *A Severed Head* are middle-aged would-be authors whose creativity is impaired by their relationships with women; Michael Meade of *The Bell* is a homosexual *prêtre-manqué*.

Iris Murdoch's epistemology, although colored by the prevailing unrest with categories and imperatives, has its foundation in the British skeptical tradition, which probably originates with Locke's *Essay Concerning Human Understanding* (1690). The long thread of British skepticism, although reasonable and persuasive in itself, has produced, in Iris Murdoch's view, an impoverished epistemology. The logical analysts, who are the intellectual heirs of figures like Locke, Hume, Wittgenstein, and Russell, have divorced philosophy from ethical or transcendent values. Although they could have constructed a theory of being based upon the mysterious, irreducible aspects of man, thus ensuring his inviolability as a thinking substance, they have turned to logic and mathematics as a means of explaining nonpsychic reality.[10]

Iris Murdoch has assented to the sufficiency and universality of logic. She adds, however, that few of us live in the domain of the purely analytical. If philosophy wants to maintain its inherited function of nourishing life, it must venture "into the cloudy and shifting domain of the concepts which men live by—and these are subject to historical change."[11] This redirection of focus from the mechanical to the human applies particularly to moral principles, which are correlative with ethics. On the assumption that man is conventional and rational, a conscious being who makes decisions according to rational criteria, the logical analysts have in recent years begun to experiment with a quasi ethics. Their departure from the original tenets of the Vienna movement of the 1930's[12] is still too patently rational to establish contact with warm centers of human experience. They eschew, for instance, questions dealing with man as a teleological being; concepts like love, human purpose, and man's place in the universe are not included in their philosophical armory. The ethical precepts that the analysts have devised are deeply rooted in linguistic structure. In brief, they study the structure of moral language without making moral judgments. Here is R. M. Hare voicing a typical attitude in his introduction to *The Language of Morals*:

> If moral language belongs to the genus "prescriptive language",
> we shall most easily understand its nature if we compare and con-

trast first of all prescriptive language with other sorts of language, and then moral language with other sorts of prescriptive language. . . . I shall deal first with the simplest form of prescriptive language, the ordinary imperative sentence. . . .

I shall then go on to discuss a kind of prescriptive language which is more nearly related to the language of morals than is the simple imperative. This is the language of non-moral value-judgments—all those sentences containing words like "ought", "right", and "good" which are not moral judgments. I shall seek to establish that many of the features which have caused trouble to students of ethics are also displayed by these sorts of sentences.[13]

Iris Murdoch's fiction reflects many of the values and attitudes of British skepticism prior to the Vienna movement and the publication of Ayer's *Language, Truth and Logic*. Jake Donaghue's progress in *Under the Net* is a farrago of misjudgments and misadventures; William Mor loses Rain Carter in *The Sandcastle* because of his failure to evaluate his relationship with her and to act in keeping with it; the cause of Michael Meade's unhappiness and his inability to establish himself vocationally in *The Bell* is his lack of self-knowledge; finally, whatever tragedy dwells in *The Unicorn* is traceable to mistaken notions about Hannah Crean-Smith's state of mind. In the spirit of Hume, Wittgenstein, and Russell, Iris Murdoch believes that everything in empirical nature is radically singular. The atoms that make up the world do not contain any reflective values. As Wittgenstein said, "In the world everything is as it is and happens as it does happen. *In* it there is no value." (*Tractatus*, 6:41.) Rather than assigning absolute values, we can approach factual truth only through probability judgments, which, based as they are on sense experience, have no logical fiat. Accordingly, any planned operation, dealing perforce with unknown shifting quantities, is susceptible to failure. Deliberate acts always reap unsought-for consequences in Iris Murdoch's pluralistic world. A paradigm case is Effingham Cooper's carefully charted attempt in *The Unicorn* to rescue Hannah Crean-Smith from Gaze Castle. The attempt fails because he overestimates his own powers and the discretion of another (Carrie, the red-haired maid at Riders). Cooper himself summarizes grimly the theoretical outcome of his knightly act; ironically, the most destructive result of his act—his being trapped in the local bog, where he nearly dies—has not yet manifested itself:

And now look where he was. He had put Hannah in peril, laying

> her open to retribution from people who had power over her,
> he had almost certainly helped Marian to get herself the sack, he
> had wounded Alice perhaps irrevocably, and worst of all he would
> himself be under sentence. He might never be allowed to go to
> Gaze again. This was a thought so agonising that he almost had to
> bend down over the pain. If they banished him he would really
> do something desperate. Yet what on earth could he do? Had he
> not now forfeited the *only* thing which he could do for Hannah?

Iris Murdoch parts company with the British philosophical tradition when it sacrifices the fragmentary nature of man to the criteria
of pure logic. The analytical approach, in her opinion, celebrates
abstract reason at the expense of the underived concreteness of
human beings:

> Philosophers have usually tended to seek for universal formulae.
> But the linguistic method, if we take it seriously, is by its nature
> opposed to this search . . . the difficulty is . . . that the subject
> of investigation is the nature of man—and we are studying this
> nature at a point of great conceptual sensibility. Man is a creature
> who makes pictures of himself and then comes to resemble the pic-
> ture. This is the process which moral philosophy must attempt to
> describe and analyze.[14]

She consents to the efficacy of logic as a mental discipline; what she
questions, similarly to Dewey, is the relevance of strictly logical
principles to the human estate. Examples from her novels show that
man is not the rational being that Ayer, Carnap, or Ryle, in *The
Concept of Mind*, suppose. The reasoning processes of Jake Donaghue, Michael Meade, and Martin Lynch-Gibbon (*A Severed
Head*) reflect a variety of mental activity that is regulated more by
caprice and emotion than by logic:

> I often use this method for deciding difficult cases. In stage one I
> entertain the thing purely as a hypothesis, and in stage two I count
> my stage one thinking as a fixed decision on which there is no
> going back.

*   *   *

> He knew that he was lost, and in making the discovery knew that
> he had in fact been lost for a long time. By a dialectic well known
> to those who habitually succumb to temptation he passed in a
> second from the time when it was too early to struggle to the time
> when it was too late to struggle.

*   *   *

> I seemed to have passed from dislike to love without experiencing
> any intermediate stage.

The dicta advanced by the linguistic analysts are too noetic to serve our ambiguous, contradictory world. The translation of knowledge to moral action is a dynamic process of which cognition is only an aspect. In that Hare and his counterparts underplay the Hamlet element in the human personality in favor of the Horatio aspect, their view of finite man is too insular and delimiting. Above all, they bypass the idea that human knowledge is a function of inter-subjectivity, that is, of personal relations. Although their program for decision making offers no intrinsic guarantees, its weighty reliance upon disembodied facts is conducive to smugness and even to solipsism. Ayer's ultimate man examines syntax and metaphor in a lonely cell, avoiding to the greatest possible extent the unforeseeable and the accidental. As we shall see, Iris Murdoch is searching for a metaphysic that is comprehensive and open-ended, not divisive and reducible to the doubt situation. The belief that meaning is more than just a function of language has prompted her to desert the British-American school in favor of the Continental tradition.

Although distinctions have grown obscure, English philosophy (Hobbes, Locke, and Hume) has usually been scientific in its orientation. Conversely, the philosophical thought associated with the Continent has disclosed a more subjective strain (Descartes, Nietzsche, and Bergson). To elucidate this contrast, we might explain it as one of physics versus psychology. Whereas one school has emphasized the object or the to-be-known, the other has stressed the subject or perceiver. The psychology-directed tradition in Western philosophy originated, of course, with Descartes. Starting with the mental properties of a finite, imperfect self, he was able to construct a valid physical world superintended by an omniscient, benevolent preserver. Nearly two hundred years later, Hegel's now-neglected *Phenomenology of Mind* (1807) labored to prove dialectically that the individual is not alienated but participates actively in a cosmic process in which the evolution of the universe coalesces and becomes one with an absolute knower. Finite consciousness develops by the accretion of ideas into a subjective thinker; subjectivity, in turn, as intersubjective relations, forms objective mind, which grows dialectically into the Absolute mind. Everything in the universe is necessary and purposive at the same time. As an historical stage in the self-explication of the Absolute, the individual is a vital ingredient. Any human mind contains the categories or concepts that make up the world drama.

Iris Murdoch endorses Hegel's view of the individual as a salient psychological entity whose perceptions can achieve the status of social principles. Perhaps the most important attribute of man's freedom is his power to conceptualize and his consequent endeavor to resemble his self-concepts.[15] Indeed, her collective label "phenomenological novelists"[16] to describe Sartre, De Beauvoir, and Camus is intended as praise. Her objection to Hegel, as Kierkegaard's, is directed to the dialectic itself: an organic being cannot be arbitrarily deposited within the tackling of a mentally derived system:

> The Hegelian self, for all its historical and psychological color, has no fundamental structure, and no fundamental predicament, for it is not ultimately an independent irreducible entity at all. In the end there will have been nothing but the different phases of the Absolute—and these phases are not phases of anything independent of the phase.[17]

Sartrean existentialism, by removing Hegel's dialectical shell, apprehends man as precious and unique. In a Godless universe, the finite standpoint is the only one; things *are* what they seem to be, regardless of how imperfectly they convey the truth of a perceivable transcendent reality (Plato) or noumenon (Kant). Consequently, each person is obliged to work out his own freedom without the help of categorical imperatives. As a creative psychic entity who cannot look for help beyond his immediate situation, each individual is the testing ground and arbiter of his personal resolves and their execution.

It is precisely with Sartre's picture of the individual as a solitary being stationed in an unreasonable, absurd world that Iris Murdoch forsakes his phenomenology. Rational precepts may fail to provide comfort and guidance when one is faced by a difficult choice, but by shelving the entire world of a priori truths along with other points of view in order to focus upon one mind at a single moment of perception, Sartre undermines any justification his work may have as social doctrine. His lonely, anguished individual, regarding everything external to him as heaving, undulating indifference, is on the way to solipsism and neurosis. Sartre furnishes no point of view or technique for studying people in their variety. The primacy of the subject, the "for-itself," disregards social values and, in the process, elevates his quirks and foibles nearly to the exalted degree of myth.

Iris Murdoch shares Dewey's belief that philosophy rises from stresses in social living. And like him, she is insistent that the complexities surrounding the most ordinary human relations will never be solved if we lack methods to control the individual's spiritual energy.[18] Sartre deserves our gratitude for defining the scope and the psychological manifestations of human freedom. His persistent brooding on personal dread and anguish, however, prevents him from illuminating problems that involve reversible social relations.[19] By refusing to regard human confrontations as encounters between conscious coordinates, the Sartrean self retains only an undignified identity. Stripped of the other-regarding impulses that could serve as the scaffolding for a theory of mutual understanding, he automatically forfeits his potential as a moral agent:

> It is on the lonely awareness of the individual and not on the individual's integration with society that his [Sartre's] attention centers. In Sartre's world rational awareness is in inverse ratio to social integration; as soon as his characters begin to reflect they detach themselves from their background.[20]

Freedom, then, is a progressive, watchful discipline that must be modified and reconstructed with reference to the freedom of others. As William Mor points out in a Marsington WEA meeting (*The Sandcastle*), freedom is translatable as virtue only when it operates unselfishly. Sartre's free individual lacks the restraining apparatus of self-discipline. His view of other people as impersonal elements to be annexed or appropriated is more than roughly analogous to Nietzsche's emancipated soul, who has arrogated to himself the license to dominate his fellows. Both Iris Murdoch and Bill Mor seem to be groping for a political liberalism that accepts man as accidental and contingent. But Mor lacks the creative energy to apply his moral principles to his personal life. Caught in a web of motives and events, he misuses his freedom by subordinating the emotional needs of Rain Carter to his own. Georgie Hands and Martin Lynch-Gibbon (*A Severed Head*) enjoy thinking of each other as not existing when they are apart, but their relationship is destroyed by the demands of the outside world. Likewise, Hugh Peronett (*An Unofficial Rose*) plans, after the death of his wife, to

resume his romantic attachment to Emma Sands on the same footing
as twenty-five years earlier.

The respective failures of Mor, Lynch-Gibbon, and Peronett can
be explained by the same principle that underlies Iris Murdoch's
political liberalism. People continue to exist without the presence
of a finite subject, framing new relations and new ideas. Man is
active, influencing and being influenced by others in an unpredictable
network of motives and acts. Any attempt to restrict this process,
whether by personal will or by political decree, presumes a tyrannical
relationship. Paul Greenfield's schemes (*The Bell*) to educate his wife
make her an object in his world and raise him to the level of a flaw-
less, omniscient subject. This static, irreversible order does not, of
course, survive. Accordingly, no political dogma can flourish that
posits superordinate and subordinate elements. Such a system necessarily violates the coordinate contingency of the world. The question
of power in a disorderly contingent world is a major theme in *The
Flight from the Enchanter; The Unicorn*, in turn, explores the consequences of existing in the immobile, mentally inert region of the
to-be-known.

Iris Murdoch's speculative writing also considers each of these
ultimately political concerns. She is, naturally, uneasy with Eliot's
rejection of political liberalism as a deterrent to unified tradition.[21]
And, although her fundamental convictions are secure, she seems
to lack at present a set of discursive principles that will yield a social
ethic commensurate with the unsponsored multiplicity of the world.
The following quotation reveals an intelligent awareness of the gaps
in her theoretical armory; at the same time, however, we observe
her insisting upon both the creativity of the individual and the re-
channeling of our impulses into new regions of moral experience:

> The technique of becoming free is more difficult than John Stuart
> Mill imagined. We need more concepts than our philosophies have
> furnished us with. We need to be enabled to think in terms of degrees
> of freedom, and to picture, in a non-metaphysical, non-totalitarian,
> and non-religious sense, the transcendence of reality. . . . We need
> to turn from the self-centered concept of sincerity to the other-
> centered concept of truth. . . . Our current picture of freedom
> encourages a dream-like facility; whereas what we require is a
> renewed sense of the difficulty and complexity of the moral life
> and the opacity of persons. We need more concepts in terms of

which to picture the substance of our being; it is through an en-
richening and deepening of concepts that moral progress takes place.[22]

Iris Murdoch has mentioned Gabriel Marcel's scorn for Sartre's
intolerance of the world's contingency.[23] In many respects, Marcel's
view of the bloated massiveness that surrounds us provides the single
major modern influence upon her ethics. St. Anselm advanced human
contingency as a proof of the existence of a noncontingent preserve.
Kant, however, refuted this proof by demonstrating the shortcomings
of the ontological argument, upon which Anselm's "cosmological
argument" depends. Nothing in experience allows us to conclude
that something known to be dependent and contingent implies the
existence of something necessary and perfect. Existence cannot be
logically deduced from a definition; although omniscience and om-
nipotence are contained in the conventional Christian definition of
God, the attribute of existence is not.[24]

Kant's refutation of the ontological argument and the skeptical
line of thought in British philosophy have ruled out, for Iris Murdoch,
the theological aspect of Marcel's Christian existentialism. She does
join Marcel, however, in rejecting Sartre's horror of the world's
contingency. There is no natural priority in a world in which all
elements have equally contingent standing. Nothing is given in logic
or experience to justify our going beyond the constituents of matter
to ratify the supremacy of a single point of view at the expense of
another. Iris Murdoch's disagreement with Sartre, as stated above,
inheres in his failure to integrate the self in a cogent social framework.
The nontheistic features of Marcel's ethics help her clarify and affirm
the potential dignity of man as a socially constructive force.

Marcel's hostility to radical individualism, as Iris Murdoch's, discovers the individual as a responsible social agent where the Sartrean
act of limitless freedom fails. Marcel regards himself as a philosopher
of being and freedom rather than as a philosopher of freedom alone.
As mere self-expression for its own sake, freedom exists as unrealized
potential, vacant form without content; freedom derives its value
as a vehicle to fuller and richer participation in being. Both Marcel's
plays and his philosophical writings reject from the start the practice
of armchair intellectualizing. To study being as an object of the cold
intellect is to misunderstand the way that objects, as sense experiences,
reveal themselves. Existence can refer only to particular existing entities. Marcel has modified Descartes' view of man as a thinking sub-

stance in favor of a closer integration between mind and body. The
senses and the flesh harmonize with the mind and the will on an
equal plane in the perceiving self:

> Being is grasped in the first instance not only through a purely
> rational determination but through its sensible presence. . . . Sen-
> sation is metaphysically important not merely as a message but as
> a means of participating in the existence universe.[25]

The philosopher, accordingly, must study being as a totality, not
as something reducible to a dualistic formula. Buber's treatment of
the Absolute Person or "Eternal Self" in *I and Thou* resembles
strikingly Marcel's "participation" theory at this point. Both men
insist that the world and its constituents are not impersonal objects,
subordinate to the philosopher's knowledge and control. The philosopher's relation to the world is one of direct participation, not one of
cognition with a set of things. One of his critics has summarized
Marcel's admiration of E. M. Forster on the basis of this criterion:
"Access to being is had through intersubjectivity."[26] Participation in
the world of beings demands a more dynamic, thoroughgoing engagement than the nonhumanistic noetic standpoint offers:

> From the very fact that I treat the other person merely as a means
> of resonance or an amplifier, I tend to consider him as a sort
> of apparatus which I can, or think I can, manipulate, or of which
> I can dispose at will. I form my own ideas of him and, strangely
> enough, this idea can become a substitute for the real person, a
> shadow to which I shall come to refer my words.[27]

In an interview with Frank Kermode, Iris Murdoch bypasses her
weighty documentation of London and Paris in *Under the Net* as
"self-indulgence" without "particular significance." Speaking of the
exhaustive technical descriptions in her novels, such as Mr. Mars's
cage in *Under the Net,* Calvin Blick's photography equipment in *The
Flight from the Enchanter,* Rain Carter's marooned car in *The Sandcastle,* and the wresting of the medieval bell from the lake in *The
Bell,* she is equally coy. These excursions into mechanical details,
she claims, reflect only "a kind of fascination with completely theoretical amateur mechanics."[28] Gindin has interpreted her "engineering projects" as satirical, designed to underscore man's failures to
execute his designs.[29] Fraser believes that her detailed descriptions
"create a sense of intractability in things, sometimes ingeniously

conquered, sometimes farcically or wretchedly triumphant."[30] As the two critics suggest, her densely descriptive passages have more artistic and philosophical justification than she admits. She herself, in her polemical writing, is fond of quoting this passage from Tolstoi's *What is Art?*: "Strip the best novels of their details, and what will remain?" The novel, as James says, is the only literary art form that offers a "solidity of specification" in the form of close observation and symbolic reference. By vividly realizing the objects of sense, Iris Murdoch is trying to bring to postwar British fiction a new, philosophically motivated blend of documented realism and poetically symbolic action.

Kierkgaard claimed that only subjectivity is truly known to exist. Sensations "appear" with the claim that they are qualities of things. They have, however, only an adjectival relation to what exists: we conceive blueness, for instance, but cannot see it. Iris Murdoch has revised the radical individualism of Kierkegaard and Sartre, in keeping with the Marcel-Jaspers-Buber theory of mutuality. The resisting thing, she insists, is as real as the effort and the striving. Toby and Dora's adventure with the winch and hawser in *The Bell* comprises a little drama in itself. The solidity of these material objects, by their resistance as counterforces to human acts, becomes inescapably present. Hugo Belfounder, in *Under the Net*, echoes his creator when he theorizes about the inexhaustibility of the world and its component parts. Iris Murdoch's idea is close to Hopkins' concept of inscape. Individual objects are more complex and fascinating than they are generally thought to be. As a novelist, however, Iris Murdoch stops here. That Rain Carter's automobile, strictly as an unthinking material thing, can shape the emotions of two people suffices to justify its solid presence in the world.

The same principle of inexhaustibility, derived in part from Marcel, governs Iris Murdoch's views on sexual love. We shall see that she is as suspicious of love's destructive powers as Sartre; the difference between the two writers lies in their basic assumptions. Sartre regards sexual love as an intransigent battle in which each party struggles to retain his identity at the other's expense. In short, the lover is rent by the exigencies of the subject-object cleavage; he wants to be the only object in his beloved's world; on the other hand, the object-status menaces his singularity and creativity. The lover's solution is to recover his lost subject-status, which he does by reducing his beloved's role to that of object. The outcome of this enormously complex reversible process is either a relationship void of emotional engagement or one in which the stronger party is polarized to the nonhuman status of instrument, manipulating and appropriating at his will.

Iris Murdoch's love relation lacks this self-conscious, complex structure. Selflessness is, in fact, its central nerve. Contrary to Shelley, she does not see the other as an idealized version of the self; accordingly, the love relation does not involve a Whitmanesque merging of personalities. Love is "the nonviolent apprehension of difference,"[31] a galvanized awareness of the inexhaustible otherness of its object. The beloved, in the tradition of Locke's epistemology, embodies an opaque particularity that transcends cognition or reflection. The realization of being in love prevents the lover from devising concepts of any sort; he is too overcome by the closely woven private qualities of his beloved to do more than admire. Content to be an object in her world, he harbors no ambitions to pre-empt or make her over. She is simply *there,* in the fullest Jamesian sense, particular and mysterious. We do not love in order to fulfill ourselves or to protect. The impulse enters forcibly and authoritatively from without. The beloved's nonsharable features, which are so perturbing because of their lawless resistance to rules or patterns, envelop her in a shifting radiance that is, simply, the sum of herself.

The following examples have been selected to reflect Iris Murdoch's steady engagement with the problem of locating transcendent values through other-directed affirmations of life. The first passage is from *Under the Net* (1954); the second is from *An Unofficial Rose* (1962):

> It seemed as if, for the first time, Anna really existed now as a separate being and not as a part of myself. . . . Anna was something which had to be learnt afresh. When does one ever know a human being? Perhaps only after one has realized the impossibility of knowledge and renounced the desire for it and finally ceased to feel even the need of it. But then what one achieves is no longer knowledge, it is simply a kind of co-existence; and this too is one of the guises of love.

*   *   *

> The lover readily imagines that he and his mistress are one. He feels that he has love enough for both and that his loving will swathe the two of them together like twin nuts in a shell. But

what one loves is, after all, another human being, a person with other interests, other pains, in whose world one is oneself an object among others.

The basis of Iris Murdoch's aesthetics, as well as of her ethics, is the proposition that the world consists of independent centers of significance. Her point of departure is Kant's theory of the beautiful. To Kant, the art object has independent self-containing existence; as a product of the imagination, it is free of conceptual codes, either moral or aesthetic. A chance assortment of flowers or interweaving lines, uncolored by an artist's moral aims, satisfies best the demands of the imagination. Iris Murdoch accuses Kant of failing to discover the link between imaginative cognition and morality: "the art object is not just 'given,' it is also thought,"[32] she insists. Kant claimed that morality, having no corresponding sense impression in the empirical world, is its own archetype; the moral will is autonomous, growing out of its own need to impose rational order. Aesthetic perception, by arresting the understanding rather than the reason, does not intersect with morality.

Kant's sublime, a mode of perception neither moral nor aesthetic, provides the pivotal concept in Iris Murdoch's *rapprochement* of morality and art. Unlike the beautiful, Kant's sublime is not associated with specific objects, and it does not occasion a feeling of harmonious repose. The sublime is an emotional experience caused by the reason's helplessness before the breadth and power of nature. Reason, the synthesizing faculty, is paralyzed before a mountain range or by the sea on a stormy night. These spectacles are too mighty and resonant to be subjected to moral order. Distressed at the imagination's failure to embrace them in their plentitude, the reason nonetheless rejoices; nature's terrifying boundlessness reinforces the reason's supremacy over the imagination as a moral instrument and, what is more important, discloses the unfamiliar depths that the reason is willing to explore in its search for unity and order.[33]

Iris Murdoch relates the sublime to morality and art where Kant fails. Mental activity, in her ethical-aesthetic scheme, provides the mainspring for both art and morality.[34] We are stunned into a cognitive grasp of ourselves as isolated beings in a chance world because of the world's opaque particularity, not its formlessness. As has been stated, Iris Murdoch, unlike Sartre, harbors no nausea for the contingent world; she likewise eschews Kant's practice of trying to impose rational order upon it. Her stress upon the world's incomprehensibility rather than upon its potential orderliness[35] grants the mind's confrontation with an art object a measure of creative activity that is absent in Kant's aesthetic. Cognition becomes virtue when it perceives the roving multiplicity of other people and their existence as minds. The realization that our imaginations can never exhaust this "otherness" allows art to assume the stature of morality. The artistic representation of other minds in operation, resisting their creator's will, counts for Iris Murdoch as an act of freedom. The artist is free when, discovering reality in others, he refrains from subordinating it to his own personal concerns. The best art is kinetic, not static as Joyce insisted. The artist abandons himself and his audience to contemplate with awe the many-faceted human personality. The social effects of this activity once again reinstate the world's complexity and the rich density of people and objects. The following statement is pivotal, for Iris Murdoch reveals here that she has eclipsed such monumental thinkers as Kant and Euclid by formulating a demonstrable first principle.

> Virtue is not essentially or immediately concerned with choosing between actions or rules or reasons, nor with stripping away the personality for a leap. It is concerned with really apprehending that other people exist. This too is what freedom really is; and it is impossible not to feel the creation of a work of art as a struggle for freedom. Freedom is not choosing; that is merely the move we make when all is already lost. Freedom is knowing and understanding and respecting things quite other than ourselves. . . . The knowledge and imagination which is virtue is precisely the kind which the novelist needs to let his characters be, to respect their freedom, and to study them themselves in that most significant area of their activity, where they are trying to apprehend the reality of others.[36]

Iris Murdoch's novels are exploratory and experimental. As did Virginia Woolf, she is trying to advance a metaphysical literature that will replace moral literature. Rejecting Leibniz's notion of a pre-established harmony, she finds truth a complex human process dissociated from divine fiat. As in Conrad, objective truth in her novels is enmeshed in a moving network of motives and acts. Her characters' numerous attitudes toward any given experience show it to be infinitely rich in meaning.[37] This is why, in spite of her continued presence in *The Unicorn,* the behavior and values of Hannah Crean-Smith remain such a mystery to us. Iris Murdoch believes that the novelist has been a more accurate portrayer of man's complexity than the philosopher. Less concerned with "ought" than with "is," the novelist subordinates explanation to description;[38] in short, his theoretical will-lessness grants him a moral insight that the philosopher often fails to achieve. The novelist's task, as Iris Murdoch explains it, is to convey "the complete reality of each of . . . [his] main characters' view of the world, and . . . their irreducible diversity."[39]

The nineteenth century was the glorious era of the novel. Scott, Jane Austen, George Eliot, and particularly Tolstoi cherished the contingency of their characters. The great author Tolstoi is confident that his tolerance will not result in banality. His refusal to condescend or to sentimentalize is the first step in the creation of solid characters who are as different from their author as they are from each other. Iris Murdoch's own novels abound with this kind of democratic activity. Honor Klein's semi-incestuous relationship with the American psychoanalyst Palmer Anderson, in *A Severed Head,* and Emma Sand's domestic arrangements with her woman secretary-companions, in *An Unofficial Rose,* have a life of their own exclusive of the reader. This same respect for personal privacy buttresses the novels down to their minor details. Mildred Finch's daughter, who never appears personally in *An Unofficial Rose,* reverses her mother's lifelong belief that she will never marry. Geoffrey writes to Marian Taylor, his former mistress, in *The Unicorn,* of his reluctant association with her remote acquaintance Freda Darsey; the beautifully modulated series of letters culminates in Marian's casual explanation that two friends of hers are getting married. Geoffrey's private life, then, gathers momentum and interest inversely to our knowledge of it.

The major abuse in fictional characterization today is the "simplified fantasy-myth" of Sartre and Beckett, which is an arbitrary and solipsistic pseudo world housing only veiled abstractions of the author's personality. These works, as "tight metaphysical objects," are closer to poetry than to the novel. Their language is nondiscursive and private, and the reader has a sense of viewing the action from the outside rather than of being invited to participate in it. Instead of conveying the impression of life in the direction of the reader's experience and social values, the self-conscious mythologizing of the simplified fantasy-myth arrogates life to itself. Although Iris Murdoch indicts no offenders, we may assume that she has in mind the representations of Roquentin, Molloy, and perhaps Golding's Christopher Martin as archetypes of modern man. The cure she recommends to arrest this practice is the reintroduction into the novel of the old-fashioned, naturalistically conceived character.[40] The application of older fictional techniques does not impose any inviolable necessity on her work. Although naturalistic methods may influence treatment, they need not delimit subject matter, style, or moral outlook. At any rate, it is better to err in the direction of character than in that of solipsism. The novel is a social transcript of sorts, submitted by various points of view and describing various layers of experience; it is not a vehicle, she insists, to record the novelist's progress toward self-discovery:

> The great novels are victims neither of convention nor of neurosis. The social scene is a life-giving framework and not a set of dead conventions or stereotyped settings inhabited by stock characters. And the individuals portrayed in the novels are free, independent of their author, and not merely puppets in the exteriorization of some closely locked psychological conflict of his own.[41]

The other threat to metaphysical literature, as suggested in the quotation, is the "loose journalistic epic,"[42] even though the critical popularity of the scenic-dramatic method of novel writing has diminished much of its force. Highly documented and often symbolic in language, works of this sort take as their motive impulse prevailing institutions. Iris Murdoch refers to this literary school as "conventional," in contrast to the "neurotic," highly self-conscious literature described above.[43] Conventional literature offers a Hegelian-Marxist view of man: the individual takes his importance as a phase in an historical program; he is subordinated to and ultimately definable by the institutions that surround him, be they social, political, or religious. Iris Murdoch again mentions no specific offenders, but she probably has in mind writers like Bennett, Dreiser, Upton Sinclair, and Sinclair Lewis. Radically undeterministic in her work, Iris Murdoch's characters are seldom fretted by hunger, the social hierarchy, or religious intolerance. They have wrested themselves from

Orwell's social mire, where the individual is flayed and butchered by a blind, rapacious mercantile society.

Didactic and satirical, Iris Murdoch declines as a moralist to depict man as a mere function of his environment. The conventional approach, which is also in the foreground of romanticism's urge for synthesis, leaves too many layers of the human consciousness unexplored. A possible fictional equivalent of her objections to an encompassing communality are the three-way relationships that some of her characters propose. Palmer Anderson and Antonia Lynch-Gibbon labor, on the grounds of "rationality," to include her deceived husband Martin in their love affair. As Honor Klein points out, this proposal stems from a moral void. The shallowness of the three-way arrangement is evinced by Martin's ability to demolish it with one punch on Anderson's jaw. Antonia, too, at the end of the novel, admits that she never told Anderson about her long-term liaison with Alexander, her brother-in-law, because Alexander "meant too much" to her. This disclosure reveals that the biologically natural bifold relation is the proper one to cultivate and that Iris Murdoch's sexual morality is more sensibly grounded in man's basic impulses than several of her critics have believed.

The entry of a third party signals the desire for power or self-justification at another's expense: Emma Sands in *An Unofficial Rose* tries to use the *ménage à trois* to control others while retaining her own independence. The inevitable failure of these patterns is that they inhibit an awareness of people as existing things. The individual's personal value, as in the loose journalistic epic, centers around his role as part of a relationship. And, although intimacy is diffused, individual will is not. Arguing by analogy, Emma Sands's physical brutalities and the complicated Lynch-Gibbon-Anderson-Klein alliances reflect in minuscule the failure of institutions to create the selfless, conceptless apprehension of the other that is the heart of Iris Murdoch's social doctrine.

Her rejection of the two theories governing the composition of novels today mirrors her discontent with Western philosophy. O'Sullivan has rightly interpreted the tension as one between objectivity and subjectivity: "Involvement is not enough, since we cannot see that with which we are involved, but detachment is not enough since we no longer relate ourselves personally with what we see."[44] The English model of close observation sustained by a relentless logic corresponds to conventional literature's program of enclosing the individual within a shell of mentally derived absolutes; in modern British philosophy and in the conventional novel, nonpsychic reality predominates. The link between the neurotic novel and the Cartesian-Sartrean line is more obvious. Obsessive self-involvement, as Virginia Woolf and T. S. Eliot insist, precludes an adequate grasp of others; Dostoevski's narrator in *Notes from the Underground* and Roquentin are too introverted to accord others equal human status. Iris Murdoch attempts to elude the shortcomings of both traditions by returning to the novel of plot, character, setting, and love interest. She brings new life to the fictional art associated with the Victorian novelists by saturating it with a multiplicity of points of view and by constructing narrative elements around specific situations; contrary to the British analysts, she believes that man is an unresolved entity who requires direct confrontations with others like himself if he hopes to ascertain the soundness and serviceability of his moral principles. Sustaining this presentation is a running pattern of imagery. Although each novel has its own imagistic strategy, the images of gold and the net form a coherent embroidery of thought that adds artistic and philosophical depth to Iris Murdoch's fiction.

The term *gold* and its cognate *golden* are vital analogues of her cordial acceptance of external reality. The perception of the finite world as rich and precious is the discovery of personal freedom. It is important to note that the aggrandizing generic terms *gold* and *golden* are never applied with a sentimental intention or withheld as a reproof. Thus, we have Anna Quentin wrapped in an aura of gold in *Under the Net*. Unrelated items like the root of John Rainborough's wisteria tree, Nina's hair, and the space illuminated by Hunter Keepe's match when he visits Stefan Lusiewicz at night in *The Flight from the Enchanter* are all described as golden. The term becomes dramatic in *The Sandcastle* as not only Demoyte's face but the particles of dust and the flaky, crumbling wood at the train station perceived when Mor discovers his love for Rain Carter are golden. The field near Imber Court, the apricots that Catherine Fawley gathers, Dora Greenfield's arms, and Toby Gashe's head appear as gold in *The Bell*. Antonia and Palmer Anderson are gold and silver, respectively, throughout *A Severed Head*. Hugh Peronett's cherished Tintoretto and his son's mistress Lindsay Rimmer are seen as golden in *An Unofficial Rose*, and Iris Murdoch refers to the "dirty golden sky" in the scene in which Ann Peronett is rent by the conflict of conventional behavior and the demands of love. The gallery of golden appearances in *The Unicorn* includes the fish at Gaze Castle, Hannah Crean-Smith's eyes, random clumps of seaweed, the hillside, the reflection of the sun in the sea, the group of people gathered around Hannah after her attempted kidnaping, and Jamesie Evercreech's face glowing above a gas lamp when he seems about to attack Marian Taylor. The most subtle use of the expression, however, takes place in *A Severed Head.* Honor Klein, the troll-like Nietzschean figure who proves to be Martin Lynch-Gibbon's final humiliation or conquest, is ambiguously associated with sulphurous fumes and hell imagery throughout the novel. This cunning inversion of imagistic strategy, if it is indeed legitimate, corresponds remarkably to our foretastes of the unexplored depths of Honor Klein's personality and to possible stages of Lynch-Gibbon's psychic development.

The net image is a legacy of Joyce. In *A Portrait,* Stephen Dedalus says that nationality, language, and religion are nets that he, as a creative artist, must elude. Iris Murdoch's use of the term is more general, although similar. Nets are commonly regarded as traps for catching fish. Symbolically, fish have a broad range of reference in Syrian, Greek, Chinese, and Christian myth. It is, however, the association of fish with Christ in Christian lore[45] that provides the symbolic justification for Iris Murdoch's net imagery: whatever threatens human dignity and transcendence is a snare to be avoided. *Under the Net,* in a way, comprises a treatise about the false assumptions we must discard before achieving a true vision of reality. As Catherine Fawley (*The Bell*) gathers apricots, her enclosure by a net mirrors her inner state. Usually seen either cowering or looking down, Catherine believes that finite sexual love has corrupted her and has invalidated her candidacy as a postulant nun. Eventually the recognition that her love for Michael Meade eclipses her spiritual fervor drives her to suicide. The net image suits Catherine, her delusion being the uncritical acceptance of terminal judgments.

Iris Murdoch's characters do not usually accept prefabricated moralities. This is one of the reasons for the deft pacing of the novels. The new situations her characters encounter are generally met with a freshness and *frisson* that both acknowledges the world's rich diversity and ensures a crisp narrative tempo. Unlike Graham Greene's heroes, Iris Murdoch's figures are not usually weighted by spiritual arrears. Each experience is seen as unique and surprising and not as a stage in a regenerative process. Hugh Peronett, for example, does not feel like a stale widower of sixty-seven when he faces Emma Sands for the first time in twenty-five years. He is as frightened and self-conscious as a high school boy. Catherine Fawley is an oddity in the Murdoch canon. Although Ann Peronett and Hannah Crean-Smith are like her, they are not so patently prisoners of an external morality. That Catherine is a netted figure explains why *The Bell* is never told from her point of view. The novel's aggressive movement, *"les quêtes, les pérégrinations, les fugues, les expéditions sérieuses ou burlesques,"*⁴⁰ in short, the quality of tragicomic restlessness, would be lost or totally confused if the narrative were filtered through her consciousness. Although her torment reaches great depths, the insularity of her vision would make *The Bell* a far less exciting novel than it is.

Other characters associated with nets convey the same general idea of human contingency being arrested and trapped. Antonia Lynch-Gibbon's words to her husband, "I must keep you in my loving net," are both vain and destructive of his freedom. The net curtains in Emma Sands's flat and Douglas Swann's advice that Ann keep *her* husband in her loving net *(An Unofficial Rose)* signal further violations of man's unsponsored equality. Emma, it seems, tries throughout the novel to achieve a kind of timelessness at the expense of others; Douglas Swann's counsel assumes the validity of an eternal scheme in which Christian marriage forms a phase. The actions of both characters, by virtue of their failure to see the individual as his own criterion, constitute a kind of anti-humanistic violence.

Iris Murdoch takes great care to dramatize the doctrine of love as nonviolent apprehension of another, within the proposition's terms. Emma Sands and Swann both seek stability in a transient world. Their attempts, lacking a basis in cognate reality, are doomed. As a social novelist, Iris Murdoch is not concerned with what may be true of the world, but with what we, as finite, imperfect beings, can know of it. But in spite of her own reluctance to take a God's-eye view of the world or to seek an external theory of personal justifica-

tion, she does recognize the impulse in others. The various quests in
the novels for a moral or a spiritual leader (Mischa Fox in *The
Flight from the Enchanter,* Michael Meade, Palmer Anderson in *A
Severed Head,* and Hannah Crean-Smith) end futilely in the uncritical reliance upon someone who is by definition just as fortuitous
and usually less stable than the searcher for values.

The need to discover reliable values is inherently human, as
demonstrated in Martin Lynch-Gibbon's search for a master. Martin is
an admitted atheist, but his self-image as an inept, ambiguous
pierrot drives him to endow others with the properties he fails to
find within himself. Iris Murdoch's irony is that life needs structure.
Complete emancipation leads to moral anarchy; on the other hand,
too powerful an allegiance to any social code chills to uncritical
acceptance (Mill) and willfully distorts the democratic contingency
of man's estate. Her characters often try to solve this problem by
retreating into a private fantasy world or, as in Martin Lynch-Gib-
bons' case, by surrendering themselves to the judgment of others. The
world's radical instability destroys both projects and reawakens the
individual to the responsibility of his freedom.

A philosophical analogue that illuminates Iris Murdoch's chaotic
world is found in Russell's 1918 lectures on logical atomism. Russell
refuses to concur with the metaphysical prejudice that if something
is real it will last for a long time, if not forever. His argument is
that although there *may* be things in the universe that last forever,
they are not empirically given. The things we know by experience
endure for only a short time; they include visual illusions and
hallucinations, in contrast to objects like tables and chairs. The latter
are not properly sense data but "logical fictions," built out of sets
of particular appearances.[47] Hugo Belfounder's manufacture of fireworks in *Under the Net* is not accidental; his author's exemplar of
the philosopher, Hugo sees the same fugacious reality in explosives
that Iris Murdoch sees in emotions and human relations. What is de-
scribable as a deeply felt existing thing, like Jake Donaghue's sudden impulses, either changes radically or suddenly disappears after
a brief, often fulgent, glow. Jake's emergence as a person in the
book's final chapter includes his cheerful acceptance of the transience
of all real things:

> Events stream past us . . . and the face of each is seen only for a
> minute. What is urgent is not urgent forever but only ephemerally.

> All work and all love, the search for wealth and fame, the search
> for truth, life itself, are made up of moments which pass and be-
> come nothing. Yet through this shaft of nothings we drive onwards
> with that miraculous vitality that creates our precarious habitations
> in the past and the future. So we live. . . .

Impermanence, then, is the essence of reality. Jake is prepared
(Chapter V) for the worst from his rival in love, Sammy Starfield,
then baffled and offended. Later Jake surmises that Madge, the apex
of the love triangle involving himself and Sammy, may be working
subtly in his behalf. Jake suggests that Sammy gamble with the
money he had offered him to compensate for the emotional loss of
Madge. In this way, Jake can salvage his integrity by refusing money
as a balm to his damaged affections, yet at the same time convert
Sammy's offer to financial gain. The two men make a battery of
telephone calls to local bookmakers and enjoy a great wave of
feeling by their mutual success with the horses. The complicated
plot does give birth to future developments, but Iris Murdoch's
basic intention is executed with mastery. Not only does she suggest
some of the subtle forces between love rivals, as in the Paul Morel-
Baxter Dawes relationship in *Sons and Lovers,* but she also compresses
a broad spectrum of human emotions within a single rhetorical
unit, Chapter V.

This same radical discontinuity and antideterminism is evident
within individuals. The character of Michael Meade testifies to the
ambiguity of the human personality and to the equally ambiguous
effects that honorable motives yield. When Othello wails that his
occupation is lost, he implies that the source of his military prowess
and his love for Desdemona are one. With the sinister Mischa Fox,
Michael embodies the truth that power for good and evil can reside
in the same human impulse. In the eyes of James Tayper Pace, who
takes the conventional standpoint, Michael is an arrant corrupter of
the young. Yet, as does Mischa Fox, he suffers, and the same motives
that attract him to Nick Fawley and to Toby Gashe incite his religious
fervor. The point and depth of interaction between human personalities is so unpredictable that even a consciously virtuous act can
yield extensive sorrow. Reversing causal explanations, Iris Murdoch
is eager to show that noble motives can and often do reap destructive
consequences.

If a mind grows more interesting as it becomes more active, then the fully engaged mind is the most interesting one. In this respect, Iris Murdoch inherits the fictional legacy of Samuel Richardson, James, Conrad, and Virginia Woolf. Her conception of reality is like Berkeley's, in that both she and Berkeley affirm the mind's centricity in nature. But where Berkeley argues that *esse* is *percipi*, Iris Murdoch insists that *esse* is *percipere*. To be is not to be perceived; it is a much more active process. Reality dwells potentially in the perceiver himself; the more reality he allows to the external world, the more substance he takes on as an operating mind. The fully developed mind is the free mind, having conferred the same status upon the objects it perceives as it has upon itself. This understanding springs from the belief that love and morality are conjoined. Iris Murdoch has probably not yet portrayed a character possessing this degree of saintlike morality, although to some readers Hannah Crean-Smith and Maggie in *The Italian Girl* may be doubtful cases. The quality that the conscious mind shares with the saint, however, is that of love. Love is the unflagging search for knowledge, a willingness to participate fully in reality.

Interaction with other selves is both unacademic and dangerous.[48] Michael Meade, together with Felix Meecham and Ann Peronett of *An Unofficial Rose,* are all capable administrators, but their progress from a supervisory to a densely personal encounter with life nearly destroys them. James Tayper Pace is able to judge Michael because James invests life with dignity through diligent work. Similarly, the love that Denis Nolan, the clerk and groundskeeper at Gaze Castle, has for animals is distorted into murder when he is personally challenged by a difficult human situation. Iris Murdoch scrupulously avoids sentimentalizing or romanticizing sexual love. There is not one happy marriage in the eight novels; her married couples, unable to create the difficult blend of romance and security, all demonstrate either a maddening clash of wills or a pallid routine. Furthermore, each of the suicide attempts that she records (five of which are successful) is grounded in imperfect love. The practically automatic power of a suicide to shift the entire emotional equilibrium of a literary work (*Hedda Gabler, The Last Puritan, The Heart of the Matter*) indicates the technical problems that Iris Murdoch is prepared to face in order to clarify her message.

Progress in human knowledge, then, requires emotional involvement and a surrender of personal order. Apprehension of the other is not merely a relation of minds. The intense encounter with life's contingency, not the fear of being engulfed by it, produces anguish. Love's demands are stern and uncompromising, even lawless, but once the commitment is made it regulates the being of the lover with tyrannical force. Martin Lynch-Gibbon seconds Iris Murdoch when he tells Georgie Hands that "in love nothing is ever reasonable." Nietzsche had advised his readers to live dangerously: "Build your cities under Vesuvius! Send your ships into uncharted seas! Live at war with your peers and yourselves."[49]

The only objection Iris Murdoch would have to Nietzsche's exhortation is the extreme voluntarism it implies. According to her, once a person has elected life he has *already* chosen to live dangerously. Rosa Keepe in *The Flight from the Enchanter,* who is nearly crushed by the psychic demands generated by her social relations, will be our representative case. On one side, she is forced to defend herself from Mischa Fox's subtle, carefully timed maneuvers to dominate her. The menace personified by the Lusiewicz brothers is much more immediate. They take turns seducing her, and later one of the brothers threatens to usurp her home. As her confusion grows into fear, Rosa, who had enjoyed with them the privileged position of teacher and "English lady," feels powerless to restore her dignity. The Poles' L-shaped room, in which their seductions of Rosa take place, suggests the interpenetration and inseparability of love, life, and loss. The Pimlico room is the scene of hilarity, compassion, cruelty, deception, and death. Mischa Fox's possible use of the Poles as instruments to torture Rosa and his own protracted suffering, which is presented obliquely, emphasize further the idea that terror and an aggressive encounter with life are inescapably joined.

Iris Murdoch's theoretical reply to the mind-body and subject-object dualisms gives rise to a third—the cleavage between knowledge and happiness. Shrinking from a Hegelian synthesis, her novels insist upon the conjunction of rich experiences and suffering, both mental and physical. The sincerity that Rosa extends to the Poles leads to her violation by them. Unhappy in his marriage, Paul Greenfield bruises and scratches himself in a gorse bush while hunting for Dora during her presumably illicit vigil with Toby Gashe. To take a different perspective on the same kind of personal confrontation, Michael Meade's unexpected gesture of love destroys Toby's efficiency at the Court and haunts him with self-doubt. Toby is, nevertheless, armed with a fresh understanding of life as he begins his first year at Oxford in the fall. The suffering described in the novels, then, cannot be called gratuitously depressing, for beside pointing up a major human failing, the agonized love relationships in Iris Murdoch also convey both a positive sense of man's perfectibility and a source of authentic values:

> What Michael had done was to Toby a tremendous revelation. His whole conception of human existence was become in a moment immensely more complex and even in a brief space had made progress.

Most of Iris Murdoch's novels take place in the summer, and each of them qualifies as a love story. Summer's heat and heavy rains enhance the illusion of intractable, teeming life. Love, as the impelling force, is always inordinate in its demands. It refuses to conform to William James's theory of truth as a new apprehension of life that we blend with an existing body of other truths. Iris Murdoch (compare with the *Phaedrus*) sees truth as specific, involving a particular human relationship and a particular situation. Love, the highest, most difficult truth, formulates its own rules. William Mor, like Shakespeare's Brutus, recognizes that his supreme cause is so interlaced with base motives that it is, finally, just another impure product of the heart's foul rag-and-bone shop:

> He saw that he had now definitely and irrevocably parted company with the truth.
>
> *   *   *
>
> In the country where he lived now, truth could not guide his choices.
>
> *   *   *
>
> He realized, with a spasm of pain, that in order to come to his beloved he would have to summon up not his good qualities but his bad ones: his anger, his hatred of Nan, his capacity for sheer irresponsible violence.

Mor's crucial error is his failure to act in keeping with love's unfair demands. The figures of the Medusa (Agnes Casement in *The Flight from the Enchanter,* Honor Klein, and Miranda Peronett) and the Enchanter (Mischa Fox and Palmer Anderson) help to develop the irrational human forces that must be included in the unique, searing confrontation with love. Love jars into wild motion not only the mind and the flesh but also the obscure, primordial elements of our personalities.

Iris Murdoch's argument reaches an inescapable paradox at this point. Once the painter is cut and the individual opts for love, he also jeopardizes all of his previous values. And, as we have seen, he will probably not be rewarded by happiness or fulfillment. The world of people and objects, Iris Murdoch agrees with Camus, is unreasonable and absurd.[50] Its absurdity becomes manifest when we confront it with expectations. Rational principles cannot harness this flaunting indifference, and our task is to assess it honestly. The lovers in Iris Murdoch's novels have the added handicap of laboring under emotional vulnerability and a vivid sense of loss.

The alternative is conveyed by Lewis Carroll's mirror image. As love is the perception of another's inexhaustibility, Iris Murdoch's lovers tighten their grasp upon reality by virtue of their emotional engagement. People only exhaust life (their own) when they decline to pass through the image of the self into the world of material objects and of other minds. As the mirror image implies, discontent with one's surface reflection promises depths of self-knowledge otherwise unavailable. By contemplating the self, one sacrifices the value of other points of view, and self-contemplation becomes its own object of thought and feeling. The false quasi-religious feeling that this activity engenders is a spiritual deadend. As in Hannah Crean-Smith's case, the perceiver is transformed into the to-be-perceived and gainsays his ability to function creatively. The process, selfish in design but ultimately self-negating in execution, dramatizes what Iris Murdoch believes to be the shortcoming of the Christian virtue of expiation. Expiation acknowledges guilt, and guilt is a variety of self-bondage, imprisoning people within themselves and within their own smugly held values. The act is a distortion of the ontological argument—that, once again, intense desire for an ideal is the same as its possession. By voluntarily locking himself within his reflected image, the individual hopes that he will purge his guilt; meanwhile, the indifferent world continues its rich, meandering course. When outsiders forsake their indifference, as they eagerly do in *The Unicorn*, they invariably violate the self-enclosed personality by projecting their own needs and values upon him. The failure, or refusal, to legislate in one's own behalf constitutes a moral decision in itself. Having relinquished the capacity to judge and act, the inert individual either stagnates or becomes the passive victim of others' violence.

A flexible theory of being, then, cannot be based on a situation involving a single person—another indication of Iris Murdoch's preference for the novel of incident and episode. Rigorously limiting her moral perspective to the social world, she confutes not only one of the main tenets of Christian morality but Sartre's belief that the self who tries to describe itself in terms of other selves is living in bad faith (*mauvaise foi*). Self-reflection begets only solipsism and self-destruction. She concurs essentially with Jaspers' theory of *zu zweien* or *community*, which insists that although the process is exceedingly difficult,[51] the individual can understand himself only through interaction with others:

> We no longer see man against a background of values, of realities, which transcend him. We picture man as a brave naked will surrounded by an easily comprehended empirical world. . . . What we have never had, of course, is a satisfactory Liberal theory of personality, a theory of man as free and separate and related to a rich and complicated world from which, as a moral being, he has much to learn.[52]

Jaspers has stated the driving principle behind his metaphysics in "On My Philosophy" (1941):

> The thesis of my philosophizing is: The individual cannot become human by himself. Self-being is only real in communication with another self-being. Alone, I sink into gloomy isolation—only in communication with others can I be revealed in the act of mutual discovery.[53]

Iris Murdoch's novels testify eloquently to the problem of self-discovery through personal relations. Significantly, our expectations of others are either unmet or outstripped; in any case, they almost always part company with reality. Our tidy predictions about the way we and others will act in a foreseeable situation run afoul of life's contradictory currents. Jake Donaghue, Michael Meade, and Martin Lynch-Gibbon have demonstrated how irrationally the human mind operates under stress. Hume pointed out that rational principles merely color and inform what is empirically given; taken by themselves, the rules of reason cannot create anything new. We have seen that our personal relations cannot be emotionally engaging and fundamentally rational in origin at the same time. This concept is,

however, but one feature of the problem of intersubjectivity. By
sacrificing rational control to emotional involvement, we surrender
ourselves to a rapidly multiplying confusion of temporary values.
Mildred Finch's methodical abandonment, in *An Unofficial Rose,*
forms a skein of disappointments and shocks:

> She had, through the years, grown used to imperfect sympathies.
> Her intimacy with Humphrey [her husband] lacked warmth, her
> intimacy with Felix [her brother], owing to his peculiar muteness,
> lacked detail. Her daughter, whom she had secretly admired, was
> now almost a stranger. She had for long had, she reflected, no
> one to whom she could open her heart. And with surprise, fear,
> and joy she noted now the extent to which, after all, she still
> had a heart. She, the clever, capable, sardonic Mildred, the
> elderly philosophical Mildred, so very much the mistress of her
> self, the captain of her very private soul, was shaken. It was, she
> thought, almost as if she were falling in love. And then she thought,
> but I *am* falling in love.

Life's untidiness and its intransigence to order and system reflect
the delicate equipoise between happiness and unhappiness. Iris Murdoch's characters plunge from serenity to gloom suddenly and without warning. Our joys are transitory, and our sorrows endure because of our emotions' susceptibility and their inability to resist
outside pressures. A love relationship is much easier to destroy than
to maintain. Honor Klein and Martin Lynch-Gibbon speak wisely
when, at the conclusion of *A Severed Head,* they allude to the great
responsibility that their love has inaugurated. Our fragile emotions
cannot usually weather life's intrusions. The beauty of Martin's relation with Georgie Hands is its secrecy, even though he refuses to
admit it. Honor Klein's surprise visit to Hereford Square deals their
love a jolt from which it never recovers. John Rainborough, con-
versely, in *The Flight from the Enchanter,* grows indifferent to
Agnes Casement by discussing her with Marcia Cockeyne. When an
outsider intrudes upon a love relationship, however accidentally,
dissociation is imminent. Palmer Anderson becomes stripped of dignity
and submits limply to Martin Lynch-Gibbon's physical violence after
being accidentally discovered in bed with his half sister. The mere
presence of an observer rends the thin subjective link between lover
and beloved. Almost unconsciously, one of them becomes objectified
as the third-person singular.

Iris Murdoch's answer to this problem is not weaker emotional ties; a relationship that is not vitally felt will slide unwatched into tepid routine. Neither does she advise lovers to enclose themselves within the brittle shell of emotion; this is merely a variety of solipsism. The best kind of love is nourished and reinforced by rich encounters with the world. Implied in her fiction and stated broadly in her philosophy is the new mode of humanistic awareness that we have already discussed: love is a central concept in morality. Unfortunately, this new vision reinstates the nettlesome head-heart dualism. The great emotional range of Iris Murdoch's characters betrays no inadequacy in the human heart to respond intensely to stimuli. The difficulty resides in maintaining the dignity of emotional engagement amid the flux of transient values. In this respect Iris Murdoch agrees with Auden on the importance of disciplined love. A feature of her novels that pertains to this idea is the striking lack of depth in personal communication. Stefan and Jan Lusiewicz can anticipate each other's moves with unflagging accuracy. They have lived together all their lives, they pursue the same profession, and they have always shared one another's women. Yet Jan reverses all expectations by stealing Annette Cockeyne's jewels and deserting his brother.

The mind's contingency and the dappled flow of life render Locke's theory of human isolation practically inevitable. Iris Murdoch's humanistic objection is that we do not try hard enough to gain access to each other. Rosa Keepe declares at times that she is stifled by the intimacy of her relationship with her brother. Yet she ignores Hunter's suffering and the more overt grief of Nina the dressmaker to pursue a doubtful goal, Mischa Fox's love, which she had wisely rejected ten years before. Nan Mor admits in a rare moment of introspection that she has never known her husband. Dora Greenfield, also, discovers to her alarm that she cannot say whether Paul believes in God. Hugh Peronett's reflections at his wife's funeral provide a final example of our natural disinclination to enter into the being of others with force and sincerity: "After more than forty years of marriage, and although his wife had not been a mysterious woman, he had not really known what was in her heart." So long as we resist passing through the mirror of the self, even our most intimate associations will be superficial and unrewarding. The redirection of thought that Iris Murdoch advocates is no less a transvaluation of values than Nietzsche's imperative. Both she and Nietzsche are self-realizationists, but the humanism that she is developing is rooted in

love and social freedom rather than in the scowling intolerance of
a master morality. Only a trained, supple intelligence can effect the
incisive emotional penetration that obliterates the subject-object di-
chotomy in social relations. It is this awareness, as palpable objective
knowledge and not as a random subjective insight discovered in an
extreme moment, that both forms the goal of Iris Murdoch's metaphysics and anchors it in everyday reality.

In addition to Auden's concept of disciplined love, she borrows
and builds on his idea that art is not a handmaid to society. Dora
Greenfield, in a moment of great doubt concerning her marriage,
visits the National Gallery and is refreshed by the great masters'
portrayals of the world's multiplicity. Bledyard, also, the ludicrous art
master of St. Bride's School in *The Sandcastle,* echoes Iris Murdoch's
sentiments regarding mimetic representation:

> When confronted with an object that is not a human being we must
> of course treat it reverently. We must, if we paint it, attempt to
> show what it is like in itself, and not treat it as a symbol of our own
> moods and wishes. The great painter is he who is humble enough
> in the presence of the object to attempt *merely* to show what the
> object is like. But this *merely,* in painting, is everything.

There is a curious point of resemblance between Iris Murdoch's views
of art and Schopenhauer's, in that they both recommend artistic
contemplation as a means of curtailing the operation of the will. In
her case, however, the will-less immersion in art does not serve to
assuage the will's bruises by offering an escape from reality. The
great painters and literary artists teach us to re-enter life with a renewed affirmation of its density and boundlessness.

Iris Murdoch does not limit her humanistic criticism of art to the
finished artifact. The art object, in fact, interests her less than art as
a human activity accompanied by personally significant reverberations. The artist's responsibility is to arrest honestly and vividly the
internal structures of existing things. She regards this Keatsian
dedication to selflessness as a great challenge but also as poor training
for normal human intercourse. The dedicated artist, like the rest of
us, is a limited being, and the demands of his vocation devitalize
him for the equally creative task of forming personal relationships.
We learn that Sidney Carter often painted his daughter Rain, but
that he seldom portrayed his wife. Perhaps the difficulty of establishing a candid, adult understanding with his wife explains her failure

to inspire him. On the other hand, it is possible that he recoiled from projecting upon canvas the personality of one he loved; the inadequacy of the two-dimensional medium and Carter's own reluctance to reflect and choose may have been symptomatic of a deeper loyalty than Rain cares to explain. Either interpretation suggests that life is an art and that the greatest artist is the individual who learns about himself through knowledge of others. In the last analysis, man is definable as a social being who discovers his individuality through interaction with other people. Although artistic ability and abstract knowledge may serve as aids, the individual's moral focus must be other persons; the only way we can achieve selfhood, Iris Murdoch insists, is to immerse ourselves in the opacity of others. After the theoretical trappings have been stripped away, the irreducible reality of other people still remains.

All of her characters who are dedicated to nonhuman goals suffer from loneliness. Their carefully developed minds are not attuned to the problems of daily life. Paul Greenfield, for instance, a specialist in medieval wood carvings and manuscripts, exercises great perceptiveness in his work. His mode of living, however, is symbolized by his Knightsbridge flat, which is "lifeless as a museum." As Iris Murdoch indicated in "A House of Theory," we need a fresh code of working principles, an ontology, in short, that will sustain the specialist, or rationalist, and the empiricist as operating units in an integral whole. The numerous examples in her fiction attest that the highly trained specialist stands to profit as much by this program as his unskilled counterpart.

Her metaphysical charter is largely incomplete. All that she has formulated to date is a body of flexible principles and a direction. An existential bias militates against her supporting any external theory of human justification like Hegel's Absolute, Comte's positivist world-state, or Marx's classless society. We have to begin with the immediate immediately; an individual is not an abstraction or a part of a system. Moral principles must be framed in accordance with his personal needs and not those of an encompassing transcendent spirit or secular organization. The merging of reason and emotion, however, cannot take place in a climate of exalted subjectivity; reality dwells ineluctably in the world external to the perceiver.

Iris Murdoch has abandoned to a great extent the Jamesian novel of patterns. (Forster has stated that a rigid fictional pattern "shuts the doors on life and leaves the novelist doing exercises, generally in the drawing room.") [54] The picaresque novel and especially the plotted novel furnish the situations needed for personalities to reveal themselves; as a progressive social entity, man discovers his being in specific frames of action, such as interpersonal encounters. The libido theory, which disregards social and religious conditioning as efficient factors in the formation of character, is as delimiting and deterministic as Marx's dialectical materialism. By reducing man's conduct to predictable patterns that will govern his life, [55] Freud's doctrines overlook the world's multiplicity and the cacophony of motives that color our simplest acts.

Life is a function of consciousness but not of a single consciousness. The anarchy of wills and emotions residing together in the world shreds any orderly, self-enclosing patterns we may advance as explanations for man's conduct. When Jake Donaghue, Martin Lynch-Gibbon, and Hugh Peronett believe that they have created an equilibrium between their conflicting interests, life intrudes from unexpected sources and directions. Iris Murdoch is working toward a metaphysics that encompasses a maximum number of possible intersections with our finite needs as social beings. Her appreciation of life as an ambiguous process will ensure a set of logical and ethical principles that are progressive disciplines—elastic enough to be revised in accord with particular situations yet rooted solidly enough in the primacy of man's contingency and social instincts to escape relativism. Our survey of the major philosophical influences upon her thought and of her own significant departures from them suggests perhaps the first serious gesture toward unifying the discordant demands of the Continental and English traditions since the early liberalism of Russell gave us essays like "A Free Man's Worship," "The Place of Science in a Liberal Education," and "Mysticism and Logic."

Notes to Chapter Two

1. Iris Murdoch, "The Idea of Perfection," *The Yale Review,* 53 (Spring, 1964), 371.

2. *Ibid.,* 342.

3. Iris Murdoch, "The Sublime and the Good," *Chicago Review,* 13 (Autumn, 1959), 51-52; the boldest statement of this theme in the novels

probably occurs in *The Bell,* during a colloquy between Michael Meade and the Abbess; the Abbess is speaking: "Remember that all our failures are ultimately failures in love. Imperfect love must not be condemned and rejected, but made perfect. The way is always forward, never back."

4. Nona Balakian, "The Flight from Innocence: England's Newest Literary Generation," *Books Abroad,* 33 (Summer, 1959), 268.

5. Murdoch, "The Sublime and the Good," *passim*; Iris Murdoch, "The Sublime and the Beautiful Revisited," *The Yale Review,* 49 (December, 1959), *passim*; in addition to the advice that the Abbess gives Michael Meade in *The Bell,* Douglas Swann's remarks to Ann Peronett in *An Unofficial Rose* are germane: "Goodness accepts the contingent. Love accepts the contingent. Nothing is more fatal to love than to want everything to have form."

6. Jean-Paul Sartre, *What Is Literature?* trans. by Bernard Frechtman (London, 1950).

7. Ved Mehta, *Fly and the Fly-Bottle: Encounters with British Intellectuals* (Boston, 1963), 54.

8. Kevin O'Sullivan, "Iris Murdoch and the Image of Liberal Man," *The Yale Literary Magazine,* 131 (December, 1962), 27.

9. Iris Murdoch, "A House of Theory," *Partisan Review,* 26 (Winter, 1959), 29.

10. The logical analysts (or positivists) framed in the 1930's a verifiability criterion of meaning that extruded questions dealing with human activity. To the exponents of the British-American school, all factual propositions, that is, propositions that describe the interacting physical world, must refer to observation statements. The truths of logic and mathematics, which are known independently of sense experience, tell us nothing about the empirical world. Philosophers like Carnap and Ayer find ethics, as value statements, cognitively meaningless. Ethical judgments assert nothing that can be proved empirically or by the a priori truths of logic and mathematics. By conveying a mood or a state of mind, ethics, as lyrical poetry, has only an expressive function without probitive force.

11. Iris Murdoch, "Metaphysics and Ethics," in D. F. Pears, ed., *The Nature of Metaphysics* (London and New York, 1957), 122.

12. See note 10, above.

13. R. M. Hare, *The Language of Morals* (Oxford, 1952), 2-3.

14. Murdoch, "Metaphysics and Ethics," 121-22; see also Iris Murdoch, "Against Dryness: A Polemical Sketch," *Encounter,* 16 (January, 1961), 18-20.

15. Murdoch, "Metaphysics and Ethics," 122.

16. "What is phenomenology? If one wanted a bold formula one might say

that it was an *a priori* theory of meaning with a psychological flavour and a highly developed descriptive technique. . . . The phenomenologist does not regard meaning only as a function of our language; nor does he, on the other hand, take it, with the Aristotelians, to be somehow inherent in things themselves, nor with the Platonists, as residing in the transcendent intelligible world. He regards it as dependent upon the activity of the subject." Iris Murdoch, "The Novelist as Metaphysician," *The Listener,* 42 (16 March 1950), 473.

17. *Ibid.*

18. Murdoch, "The Sublime and the Beautiful Revisited," 255.

19. Iris Murdoch, *Sartre: Romantic Rationalist* (New Haven, 1953), 70-71.

20. *Ibid.,* 26; see also Iris Murdoch, "Hegel in Modern Dress," *The New Statesman and Nation,* 53 (25 May 1957), 675.

21. Iris Murdoch, "T. S. Eliot as a Moralist," in Neville Braybrooke, ed., *T. S. Eliot: A Symposium for His Seventieth Birthday* (New York, 1958), 159-60.

22. Murdoch, "Against Dryness: A Polemical Sketch," 19-20.

23. Murdoch, *Sartre: Romantic Rationalist,* 26.

24. For a modern view of the ontological argument, see G. E. Moore, "Is Existence a Predicate?" *Philosophical Papers* (New York, 1962), 114-25.

25. James Collins, *The Existentialists: A Critical Study* (Chicago, 1952), 140.

26. Kenneth T. Gallagher, *The Philosophy of Gabriel Marcel* (New York, 1962), 67.

27. Gabriel Marcel, "Ego and Its Relation to Others," *Homo Viator: Introduction to a Metaphysic of Hope,* trans. by Emma Craufurd (Chicago, 1951), 17-18.

28. Frank Kermode, "The House of Fiction: Interviews with Seven English Novelists," *Partisan Review,* 30 (Spring, 1963), 65.

29. James Gindin, *Postwar British Fiction: New Accents and Attitudes* (Berkeley and Los Angeles, 1962), 186.

30. G. S. Fraser, "Iris Murdoch: The Solidity of the Normal," *International Literary Annual,* II, John Wain, ed. (London, 1959), 48.

31. Murdoch, "The Sublime and the Good," 54.

32. *Ibid.,* 51.

33. Murdoch, "The Sublime and the Beautiful Revisited," 249.

34. Murdoch, "The Sublime and the Good," 51-52; Murdoch, "The Idea of Perfection," 376-77.

35. Iris Murdoch, "Vision and Choice in Morality," *Aristotelian Society: Dreams and Self-Knowledge,* Supplementary Volume 30 (London, 1956), 50.

36. Murdoch, "The Sublime and the Beautiful Revisited," 270.

37. Iris Murdoch, "Nostalgia for the Particular," *Proceedings of the Aristotelian Society,* 52 (London, 1952), 255.

38. Murdoch, *Sartre: Romantic Rationalist,* ix-x.

39. Alasdair Clayre, "Common Cause: A Garden in the Clearing," *TLS* (7 August 1959), xxxi.

40. Murdoch, "Against Dryness: A Polemical Sketch," 20.

41. Murdoch, "The Sublime and the Beautiful Revisited," 257.

42. *Ibid.,* 264.

43. Murdoch, "The Sublime and the Good," 53.

44. O'Sullivan, 27.

45. Eva C. Hangen, *Symbols, Our Universal Language* (Wichita, Kansas, 1962), 105-6.

46. René Micha, "Les Romans à machines d'Iris Murdoch," *Critique* [Paris], (April, 1960), 295.

47. Bertrand Russell, *Logic and Knowledge: Essays 1901–1950,* Robert Charles March, ed. (London, 1956), 274-75.

48. Murdoch, "The Sublime and the Good," 51-52.

49. Friedrich Nietzsche, "The Gay Science," in Walter A. Kaufmann, ed., *Existentialism from Dostoevsky to Sartre* (New York, 1956), 106.

50. Albert Camus, *The Myth of Sisyphus and Other Essays,* trans. by Justin O'Brien (New York, 1955), 45.

51. Karl Jaspers, "On My Philosophy," trans. by Felix Kaufmann, in *Existentialism from Dostoevsky to Sartre,* 145.

52. Murdoch, "Against Dryness: A Polemical Sketch," 18.

53. Jaspers, 147.

54. E. M. Forster, *Aspects of the Novel* (New York, n.d.), 163.

55. Karen Horney, *New Ways in Psychoanalysis* (New York, 1939), 44.

Three

UNDER THE NET

The Novel as Philosophical Criticism

IN THAT *Under the Net* treats fiction's ability to portray reality and, in passing, attempts to describe that reality, it is certainly one of the most ambitious first novels of the century. Its bold dramatization of weighty philosophical ideas testifies to an eager intelligence reorienting and rediscovering itself in a new medium. The hearty critical acceptance the novel has earned rests largely in Iris Murdoch's affirmation of the English comic novel as a vehicle for the presentation of philosophical concepts. She herself has called *Under the Net* "a rejection of all forms of thought and language which act as barriers."

> It plays with a philosophical idea. The problem which is mentioned in the title is the problem of how far conceptualizing and theorizing, which from one point of view are absolutely essential, in fact divide you from the thing that is the object of theoretical attention.[1]

The major influence behind Iris Murdoch's examination of a reality that defies theorizing and classification is Wittgenstein's *Tractatus*. Wittgenstein asserts that reality is logical and that a proposition is a "picture of the facts." We have no way of picturing this picturing relationship, however. The common "form" or "structure" shared by the proposition and the reality it stands for cannot be represented (*Tractatus*, 2: 17, 172). Wittgenstein calls the relationship between propositions and factual reality "the inexpressible" ("*Das Mystische*"). Empirical data cannot be expressed by propositions or, in fact, by any means whatever; it is fatuous to define reality ("that which is the case") by means of an agent that is not reality, the sounds or signs of speech. Iris Murdoch had addressed herself to this same problem in a paper read to the Aristotelian Society in 1952 and agreed in spirit with Wittgenstein's conclusions:

> Nothing can reproduce an experience (even a very good photo is only a reminder) and nothing can be really like an experience except another experience; and here what we want is an infallible criterion of sameness and this is just what we cannot find.[2]

Wittgenstein's purpose in the *Tractatus* was to show that, because we cannot discover the organic link between a particular existing thing and its linguistic surrogate, traditional metaphysics is impossible— not merely false, but nonsense. Without gainsaying the salience of his attempts to dissolve philosophy into linguistic analysis, Iris Murdoch, in a 1962 review of Elias Canetti's *Crowds and Power,* redirects his conclusions to the problem of establishing human values:

> The paradox of our situation is that we must have theories about human nature, no theory explains everything, yet it is just the desire to explain everything which is the spur of theory.[3]

To avoid theorizing and generalizing is, ironically, itself a theory. It is, moreover, a theory limited to the pragmatic world of facts and physical reality. Philosophy may not have yet devised a means to objectify objectivity, but our erratic mode of stimulus-response activity, personified in *Under the Net* by Jake Donaghue, reveals that raw experience does not constitute the test and end of human activity. Iris Murdoch's representative of the antimetaphysical philosopher in *Under the Net* is Hugo Belfounder. Discussing the irrevocable cleavage between language and reality, Hugo insists that all description falsifies and misrepresents:

> "There's something fishy about describing people's feelings," said Hugo. "All these descriptions are so dramatic. . . . "
> "But suppose I try hard to be accurate," I said.
> "One can't be," said Hugo. "The only hope is to avoid saying it. As soon as I start to describe, I'm done for. Try describing anything—our conversation, for instance—and see how absolutely instinctively you——"
> "Touch it up?" I suggested.
> "It's deeper than that," said Hugo. "The language just won't let you present it as it really was."

"Suppose, then," I said, "that one were offering the description at the time."

"But don't you see," said Hugo, "that just gives the thing away. One couldn't give such a description at the time without seeing that it was untrue. All one could say at the time would be perhaps something about one's heart beating. But if one said one was apprehensive this could only be to try to make an impression—it would be for *effect;* it would be a lie."

I was puzzled by this myself. . . . "But at this rate almost everything one says, except things like, 'Pass the marmalade,' or, 'There's a cat on the roof,' turns out to be a sort of lie."

Hugo pondered this. "I think it is so," he said with seriousness. . . .

"All the time when I speak to you, even now [said Hugo], I'm saying not *precisely* what I think, but what will impress you and make you respond. That's so even between us—and how much more it's so where there are stronger motives for deception. In fact one's so used to this one hardly sees it. The whole language is a machine for making falsehoods."

Hugo's attempts to escape the snares of language provide Iris Murdoch with both an apologia and a metaphysic for the novel. Both Hugo and his author subscribe to the atomistic plurality of the world. Hugo conveys Iris Murdoch's philosophical convictions by devoting his practical skills to the creation of fireworks. The uniqueness of the pyrotechnical effects of each set piece constitutes for Hugo a work of the highest art. As soon as his rockets become popular, he gives them up, convinced that increasing public demand will diminish their quality as honest copies of ephemeral, rigorously particular reality. An artist as well as a philosopher and a craftsman, Hugo turns to the silent film and the mime theater as new ways of conveying the irreducible particularity of the world. But in their practical execution, these "pure" art forms contain unforeseen limitations. The silent film eliminates the layer of language that divides action from reality; accordingly, the masked mime, here Lazemnikov's *Marishka,* does away with misleading facial expressions as well as with dialogue. But an art that restricts itself to transcribing physical events fails in that it reduces life to stimulus-response behaviorism. The first noticeable weakness of mime and of expressionistic cinema is their built-in endorsement of outdated, or at least no longer sharable metaphysical principles. Jung's idea of synchronicity as meaningful coincidences linked acausally[4] has quickened a new suspicion concerning cause-and-effect reasoning, as has

Russell's essay "On the Notion of Cause." As Douglas Hewitt notes in his study of Conrad, causality is less important in literature today than it was in the work of Jane Austen.[5] Emma Woodhouse's personality assumes contours through social interaction; the same cannot be said of Miriam Henderson, Durrell's Justine, or Jake Donaghue.

A second weakness of Hugo's theory of art, implicit in the first, resides in the sheer inadequacy of behaviorism to portray reality. Behaviorism and dumb-show techniques may operate well in a farce, a melodrama, or an expressionistic film—art forms in which symbol, motive, and surface action fuse. They do not operate well, however, in a subtler medium that tries to present various levels of moral consciousness. Besides, action and gesture do mislead, in addition to disguising the ironies and contradictions of human acts, for example, Conrad's Brierly in *Lord Jim* and E. A. Robinson's Richard Cory. Intruding upon a performance of *Marishka,* Jake Donaghue recognizes Hugo as a member of the cast but misinterprets the nature of his attachment to Anna Quentin, his leading lady—an error that causes most of the needless sorrow that Jake experiences throughout the novel:

> This also explained the Mime Theatre. This doubtless was some fantasy of Hugo's which he had recruited Anna, against her will maybe, to realize. That she had picked up in the process a crude version of his ideas was not surprising. Anna was sensitive, and Hugo was impressive. . . . I was reminded of the silent expressionism of Hugo's early films. The speechless purity of the mime might well have become a genuine obsession for Hugo. But the beautiful theatre itself—this was a house for Anna, a house which Hugo had built and in which Anna would be queen.

As a person, as well, Hugo dramatizes the shortcomings of remaining cognitively transfixed by the doubt situation. Iris Murdoch has called him "a sort of non-philosophical metaphysician who is supposed to be paralyzed in a way by this problem [the problem of representational language]."[6] Hugo's tenacious detachment and objectivity render him a living paradox. Gifted with great physical and intellectual power—Iris Murdoch associates bear imagery with him on numerous occasions in the novel—he rarely accomplishes anything aside from divesting himself of his money and his property. At the conclusion of the novel he has only personal suffering to show for his objectivity. After leaving London to pursue the trade of watchmaking, Hugo reveals that he is unequipped emotionally for dense

personal involvements. Powerless to act decisively in his own behalf, he functions positively only as an influence on others, which, of
course, reverses the major tenets of his antiphilosophical program.

The flocks of Holborn starlings that sport in the area between
Hugo's living-room window and the building's sloping roof symbolize
his intellectual dedication. But Hugo's departure from his sumptuously
appointed flat suggests that mental activity alone, divorced from
warm human ties, is not sufficient. Allowed complete freedom, the
starlings befoul and desecrate the flat, thereby repudiating their
symbolic value as affirmations of intellectual activity. Iris Murdoch
approaches Bloomsbury personalism with her insistence upon human
involvements as a regulating principle to guide and enrich our
rational pursuits:

> As I entered Hugo's sitting-room there was a sudden wild flurry.
> The room was whirring and disintegrating into a number of black
> pieces. I grasped the door in a fright. Then I saw. The place was
> full of birds. Several starlings which had not found the window
> in their first dart fluttered madly about, striking the walls and the
> glass panes. . . . Hugo's flat seemed already more like an aviary
> than the abode of a human being. White dung spattered the carpet,
> and through the open window the rain had come in and made a
> deep stain upon the wall. It looked as if Hugo had not been there
> for some time.

Several other characters in the novel personify moralities as unsatisfactory and sometimes as self-defeating as Hugo's. Lefty Todd,
the efficient oratorical leader of the New Independent Socialist
Party (NISP), exemplifies a political dedication that tries to blend
theory with practice. To Jake, however, Lefty's explorations of England's socialist consciousness have little appeal; before Jake can
engage in collective action, he understands that he must first formu-
late and test his own standards. Dave Gellman, Jake's occasional
roommate, is a metaphysical foil to Hugo. A professional philosopher
and a contributor of articles to *Mind,* the leading philosophical
journal in the English-speaking world, Dave labors to treat life objectively, as if it were a problem in logic or semantics. In Chapter
XIII, he determines precisely Jake's legal position regarding the
kidnaping of both Sammy Starfield's canine film star Mr. Mars
and Jake's stolen translation, then in Sammy's hands. As does Hugo,
Dave opts for a bare, Spartan life, stripped of sympathetic ties, and,
also like Hugo, his residence reflects his mode of living.

Malcolm Bradbury has developed the link between Dave's anti-personalist philosophy and his symbolically suggestive Goldhawk Road flat: "His flat is next to, and dominated by, the cold walls of a modern hospital; he represents a spare, utilitarian view of the world."[7] Dave, furthermore, is as much a victim of contingency as his Wittgensteinian counterpart. (There is a comic scene in the novel in which Dave periodically interrupts his typing of a philosophical article to hold up his two hands and look at them; Iris Murdoch's philosophical joke is that G. E. Moore adduced the existence of a material world by doing roughly the same thing in his "Proof of an External World.") Dave scorns charitable acts as aids to moral promiscuity; yet in spite of his efforts to be unpersonable, his flat in "contingent" London attracts many followers, including Jake and Finn, who remain there for weeks. It is doubtful that Dave would be able to reason so flawlessly in his own extremity as he had done in Jake's or, presumably, in the *Mind* article. Furthermore, rational principles, as Hume insisted, may regulate personal conduct but cannot constitute it. Jake's refutation of Dave's chilly mentalized approach to life is contained in *The Silencer*, a philosophical essay Jake writes in the form of a dialogue:

> When you've been most warmly involved in life, when you've most felt yourself to be a man, has a theory ever helped you? Is it not then that you meet with things themselves naked? Has a theory helped you when you were in doubt about what to do? Are not these very simple moments when theories are shilly-shallying?

Contrary to Hugo and Dave, Jake's quasi retainer and *valet de chambre* Finn is too empirically unreflective to serve as a model. He is Iris Murdoch's parody of Rousseau's natural man, unpretentious, compassionate, and able. Like Mars the Alsatian (a breed that corresponds closely to the German shepherd or police dog), Finn is able to deal with awkward practical matters, such as picking a lock or finding a place to live in an embarrassed moment. But Finn is no more capable than the star of *Red Godfrey's Revenge* and *Five in a Flood* of learning from experience or of erecting a moral code. Madge, or Magdalen, who dismisses Jake and Finn from her garret upon her engagement to Sammy Starfield, practices, as Finn does, a will-less mode of existence. By allowing others to legislate for her, Madge achieves the prestige and social power she had always yearned for. In the process, however, she relinquishes her personal freedom; down to the fineries of her clothing and cosmetics, she is first Sammy's creature and then that of the anonymous owner of the huge Anglo-American film syndicate she represents. Though the reader never learns whether Madge's surrender to the will of others is deliberate, it is odd that both times she appears in the novel she performs a decisive act—first, in London, she evicts Jake and Finn, then, in Paris, she offers Jake a high-salaried job as a script writer.

Jake's refusal of her offer takes place simultaneously with the Bastille Day celebrations in other quarters of the city. The relevance of Jake's act to the historical event embraces a good deal more than the common theme of human freedom. Both occasions presage the terror and the personal responsibility of encountering life without intermediaries; both constitute, from another standpoint, comic, sentimental histrionics that turn out to have more long-range symbolic value than immediate importance. Jake's state of mind, when he leaves Madge's hotel room, reflects the age's distrust of received moral and philosophical doctrines. He finds that he has traveled from London to Paris to spurn an offer of love, a way of life, and a high salary for doing the kind of work he had already been doing, when it was available, for much less money. His discovery of personal freedom demands his depriving himself of a lucrative, easy-going life of subjection.

The quest motif is clear, but more important is the manner in which Jake's artistic and personal independence manifest themselves to him. In the chaotic modern world, where abstract rationalism has been either scrapped or renovated, principles like cause-and-effect, motive-and-act, and ground-and-consequent[8] have been distorted, inverted, or turned inside out. Jake does not experience a benign wave of euphoria when he leaves the Hotel Prince de Clèves; on the contrary, his first reaction is regret for having foolishly rejected the chance to give up the starveling, catch-as-catch-can life of a literary hack. He only becomes aware of his self-legislating gesture of freedom a few hours later in a spontaneous act of delayed understanding:

> All that mattered was a vision which I had had of my own destiny and which imposed itself upon me as a command. What had I to do with script-writing? . . . The business of my life lay elsewhere. There was a path which awaited me and which if I failed to take it would lie untrodden forever. How much longer would I delay? This was the substance and all other things were shadows, fit only

to distract and deceive. What did I care for money? It was as nothing to me.

Under the Net represents a new kind of social comedy. The discrepancy between aim and execution, motive and theory, and appearance and reality reaches original artistic depths in this *"boîte à
surprises."*[9] Without explaining social life by a priori notions, Iris
Murdoch presents it somewhat blithely and unapologetically as it is—
ambiguous and fragmented. A good deal of the novel's sprightly
tone can be accounted for by Jake's knowledge that reality exempts
him, the philosophical narrator writing in retrospect, from positing
orderly ontological systems. After suddenly realizing that his judgments
concerning the complicated relationship involving Hugo, the Quentin
sisters, and himself have been mistaken, Jake exclaims to himself,
"A pattern in my mind was suddenly scattered and the pieces of it
went flying about me like birds."

Iris Murdoch dramatizes rather than explains life's inherent resistance to patterns of knowledge or control. The theorizing of Hugo
and Dave Gellman is nullified by the inevitability with which human
contingency and sheer messiness rush into their lives. She also employs
the classic "biter-bit" device to demonstrate the frailty of our enterprises in a world that sustains numerous points of view and personal
values. While Sadie Quentin sits under the hair dryer in her Mayfair
beauty parlor, ministering to her vanity, her vanity is piqued by
Jake's mention of her sister Anna. Jake, also, in a later episode, discovers that he is being watched by the neighbors as he eavesdrops
upon Sammy and Sadie while the two discuss his purloined translation. To reflect further the transience and discontinuity of all values,
Iris Murdoch shows that even our most magnanimous acts can have
damaging consequences. Hugh Peronett's giving of his Tintoretto to
his son Randall, in *An Unofficial Rose,* Madge's offer of a job to
Jake, and Jake's own act of helping Hugo escape from the hospital
all result in the severing of a vitally felt relationship. As far as the
reader knows, the persons involved never see each other again.

Our personal standing (as well as our conscious choices) is also
liable to radical dislocation; as his own legislator and judge, finite
man erects his own standards and responds to them with as much
energy and originality as he feels they warrant. Thus Jean Pierre
Breteuil, after writing several commercial pot-boilers, produces a
first-rate novel in *Nous les Vainqueurs,* and Finn upsets Jake's

mental image of him by returning to Ireland with his race-track winnings and to a possibly more religious life. Deriving from one whose intellectual depth and imagination are certainly greater than average, Jake's diagnoses of situations and personalities are almost infallibly wrong. The image of the Pont Neuf overhanging the Seine (the bridge's "round arches make their reflexions a perfect O, in which one cannot tell what is reflected and what is not") conveys our tenuous understanding of the rift between solidity and illusion. The world houses too many independent centers of creative activity (operating minds) for any single explanation to retain its validity.

Fraser has interpreted the novel's title in accordance with our inscrutable social relationships:

> Society is seen as precisely the net which is always coming down
> to catch us, but which has large or coarse meshes which we can
> easily escape through if only to be caught in other, finer meshes.[10]

Although Fraser's remark conveys some of the important developments that arise from social interaction, it seems to bypass the question of the individual as a conscious social ingredient. Each of us is imperfect and drastically limited; many of the meshes Fraser refers to are of our own making and are woven by our inability to avoid snags and flaws. One of the reasons for the dread that the existential philosophers say accompanies the decision-making process is that any human choice cannot account for more than a small number of foreseeable consequences. Lacking a superintending benign preserver, we are condemned to enact our own freedom, and each situation generates its own exigencies and rules. Hugo's escape from the hospital exposes the thinness and instability of the line between dignity and broad farce:

> There was not a sign of life from the Night Sister and not a sound
> of any kind to be heard. I slid out and Hugo followed, making a
> noise like a bear, a mixture of grunting and lumbering. . . . Then
> I turned back again, and nearly laughed out loud. Hugo had got
> his two boots gripped by their tongues between his teeth, and was
> negotiating the passage on hands and feet, his posterior rising
> mountainously into the air.

Recording his own experiences, Jake respects life's contingency enough to deny that he is telling the whole truth; even if we know "what is the case," we know only a limited aspect of it for a brief time:

> Subtle people, like myself, can see too much ever to give a straight answer.
>
> *   *   *
>
> If I spoke now there was always the danger of my telling the truth; when caught unawares I usually tell the truth, and what's duller than that?
>
> *   *   *
>
> That's another story, and I'm not telling you the whole story of my life.

Jake, as we have seen, disavows the practical public features of Lefty Todd's socialist creed. His literary and philosophical values, nevertheless, incorporate many of Lefty's ideological tenets. Lefty's political zeal is not inflammatory and blatantly reformist; the unity of theory and practice that he visualizes is admittedly a distant goal. Speaking of his NISP, Lefty states, "Our role is to explore the socialist consciousness of England." The novelist and the politician alike, both lacking complete knowledge, must describe reality before voicing claims and imperatives.

The remarkable number of surprises and reversals that occur in *Under the Net* shows this task to be extremely difficult. Jake regards the publication of *The Silencer* as a betrayal of Hugo, and the ensuing guilt that Jake suffers damages their friendship; ironically, several years later, Hugo acknowledges Jake's originality. By coloring Hugo's reactions with his own emotions, Jake forfeits a vital, mutually profitable association. Likewise, his and Finn's failure to account for Mars's native intelligence, as the two attempt to remove the dog and his cage from Sammy Starfield's flat, costs them unnecessary labor and anxiety. Had Jake acknowledged the perceptions of Hugo and Mars, he could have spared himself needless worry and toil. Human freedom, once again, recognizes the freedom of others (even of dogs, it seems) as independent centers of significance. The core of humanistic awareness, for the politician and the novelist, is the need to understand that the world consists of a multiplicity of minds acting without reference to our concepts or emotional stresses:

> It will be noticed that *Under the Net* is in the deepest sense a paradoxical work: the point is made that reality is incommunicable, just *there,* and at the same time a whole, highly conscious and sophisticated novel is devoted to saying this.[11]

The novel's complicated plot serves further to objectify life's in-

communicable, irreducible quality. Iris Murdoch dramatizes without
accounting for such happenings as Jake's sudden yearnings for the
company of either Anna or Hugo despite his not having seen either
of them for years. The author's silence contains, nevertheless, its own
message. As social beings, people are inescapably related to one another, even when the interlocking rings of knowledge, intimacy, and
power that join us are temporarily concealed. Perhaps Jake's difficulty
of getting in and out of places (the Riverside Theatre, Sadie's lux-
urious flat, the Bounty Belfounder film studio, and the hospital)
symbolizes our initial reluctance to frame human relationships and,
at the same time, our helplessness to disengage ourselves once the
relationships have congealed. Our inability to convey the depth and
the extent of interpersonal dynamics may be related to Wittgenstein's "the inexpressible." The only decisive statement Iris Murdoch
seems to make concerning our relationships is that they are inevitable
and that they are not inert. As in Powell's *The Music of Time,* persons
keep returning into our lives involuntarily, unpredictably, and with
new claims upon us. We can only intuit vaguely the nature of our
personal ties. Our moral perceptions, Iris Murdoch insists, are tenta-
tive, fragmentary, and almost always subject to radical revision:

> My typescript has been stolen. Stolen? Madge shows it to Sammy,
> who shows it to H. K. Stolen? What's Madge up to anway? Madge
> is being double-crossed by Sammy, who ditches her for Sadie.
> Sammy uses Madge and Sadie uses Sammy to get her revenge
> on Hugo and make a fortune in dollars at the same time. I began to
> see the whole picture.
>
> *   *   *
>
> I began wondering how sorry I'd felt for Madge, and then it oc-
> curred to me that Madge had probably started double-crossing
> Sammy even before she knew that Sammy was double-crossing her.
>
> *   *   *
>
> Hugo's head was down. . . . I observed him closely as one might
> observe a picture of a dead man. I had a strange sense of his being
> both very distant and yet closer to me than he had ever been or
> would be again. I was reluctant to speak. So we went for a long
> time in silence.
>
> *   *   *
>
> I began thinking about Hugo. . . . He was a man without claims
> and without reflexions. Why had I pursued him? He had nothing to
> tell me. To have seen him was enough. He was a sign, a portent,

a miracle. Yet no sooner had I thought this than I began to be curious again about him.

The structure of *Under the Net* demonstrates the strength of Iris Murdoch's grasp of her theme and her unity of method. The organization of a novel that proclaims the world's diversity, it scarcely needs saying, poses unique problems. Total formlessness and opacity would reflect with some accuracy the particularity of things and their defiance of classification and pattern. But a novel built out of obscurely related particulars would be artistically unsatisfying, a casual celebration of chaos for its own sake. On the other hand, a rigid organization would suggest that Iris Murdoch presumed to index and codify the nonclassifiable, thus impairing the novel's central theme. Her evasion of the twin evils involves her taking a middle course, but a middle course that is augmented and modified by her philosophical interest. Chapters IV, VIII, XII, XVI, and XX in this twenty-chapter book constitute provisional climaxes. The symbolic or psychological heights attained in these pivotal chapters are all either enriched or revised in succeeding episodes. Chapter IV, in a way, generates its own dialectic; it is here that Jake meets Hugo and later comes to publish *The Silencer*. The chapter's closing pages show Jake's motives degenerating from the quest for objective truth to deception and thirst for public glory. In addition, the next chapter introduces the professional gambler and night-club owner Sammy Starfield, whose display of financial power and whose crass ignorance influence Jake for a time as vividly as Hugo's lucid objectivity.

Chapter VIII, the next plateau, is a paradox for anyone reading the novel for the first time. The wealth of religious symbolism directed to social reform suggests an engagement on Jake's part that almost insists upon forming the emotional nucleus of the novel. Apparently, however, just as forcibly as the theme of society's rebirth is affirmed, it wanes in the following chapters, only to reappear transmuted at the end of the book. In Chapter VIII Jake becomes acquainted with Lefty Todd, who is always represented as dedicated and methodical, yet also fun-loving and gifted with the perceptiveness to confront life in all its phases with gusto and cheer. He is twice associated in the chapter with Orion, a hunter of great powers who is always defeated by some sort of guile. After their meeting in a Ludgate pub, Lefty catechizes Jake on his knowledge of Marx. The two men, joined by Finn and Dave Gellman, then wander drunkenly through London's streets and to the General Post Office, where they are dismissed for shouting and singing. Following the symbolic night journey and hymn ritual, they swim in the Thames; Dave, significantly as a Jew and an antimetaphysical analyst, does not participate in the baptism ceremony. As their last act of the night, the men feast on biscuits, *foie gras,* and brandy. The end of the chapter is heralded by the ringing of church bells in various parts of the city as dawn breaks.

It is difficult to see any immediate spiritual progress in Jake as a result of his symbolic vigil with Lefty Todd. Jake fails to keep future appointments with Lefty; he is seen as a thief in Chapter IX, stealing flowers in Covent Garden Market; in the same chapter, he hides in the truck that carries away the stage properties from the defunct Riverside Theatre; and later, he descends to eavesdropper, housebreaker, and kidnaper of Mr. Mars. The removal of the regal, softly undulating trappings that Jake had mentally associated with Anna Quentin creates a mental clearance and anticipates Hugo's final unmasking of the reality of the Anna-Hugo-Sadie-Jake relationship. As far as the reader learns, Jake never returns to collect Anna's coronet from the Left Luggage office where he leaves it. His renunciation of his illusions about Anna proves to be congruent with his social-artistic development. At this juncture in the novel, however, owing to Iris Murdoch's discontinuous presentation, the connection is barely perceptible.

Chapter XII takes place at the Bounty Belfounder film studios, where Jake finally manages to find Hugo. The chapter blends the old and the new, idealism and violence, classicism and romanticism, splendor and tawdriness, and seriousness and farce. On a set for filming a picture about Catiline, Lefty Todd, another political separationist and subversive who may also be misrepresented by his detractors (Iris Murdoch telescopes Cicero's Catilinian orations with the news reports in the *Evening Standard*), eloquently preaches Marxism. Lefty's audience, clad in overalls and togas, disperses when the meeting is raided by a rightist faction and then by the police. In his attempt to help Jake and Lefty escape, Hugo blows up the towering plastic and Essex-board model of ancient Rome that serves as a backdrop for the film.

Iris Murdoch's intention in this episode is to convey the sameness between antiquity and today. Unlike Kierkegaard, she does not portray man as an eternal pilgrim searching for the Heavenly Kingdom. The Eternal City, as with Nietzsche's eternal recurrence doctrine, is the here-and-now. Iris Murdoch's mythologizing is directed to the universal and the basically human. The human limits and situations governing man's attempts to discover freedom, she believes, remain the same through all ages.[12] Her gravity of purpose does not, however, destroy her sense of humor or her acute artistry. In a riotous parody of *The Iliad*, she confounds Homer's warriors with modern man in order to blend man's perpetual search for liberty with the frank absurdity of the measures he is often forced to take:

> The ground was strewn with legless torsos and halves of men and others cut off at the shoulders, all of whom, however, were lustily engaged in restoring themselves to wholeness by dragging the hidden parts of their anatomy out from under the flat wedges of scenery, which lay now like a big pack of cards, some pieces still showing brick and marble, while others revealed upon their prostrate backs the names of commercial firms and the instructions of the scene-shifter.

The pagan element in Chapter XII is no doubt included to balance and augment the Christian motif developed in Chapter VIII; and, once again, Jake fails to benefit visibly. Perhaps the fracas at the studio does arm him with a new sense of freedom, but there is no way of affirming this other than by pointing vaguely to his rejection of Madge's job offer in Chapter XIV. At any rate, his raw physical encounter with practical politics does not cure Jake of chasing the shadowy, evanescent image of Anna Quentin. The folly of pursuing his illusions ("I could now have caught her easily. But something made me pause.") is brought home to him only in Chapter XV, when he follows Anna through the streets and parks of Paris only to lose her near an avenue of trees ("Every tree had blossomed with a murmuring pair and every vista mocked me with a stone figure.").

Iris Murdoch's artistic execution of life's dialectic in *Under the Net* may be relentless, but her unflagging patience often rankles. The loose thematic strands that she expects the reader to join are often buried in the coils of new events and developments. The organization of *Under the Net,* perhaps more than any other feature of the novel, demonstrates overtly the truth that good philosophy is not always identical with good fiction.

The plateau reached in Chapter XVI is effected simply and directly. After nearly a week of convalescence following his exertions in Paris, Jake pauses before the hospital situated across from Dave Gellman's flat. "I stood for a while watching the cars coming and going in the square courtyard in front of the main entrance. Then I crossed the road and went in and asked for a job." It is significant that the business arrangement is reported in the most businesslike manner available; we are not even shown Jake being interviewed—a development that, incidentally, would have necessitated the introduction of another character into the novel. The hospital orderly job is Jake's first in spite of his thirty-odd years, but because of it he gains a sense of proportion and vocation that he retains and builds on in later sections of the novel:

> At some time in the future, I decided, I would arrange to work, whether here or elsewhere, only half-time. Then in the other half of the day I might do some writing. It occurred to me that to spend half the day doing manual work might be very calming to the nerves of one who was spending the other half doing intellectual work.

Although Hugo's entry as a patient into the hospital (Chapter XVII) dissolves Jake's prospects of converting his ambitions to acts, his dedication remains with him, gaining final expression in the last chapter (XX), where he discovers his vocation as a writer. Iris Murdoch does not delineate the relation between Jake's prior experiences and his final vision of himself as a literary artist. Her message is that life establishes its own incommunicable dialectic, from which we can emerge with a fresh understanding.

Under the Net begins with a premonition that something has gone wrong and ends with a miracle. Jake, observing Mrs. Tinck's two pure Siamese kittens and two tabbies, cannot explain why they do not share equally the inherited physical traits of their parents: " 'I don't know why it is,' I said. 'It's just one of the wonders of the world.' " In its profoundest phases, life defies analysis; Jake's erratic progress concludes with the realization of this truly creative principle. His own life up to this point had been a chronicle of failures, sorrows, and needless expenditures of effort, all arising from his inability to recognize the temporality of things and the multiplicity of awarenesses in the world. As the novel's epigraph, extracted from Dryden's "The Secular Masque," recommends, once the mistakes of the past are unveiled, we must establish a new beginning. Jake's new beginning is celebrated first by *The Silencer,* the product of Jake's first hospital association with Hugo, and next by *Under the Net,* the result of their second accidental meeting in a hospital. The lesson of both books is the linguistic and fictional difficulty of transcribing reality with depth and honesty. *Under the Net* represents a humanistic advance upon the earlier work by projecting its philosophical message against the interplay of contingent human life. The result, an inevitable corollary of man's imperfection, is the new humanistic-aesthetic concept that our subjective apprehension of the world has no bearing upon it; reality remains untouched by our efforts to structure or explain it.

Jake is Iris Murdoch's persona in the novel, but he does stand forth, nonetheless, as a character in his own right. Although his development represents a conscious working out of her philosophical views, she both treats him critically and allows him to take charge of the action; it is through him, as the semideluded narrator and densely involved participator—two solid Jamesian devices—that she makes some of her most telling comments about the estate of modern man. O'Connor has related the novel's light-and-dark imagery and the uncertain, mournful atmosphere it generates to this very problem:

> *Under the Net* introduces a half-world of writers and actors and left-wingers who are out of touch with the mores of both the lower classes and the middle classes. The characters come alive or pursue their dreams most ardently when twilight falls, or most soulfully when the dawn is breaking. There is something touching and pathetic about their lostness.[13]

Jake himself is the same kind of social anomaly as Larkin's John Kemp (*Jill*), Amis's Jim Dixon, Wain's Charles Lumley (*Hurry on Down*), and Osborne's scowling Jimmy Porter.[14] These products of the Butler Act have been given the educational opportunities to become different from their neighbors and their fathers, but their academic training has not helped them to form relationships outside their social class. As a social interloper, Jake is extremely self-conscious and is often unstrung by the imagined presence of disembodied eyes scrutinizing him. He is forced, as is Büchner's Wozzek, to hire himself out for medical experiments, submitting to cold toxin and vaccine. A reader of Beckett's *Murphy* and Raymond Queneau's *Pierrot Mon Ami,* Jake resembles the pathetic central figures of these works. He is foolish and naïve, a chronic harlequin figure chagrined by unrequited love. As with Murphy and his rocking chair and Molloy and his sucking-stone, Jake attaches great significance to ludicrous acts or preoccupations; he is completely engrossed by the worthless project of removing Mars's cage from Sammy's apartment, and for no discernible reason finds himself, as has been stated, convulsed with the desire to be with Anna or Hugo at unpredictable moments. Jake's Sherlockian knowledge of a ruined London and his readiness to expend more energy avoiding a regular job than most jobs would demand testify further to his comic homelessness.

Yet, in spite of his ludicrous behavior, Jake is mentally free, a buffoon and a failure whose stubborn naïvete imparts to him an obscure dignity. As does Murphy, sitting naked in his rocking chair, Jake, squatting cross-legged, reflects some of the vague, mysterious splendor of an Eastern idol. And although he is lazy and parasitic, he does seize opportunities when they are available. The one important occasion that he shuns, Madge's offer, grates against his instincts; contrary to Hugo, who censures him for trying to interpret life sympathetically instead of objectively, Jake proves that his impulses can be reliable. His volatile personality figures largely in his development as a creative artist; after accompanying him on his irresponsible excursions through two cities, the reader is neither surprised nor offended by his moral growth. It is natural to Jake, as well, to indulge his fantasies about Anna and Hugo even after Hugo shatters them. Surrendering to a different version of life's inevitable dialectic, Jake's breaking into Hugo's safe to find Anna's love letters represents a final, gratuitous farewell to the life of chimera.

Early in the novel Jake says, "I hate contingency. I want everything in my life to have a sufficient reason." His parody of Leibniz can be interpreted as a desire to reduce experience to an identity statement. The understanding he gains at the end of the novel both repudiates this earlier wish and guarantees a mode of emotional response that will objectify his feelings. His development has reached the point at which his emotions will be specifically directed to the events and people he had previously seen as projections of his understanding and of his private fantasies. The critics have unanimously agreed in their interpretations of Jake's final revelation as a decisive advance from his earlier logical positivism. Bradbury's remarks about the novel's closing pages will serve as our representative example:

   In particular, two things have altered for the better: he [Jake] has developed from being a literary hack, a man who sees words and things as separate things, to being creative in his own right; and he has developed from having "shattered nerves" to being able to encounter life and loneliness.[15]

Under the Net constitutes Iris Murdoch's dedication to literary art as well as Jake Donaghue's. The two figures coalesce in subtle but identifiable thematic motifs. Jake's friends find anti-Semitism in his unfinished epic poem *And Mr. Oppenheim Shall Inherit the Earth;* his rejoinder is that Oppenheim symbolizes Big Business rather than Judaism; accordingly, Iris Murdoch's first ambitious imaginative work contains an American film mogul named H. K. Pringsheim. She invites the reader to draw the same kind of analogy through her manipulation of the Prometheus myth. By using Hugo Belfounder's ideas, Jake, in a way, "steals" a book from him (*The Silencer*); Sadie and Sammy literally do steal Jake's translation; Jean Pierre Breteuil, who proves himself to be a distinguished novelist, steals *Nous les Vainqueurs* from the gods. This thematic repetition, however muted, when combined with the novel's critique of linguistic analysis, invites the reader to posit the same kind of Promethean relationship between Iris Murdoch and Wittgenstein. This idea is underscored by other Joycean elements in the novel. Jake's wanderings through London and Paris, no less than those of Stephen Dedalus through Dublin, prove to be a symbolic escape from a labyrinth ("Finn and I lived on the fourth floor in a maze of attics"); Jake's vision at Mrs. Tinck's—the reproductive habits of her cats suggest life as adequately as the Irish Sea—corresponds roughly to Stephen's epiphany. The first halves of both *A Portrait* and *Under the Net* contain a formal religious ritual, and Jake follows Stephen's examples of eschewing political associations and repudiating father-surrogates. In keeping with Iris Murdoch's belief that today's world is much more complex than Joyce's was at the turn of the century, the epiphany symbolically prepared for in Chapter VIII does not take place until Chapter XX. Lefty Todd's social awareness is still the vital ingredient of Jake's revelation, but it is as a writer, and not as a politician, that Jake will employ his creative talents.

Under the Net is an impressive first novel. Jacques Souvage's objection to the novel, however, is worth considering as an aid in isolating its serious shortcomings. Souvage complains that *"Under the Net* combines elements of the *picaresque novel* and of the *Bildungsroman* without succeeding in blending them."* And although he calls the Jake-Hugo-Quentin sisters relationship "profound," "three-dimensional," and "the emotional and spiritual core of *Under the Net,"*[16] it is precisely this element that flaws the novel's quality and indirectly accounts for most of its other faults. In that Anna and Sadie each make only one brief appearance, they cannot sustain much narrative weight. The psychological impact they have on Jake is largely unaccounted for dramatically and presented with little scenic depth. In her apprenticeship, Iris Murdoch was not able to infuse the first-person narrative with the energy and the suppleness to create convincing emotional relationships. The shifting-point-of-view technique seems to be a more congenial method and one more clearly in line with her central tenets. Another improvement in the later works is her acquired talent for representing life as transient and unstable without including such an abundance of physical motion. She is not at her best when tracing the erratic progress of social vagabonds. Her Jake Donaghue, as well, presents special problems as a picaresque hero: he must be reflective in order for his awareness to be personally significant; on the other hand, to guard against the novel's slackening in pace, he must be physically nimble and restless. It is surprising that the problems of character representation that Iris Murdoch faced with Jake did not destroy the entire effect of the novel.

The strong satirical interest and wide social sweep generally associated with the picaresque novel demand that the hero be roguish and cunning, but not meditative. If he reflects deeply, narrative movement is choked and the social panorama diminished and blurred. Jake's defect is that he is simply not rascal enough. Iris Murdoch has to strain to make his reckless conduct convincing and true to character. His interests in judo and in swimming are more intellectual than recreational. Elsewhere, the reader is driven to question whether someone of Jake's theoretical training is behaving naturally when he acts so irrationally. This discomfort is embarrassingly conspicuous in Jake's manner of addressing the reader. Jake occasionally employs a philosophical trope originally and humorously:

> I pictured Jean Pierre with his plump hands and his short grey
> hair. How could I introduce into this picture, which I had known

so long, the notion of a good novelist. It wrenched me, like the changing of a fundamental category.

Often, however, Jake's attempts at humor are maladroit: "Perhaps she smokes all night, or perhaps there is an undying cigarette which burns eternally in her bedroom." "I began to have the feeling of responsibility again. After all, she had no father, and I felt *in loco parentis*. It was about the only locus I had left." Furthermore, there seems to be no thematic justification for Jake's self-dramatizing poses. Passages like the following could have been deleted had Iris Murdoch been able to diffuse more evenly their emotional equivalents into the action through character interplay, indirect statement, or symbolism—three devices she skillfully employs in her later fiction:

> My appetite for Hugo's conversation was not blunted. There might be more speech between us yet. Was it this then that made me seek him with such a feverish urgency? It seemed to me that after all I wanted to see him because I wanted to see him. The bullfighter in the ring cannot explain why it is that he wants to touch the bull. Hugo was my destiny.

These flaws do not make *Under the Net* a stylistic misfire. Iris Murdoch's attempts to endow her narrator with a dense, many-faceted personality creates stylistic problems that a more experienced novelist writing from the first person could have avoided. The novel's style is uneven, to be sure, but its virtues are as striking as its faults. Iris Murdoch captures through language some of the mysterious, sensory qualities of Mrs. Tinck's cats ("An ever-increasing family of tabbies . . . somnolent and contemplative, their amber eyes narrowed and winking in the sun, a reluctant slit of liquid in an expanse of hot fur.") and, by a bolder use of assonance, those of Mars the Alsatian ("I received the enormous warm sleek beast into my arms"). She also employs traditional imagery in surprising ways; while Finn and Jake are kidnaping Mars, it is Finn's eyes and not those of the dog that are described as "growing as round as saucers." And, despite the lack of artistic finish and depth in her portrayal of Sammy Starfield, she acquits herself to some extent by suggesting the character of her ambiguous, semiunderworld figure through original, but decidedly characteristic speech habits:

> "I suggest," I said, "that you tell we a winner in the three o'clock race, and that you phone the bet for me to your own firm or wherever you keep your betting account. . . ."

Sammy was overjoyed. "Done!" he said. "What a sportsman! But we'll make a sight more than fifty pounds. I know to-day's card like my own daughter. It's a poem."

It is noteworthy that *Under the Net*'s stylistic merits appear in places where the author is least conscious of Jake as a narrator. Her uneasiness with him, as we have seen, accounts for most of the novel's blemishes. The book's aesthetic and, at the same time, humanistic scopes justify soundly, however, the inauguration of Iris Murdoch's career as a novelist. After finishing the book, the reader is convinced of her faith in fiction as a reliable description of social morality. Without enlisting social or supernatural manifestoes, she transforms her paradoxes into socially tenable principles. If *Under the Net* blunders as literary art, it is a distinguished blunder, the imperfect product of an apprentice's zeal. Without excusing its dramatic omissions and occasional clumsiness, we are forced to acknowledge its richness of idea and the boldness with which Iris Murdoch projects philosophical weight upon the novel's slender picaresque frame. It is not until *A Severed Head* that she returns, as a more adroit professional, to the first-person narrative. *The Flight from the Enchanter*, *The Sandcastle*, and *The Bell* put forth many of the ideas first presented in *Under the Net*, but more evenly and through more lucid psychological interpenetration. *Under the Net* can, however, claim originality and merit on its own behalf. Its coherence of form and over-all meaning and the frankness with which it represents man's ambiguity make the novel a secure mythological statement of idea. Where it fails in dramatic execution, it compensates in some measure by its sincerity and by the humanistic depth of its single predominant message.

Notes to Chapter Three

1. John Barrows, "Living Writers—7: Iris Murdoch," *John O'London's*, 4 (4 May 1961), 498.

2. Murdoch, "Nostalgia for the Particular," 254.

3. Iris Murdoch, "Mass, Might and Myth," *Spectator* (7 September 1962), 337.

4. Carl G[ustav]. Jung, "Synchronicity: An Acausal Connecting Principle,"

The Structure and Dynamics of the Psyche, trans. by R. F. C. Hull (New York, 1960), 419.

5. Douglas Hewitt, *Conrad: A Reassessment* (London, 1952), 132.

6. Kermode, 65.

7. Malcolm Bradbury, "Iris Murdoch's *Under the Net,*" *The Critical Quarterly,* 4 (Spring, 1962), 48-49.

8. Schopenhauer introduced this logical method in *The Four Fold Root of Sufficient Reason,* first published in 1813.

9. Micha, 291.

10. Fraser, 38.

11. O'Sullivan, 28.

12. Hazel E. Barnes, *Humanistic Existentialism: The Literature of Possibility* (Lincoln, Nebraska, 1959), 30-31.

13. William Van O'Connor, *The New University Wits and the End of Modernism* (Carbondale, Illinois, 1963), 70.

14. Gindin, 87-108.

15. Bradbury, 48.

16. Jacques Souvage, "The Unresolved Tension: An Interpretation of Iris Murdoch's *Under the Net,*" *Revue des langues vivantes,* 26 (1960), 426-27.

Four

THE FLIGHT FROM THE ENCHANTER

The Fragmentation and Fusion of Society

T HE THEME OF *The Flight from the Enchanter,* as of *Under the Net,* is human freedom and the obstacles we must overcome in order to be free. Once again, freedom is depicted as an active process of becoming and as an intensely private responsibility with public ramifications. Although Iris Murdoch's argument is basically the same in her first two novels, the terms and the method differ radically in each. Where *Under the Net* traced the dangers of subscribing to various mental categories or prejudices, *The Flight from the Enchanter* studies the social dangers that curtail our freedom. *The Flight from the Enchanter* coincides in several important respects with Edwin Muir's formula for the novel of character:[1] the figures do not develop appreciably; there is a good deal of movement and scene-shifting, ultimately intelligible as social criticism, within a loose plot; and the plot itself, finally, is subservient to the characters. Iris Murdoch's withdrawal from the first-person narrative produces in *The Flight from the Enchanter* a richer and broader social panorama that is less immediately reducible to her commanding philosophical interest. As the novel becomes more artfully rendered, abiding moral concerns are diffused into closely observed character interaction, story movement, and thematic congruity. By dramatizing its basic message through many points of view instead of merely one, *The Flight from the Enchanter* conveys a denser social reality than its predecessor and a more incisive penetration of human psychology in its various phases.

The Flight from the Enchanter presents a social and a vocational map of modern London; we meet and become acquainted with public administrators, magazine editors, factory laborers, carefree international society people, and harried refugees from Iron Curtain persecution; professional interests range from ancient history and the deciphering of Mongolian scripts to dressmaking. What all the characters share in common is the quality of innocence and a sense of moral fragmentation that would disturb them more were they armed with greater self-knowledge. Nothing is stable in Iris Murdoch's contemporary London—private relationships, institutions, and even physical landmarks are imperiled by mutilation and extinction. John Rainborough's family garden and his position as a high-ranking civil administrator are no more secure than his volatile love affair with Agnes Casement. The Lusiewicz brothers, at first abject and submissive to Rosa Keepe, repay her affection by alternately seducing her and then by attempting to move into her home.

Iris Murdoch does not advocate an English aristocracy or a courtly medieval social order that exalts and enshrines women as semi-divine objects of self-deprecating masculine love. Her interest is to show how thin, shadowy, and unprotected all contemporary modes of social life are. All of the characters in *The Flight from the Enchanter* are menaced, retaining their values and their self-dignity by pure chance or by the blundering caprice of others. Personal isolation is often so extreme that overt conflict is impossible. Nina the dressmaker, for instance, dies because of the vagueness of her relationship to Mischa Fox:

> Nina had given up some time ago the attempt to define what her relation was to Mischa Fox. When Mischa had appeared in her life she could, from the first moment, have refused him nothing. . . . She was ready from the first to be his slave, though it never occurred to her to think that she might take more than a very minor part in his life. She had been prepared to be neglected and even in the end abandoned. She had not been prepared for the curious role which she found herself in fact forced to play.

Mischa pays Nina's rent and supplies her with a generous monthly allowance; the demands he makes upon her in return are not, to all appearances, heavy. Nina is expected only to accommodate his friends and make herself available to him at rare intervals. This regimen, however, deprives her of a private life and of the opportunity to be vocationally self-sustaining. The image that Iris Murdoch uses to characterize Nina's dressmaking shop is the Dantesque forest. Accordingly, Nina's fears are nonspecific and hallucinatory. Her chaste, obscure imprisonment in her top-story tower contrasts stridently with Rosa's brief period of raw physical captivity by the Poles. But, while Rosa can overcome the Poles, the sporadic random nature of Nina's quasi-romantic arrangement with Mischa drives the dressmaker to suicide. Whereas Nina could have parried or even absorbed Mischa's open hostility, she cannot defend herself against his indefinable, yet insistent remoteness.

The radical disjuncture between people is underscored in a brief episode that describes Nina unsuccessfully trying to get Rosa's attention as they walk toward Kensington; instead of noting the urgency of Nina's entreaties, Rosa salutes the wealthy dowager Ada Carrington-Morris without being recognized or acknowledged herself. Our humane principles, which we jealously adhere to in theory, are easily nullified when they run counter to matters of personal convenience. If our age is beset by moral loneliness, Iris Murdoch insists that we, as individuals, are often culpable. Our lack of openness to the being of other people is creating a social order in which we are not safe from the will or the apathy of our fellows.

O'Connor states that *The Flight from the Enchanter* makes sense only as allegory.[2] Mischa Fox's appetite for power does admittedly embrace nearly all of society, but this theme is more immediate and urgent than allegorical. Another argument against O'Connor's inference that the characters in the novel personify abstract ideas is the psychological penetration afforded by the shifting- (here, freely shifting) point-of-view technique. All novels that have a wide social sweep and at the same time depict the discovery of freedom by several individuals (*U.S.A., Orient Express, The Alexandria Quartet*) consider a diversity of characters who can be explained as representative. O'Connor's observation that *The Flight from the Enchanter* contains a multiplicity of characters with discernible values does not prove that the novel is an allegory. Each character is seen in depth, even though the depth is not uniform, and each suffers physical pain as well as mental anguish in his halting, often self-defeating gestures toward freedom and integrity. These voyages of self-discovery, whether consciously or unconsciously waged, are not quiescent mental operations; one's entire being is engaged in the struggle. The frustration of Nina gathers to paroxysms of grief, and Hunter departs bruised and burned from his confrontations with Calvin Blick and Stefan Lusiewicz.

The theme of personal freedom is stated in the novel's opening paragraph as Annette Cockeyne decides, during an Italian lesson, to leave Ringenhall's Ladies' College in favor of educating herself independently. To celebrate her resignation from Ringenhall, Annette performs the defiant, heedless acts of swinging from the dining-room chandelier and stealing a book from the school library. Although Iris Murdoch's tone and attitude are affectionately comic, she nonetheless emphasizes Annette's buoyant solipsism at this stage in her development. Nor can Annette boast of moral growth after her entry into the School of Life:

> She stood there in the silence until it began to look to her like a library in a sacked city. No one owned these books now. No one would come here again; only after a while the wall would crumble down and the rain would come blowing in. It occurred to Annette that she might as well take away one or two books as souvenirs.

> * * *

> There was no feeling Annette liked so much as the feeling that someone else was making or doing something for her the fruit of which she would soon enjoy. This feeling was perhaps for her the essence of freedom.

Appropriately, Miss Walpole, the headmistress, orders Annette down from the chandelier and reclaims for the library the book Annette, in her euphoria, had stolen.

The passage from the *Inferno* that the Italian class had been studying when Annette decided to leave school is equally suggestive. She pities the Minotaur, which Virgil and Dante address and allude to so scornfully in the twelfth canto. As half man and half beast, the Minotaur symbolizes human reason perverted by bestiality; this state of being is most closely approximated in the novel by Mischa Fox, whose name implies both elements and to whom Annette gravitates through the maze of contemporary London. Mischa's huge Kensington house is also called a maze.

Perhaps Iris Murdoch weights her characterization of Annette with too many symbolic accoutrements: her dominant guise is that of a mermaid; she sees Mischa for the first time while she is trying on the elegantly seductive dress she later wears to his party; struggling with Rainborough, her body exposed above the waist, she reminds him of a fish; and Rosa tells Annette that she looks like a mermaid. Gindin offers an explanation of this symbolism in the novel: "In *The Flight from the Enchanter* . . . references to fish are often indications of the natural forces man tries to capture, possess, construct."[3] Another possible meaning, as has been stated,[4] is the standard Christian symbolic interpretation of fish. Denoting baptism and Christ Himself, fish are readily reassignable as symbols of man's transcendence and of the sacredness of his person. The panoply of whirling colors associated with Annette, namely her petticoats and her collection of unset precious jewels, augments, however gratuitously, Iris Murdoch's portrait of her as an exuberant, somewhat pampered sprite whose graceful innocence and aplomb cannot be expected to survive intact in the modern world.

Relying on her own resources, Annette nearly perishes of foolishness; she can take no credit for mistaking Rosa's milk-of-magnesia tablets for sleeping pills. Her staging of her suicide as a party reveals that Rosa's cruelty, Mischa's contemptuous aloofness, and her brother Nick's inflated self-importance have taught her little about her moral estrangement. That she does not even bear a scar of her leg injury is more a matter of luck than of her own conscious efforts; no less than Nina the dressmaker, she is driven to the nadir of loneliness and self-despair. We see Annette at the end of the novel stroking her uplifted legs above a polychromatic rustle of petticoats; her earlier fascination with her body has not ripened into a selfless apprehension of life's diversity. The only gem surviving from her jewel collection is the white sapphire, which perhaps forecasts a clearer, more incisive moral vision. In any case, she has not yet attained a fresh understanding of reality. Her experiences will serve only as stories to tell Nick, which he will neither listen to carefully nor believe, because of his own self-absorption.

The idle luxury of the wealthy, international Cockeyne family recalls the legendary utopia of the English medieval satire, *The Land of Cockaygne*. But although the carefree, lavish life of Annette and her family does ridicule the struggles of the British middle class in its various guises, the charming opulence of the Cockeynes would not suffice normally to shield them from the indifference and the selfishness of others. It is suitably ironical that the volume that Annette tries to steal from Ringenhall's library is Browning's *Collected Poems*. As the poet of joy and vigorous achievement, Browning's literary career advanced from self-absorbed introspection (*Sordello*) to highly dramatic psychological monologues (*The Ring and the Book*). Fra Lippo Lippi's objections to the one-dimensional techniques of medieval painting derive from Browning's view of spiritual growth as the product of a selfless, loving immersion in sensory life. Annette is certainly enthralled by the objects of sense perception, but, unlike Browning or Iris Murdoch, she is still too immature to translate them into a sustaining metaphysic.

John Rainborough, another figure from the upper classes, fares less well than Annette. Representing the obsolete, exhausted elements of modern British society, this relic of Edwardianism finds himself rebuffed at every turn. Rainborough, although independently wealthy, has been working for years as a comfortably high-ranking official in the Civil Service. But a shift in bureaucratic policy sends him from the drowsy feudal security of the Home Office to the newly created Special European Labor Immigration Board (SELIB), where he is beset by streamlined operational concepts, inefficiency, and a mysterious system of promotions. Instead of having trained men with university educations as his colleagues, Rainborough is surrounded by predatory young women who have elevated themselves from the position of secretary to that of Organizing Officer.

Personally, Rainborough is tactless and devoid of self-control. His goal is self-knowledge, but in spite of his moments of insight and illumination he cannot act. Meditating upon his engagement to Agnes Casement, he tries to convince himself that his decision to marry her is the right one:

> Need ballast. All this wandering about no good. Must root myself in life. Children and so on. Marriage just what I need. Must have courage to define myself. Naturally, it's painful. But best thing really. That's my road, I knew it all along.

Not only is Rainborough unable to face his rationally justified emotional commitment, but he allows Marcia Cockeyne to perform the duty of ending his engagement to Agnes. The conversion of moral principles to conduct seems to be a challenge in which Rainborough, like so many of the other characters in the novel, is unable to acquit himself honorably. Although he understands Mischa Fox and Calvin

Blick more intelligently, perhaps, than any of the others—most of the
exposition concerning them is presented by Rainborough in dialogue—
his transparency makes him their easy victim.

For years his refuge from the outside world, even his stately family
home near Eaton Square is threatened; the adjacent hospital—
symbolic of a lean, hard, utilitarian practicality—plans to tear down
his garden wall and uproot the ancestral wisteria tree, a traditional
emblem of gentleness and devotion,[5] in order to make room for a new
X-ray department. (Is Mischa a member of the hospital's Board of
Directors?) Morally inert, Rainborough is like a vacuum; others
perpetually call upon him uninvited, and Agnes Casement exercises
her professional and matrimonial ambitions with astonishing speed
at his expense. (Her name suggests an outlet to new experience.)
Her unauthorized report to the Director of SELIB and her request
that Rainborough accompany her to Mischa's party soon thrust
her to the center of Rainborough's troubled mentality. In a scene
symbolizing his helpless frustration and the inevitability of his reluctant attachment to Agnes, Rainborough asks her to help him pull
the storied wisteria out of the ground. In spite of himself, he finds
that he is forcibly united with her in an act that both celebrates the
destruction of a tidy, orderly past and augurs a chaotic future of
shocks and surprises:

> He stood with Miss Casement, their feet deep in the earth, and
> side by side they began to pull. Rainborough inhaled a powerful
> smell of soil and Bond Street perfume. His bared left arm was
> braced against the tweedy sleeve of her coat, and their shoulders
> were glued together. . . . Then suddenly with a rending sound the
> trunk gave way and the great fan of branches came heeling over
> away from the wall. Rainborough and Miss Casement fell sharply
> backwards into a heap of unturned earth and uprooted flowers, and
> a great network of tiny leaves and twisted branches subsided to
> cover them.

The demolition of the garden wall, Rainborough's short-lived
engagement, and his resignation from public administration occur
practically simultaneously. And despite Agnes Casement's ability to
act quickly and take chances, she, too, becomes a victim of Rainborough's timorous inertia. His brief association with the aggressively
chic Marcia Cockeyne exposes the natural shortcomings of this
energetic civil servant from the middle class:

> After the harsh sweetness which emanated from Miss Casement . . .
> the scent of Marcia was a celestial subtlety. . . . It occurred to
> him suddenly that the whole extraordinary ensemble of powder, per-
> fume and paint which gave so artificial a surface to Miss Casement
> lay upon Marcia as a natural bloom.

As a woman screened from him by marriage, Marcia Cockeyne is
a suitable object of Rainborough's romantic contemplation. He up-
roots the wisteria, tramples his flower bed, and kills the moth that
Mischa had permitted to escape, but he cannot act constructively.
Most of his observations are rational, generalized, and directed to
himself. His theory of love is abstract and void of other-regarding
sentiments. Fascinated with Agnes Casement at a distance, he can
think of her only as "Miss Casement." He is too self-absorbed to
admit her into his life other than as a disembodied fantasy conform-
ing to his private conception of romantic love:

> Rainborough was not averse to being unhappily in love; indeed, an
> arrangement of this kind would have suited him very well. . . . As
> a lonely and unfortunate admirer Rainborough could, he thought,
> have found in the tension of such a relationship a mode of being
> both apart from and together with the beloved: such a combination,
> in short, of security, yearning, and rapture, as had now become his
> ideal conception of partnership with a woman.

Finite reality, as Iris Murdoch interprets it, is a reversible flow.
Seen at the end of the novel as a moral void, Rainborough is able
only to escape from life or destroy it. Because Miss Casement explodes into his life as a forcible presence and not as a dim extension
of his private love allegory, he flees from her. His fear of measureless, disorderly attachments renders anyone linked with him romanti-
cally as vulnerable to sorrow as he himself; ironically, his failure to
meet adversity or inconvenience makes him as much an agent of
destruction as the notorious Mischa.

Although Rainborough becomes a power of evil by default, his
manner and outward bearing are certainly pleasant; the reader confronts him always with a tolerant, bemused attitude. Rainborough
is a witty, somewhat pathetic character who gets what he deserves,
but the reader is never greatly moved by his farcical gestures to
loose himself from difficult situations.

Evil does not wear its traditional masks in the fiction of Iris
Murdoch. Her "villains" all suffer and frequently damage others
without being aware of the implications of their acts. Her definition

of sin revolves around the failure to see the needs and desires of others as vividly as one's own. Like Sartre, she is distrustful of motives and is especially suspicious of moral absolutes or imperatives. The particularity of each situation in our unsponsored world gives rise to its own morality. The specific actions that grow out of both Rainborough's self-deception and the heartiness of the Lusiewicz brothers reveal that these men have offended the freedom and dignity of others. Both Agnes Casement and Rosa Keepe suffer because of their associations with Rainborough and the Poles. Ironically, Rainborough, at least, has not deliberately interfered with Miss Casement's independence. A person must interact with others in order to gain the wisdom that comes only from an objective understanding of reality. The social requirement that Rainborough and the brothers violate is the need to conduct one's relationships without the barriers of theory, dogma, or personal comfort.

Regardless of motives, Iris Murdoch seems to think that all of us are well equipped to cause others great pain. As individuals, Stefan and Jan are attractive, talented, and ebullient. They have won the affection of their fellow workers at the factory, and their primitive Slavonic mystique suggests unexplored layers of creativity:

> The brothers had meanwhile been achieving a startling degree of success. They had both had some training in engineering before they arrived and they rapidly showed a remarkable aptitude with machines. They learnt to speak English with confidence and charm. . . . Their appearance improved. . . . At the factory, their beauty, their awkward English, which they soon learnt to make into an instrument of seduction, and their curious resemblance to each other soon commended them to the women. . . . To the men, their mechanical skill and willingness to learn soon commended them just sufficiently to compensate for the irritations caused by their success with the women. They became popular.

*   *   *

> It gave her [Rosa] a particular joy to teach them English. . . . As her pair of princes awoke into the English tongue and as they were able more and more to reveal themselves to her, she found in them a hundred-fold the intelligence, the humour and the joy at which she had at first only guessed.

*   *   *

> On most evenings when they met, one or other of the brothers would tell a story about Poland. The stories would always begin with the words. "In our village . . ." Rosa never tired of hearing

these stories. What they conjured up for her was something very remote yet crystal clear, like a vision procured in a fairy-tale.

Despite her awkward relationship with the brothers, Rosa is unwilling to give them up. Representing the coltish heroic ardor of an innocent mythical utopia, they refresh and enrapture us in the same way as they do her. The following idea is drastically overstated, but it contains enough truth to convey the difficulty of framing accurate judgments about the Poles:

> The Poles are magnificent creations . . . they are presented with verve, we respond clearly and strongly to them, and the author's sheer pace overrides any objections we might want to make. By a violent but acceptable transition we pass from finding them as harmless and lovable as Rosa did, to feeling them dangerous, cruel and hateful. . . . But they are simple. Being uncivilized, they are not warped. They are so directly and basely self-seeking that in a law-abiding community, with an adequate police force, ordinary people need not fall foul of them, and people who fall in with their wishes can gain from contact with their beauty and vitality.[6]

Allsop is correct when he states that Mischa Fox is the enchanter or devil of the title, *The Flight from the Enchanter*.[7] To justify and partially to qualify Allsop's interpretation, it is important to understand the operation of Mischa's mind and to assess his place in the novel's social milieu. The celebrated owner of several newspapers and magazines, Mischa, personally, is a figure of mystery. As he explains to Annette Cockeyne, he is famous for nothing in particular; he is merely famous. Like that of the redoubtable Professor Moriarty, Mischa's face and his specific business transactions remain largely out of direct view; Mischa is seen either at a distance or with his face partially obscured by shadows, and although we know that his influence in Parliament causes the deportation of Stefan Lusiewicz we are never told precisely how. Mischa descends from the literary tradition established by Robert Sherwood's Achilles Weber of *Idiot's Delight*, Greene's Sir Marcus of *This Gun for Hire*, and Powell's Sir Magnus Donners. The origin of each of these financial moguls is unknown, available information about them is widely contradictory, and their names do not appear in places like *Who's Who*, trade magazines, or business registers. The aura of mystery that screens Mischa from even his closest associates is best summarized by Rainborough:

> "Who knows?" said Rainborough. "No one knows Mischa's age. One can hardly even make a guess. It's uncanny. He could be

thirty, he could be fifty-five. Have you ever met anyone who knew . . . ? No one knows where he came from either. Where was he born? What blood is in his veins? No one knows. And if you try to imagine you are paralysed. It's like that thing with his eyes. You can't look into his eyes. You have to look *at* his eyes. Heaven knows what you'd see if you looked in."

Like Fellini and Antonioni, Iris Murdoch is interested in capturing the psychic reality and moral substance of notable public celebrities. Sammy Starfield, in this respect, is a preliminary exercise for her fuller characterization of Mischa. As a social novelist, she finds no observable link between inner strength and rectitude of conviction, on the one hand, and personal power, on the other. R. J. Kaufmann furnishes some sound premises concerning Mischa's perplexing character:

> Like many people who assiduously seek power, he seems not so much to want everything as to leave nothing free that he might want. . . . Along the way, he casually wrecks a bunch of lives, remotely occasions a suicide, and at the end rejects a penitent Rosa. Yet he seems passive and puzzlingly guiltless.[8]

There is no disputing Mischa's charm and appeal. His boyish, perhaps slightly feminine, habits and his apparent guilelessness are disarming in the same way as the lucid exuberance of Stefan and Jan. Iris Murdoch's argument is that evil can exert a fascination that easily overshadows ordinary virtue. Calvin Blick forces Hunter Keepe to pursue *him* through Kensington before unleashing his scheme to blackmail Hunter. And, at the end of their interview in the photography laboratory, Hunter is stunned into acquiescence while Calvin combs his hair and dries him with a towel. Nina's tragic problem is that she cannot endure waiting for Mischa's irregular visits and that she is also forbidden to arrange meetings herself. The object of her love, of Rainborough's aspirations to social prestige, and of Hunter Keepe's nascent homosexuality, Mischa occupies the most privileged and the most influential position in the novel. Most of the action and countermaneuvering can, in fact, be traced to his personal will. Rosa directs most of her ingenuity to the task of concealing from Mischa her relationship with the Poles; ironically, he probably paid them to seduce her in the first place and certainly knew about the relationship well before Rosa began to think of protecting herself from them.

Perhaps the most trenchant irony in *The Flight from the Enchanter* is that, if all the characters derive their social identity ultimately from Mischa, they are all potential slaves to his commanding neurosis. The motive force behind all of his conscious acts is a terrified pity for the finite world. Mischa unconsciously transforms his obsessive compassion for the fragility and evanescence of contingent life into sadistic cruelty. His outward display of mildness and affectionate charity is a ruse for his frankly morbid psychic impulses;

> "Someone gave me a little kitten once," he said, "and I killed it. I remember. . . ."
>
> *   *   *
>
> "So poor and defenceless," Mischa murmured. "That was the only way to help it, to save it. So it is. If the gods kill us, it is not for their sport but because we fill them with such an intolerable compassion, a sort of nausea. Do you ever feel . . . as if everything in the world needed your—protection? It is a terrible feeling."

Mischa is unable to establish a balanced, candid relationship based on a respectful mutuality. The first statement we hear him make in private conversation is an expression of sorrow at seeing a one-footed bird. It is, moreover, partially because the *Artemis,* a small independent magazine, is so helpless and forlorn that he covets it. In a very rich scene, Mischa explains *his* philosophy of love to Rainborough; curiously, this self-disclosure of the novel's guiding spirit is stated in a situation in which it appears secondary, as the reader and Rainborough are both absorbed with the presence of Annette in Rainborough's china closet. Likening women to fish, Mischa ascribes to them a three-phase development. In the first, the young girl's passion for reforming men leads her to the most wicked, who is forced to demolish her; for every destroyer, Mischa insists, there is someone who courts destruction. The battered unicorn-girl then recovers from her bruises to become the siren and sets out to devastate men herself. If she can survive her own heart's destruction a second time and still have the capacity to love, she is a suitable life's mate.

The obstacles and degradations that Mischa throws in the path of Rosa Keepe indicate that he has precisely these plans for her. What he fails to see is that this kind of predatory arrangement will result either in further oppression or in hostile revolt. A relationship based on a tyrannical disregard of the other's independent dignity is bound to foster continued tyranny.

The moral absolutism that Mischa arrogates to himself is reflected in the trappings of his huge residence. His ballroom is draped with tapestries depicting insects, birds, and animals. The only human beings in the *décor* appear together with animals in the netsuke atop Mischa's mantelpiece. Nowhere are people shown with other people. Mischa drives to the edge of the sea to release the melancholy that seizes him after Rosa smashes his aquarium. Annette, who accompanies him, is too naïve and untutored, however, to apprehend his posturing on the shingle as the silly, self-dramatizing gestures of a petulant, distorted spirit. Mischa, no less than his victims, is frail and haunted. But it is his refusal to overcome his neurosis that deprives all of the characters, including himself, of realizing their social responsibility as free, independent psychic units whose private acts constitute public morality.

Mischa's aide-de-camp Calvin Blick is called by Rainborough "the dark half of Mischa Fox's mind. . . . He does the things which Mischa doesn't even think of. That's how Mischa can be so innocent." Blick, as his name suggests, is associated with the photography equipment in Mischa's basement, and he certainly qualifies as an enchanter in his own right. Without compunction, he schemes to intimidate Rosa with the same story in reverse that he had used to blackmail her brother. According to Olga McDonald Meidner, Iris Murdoch wanted to demonstrate, through Mischa and Calvin Blick, that any great social power is inescapably an agent of evil. Given the contagious nature of power (a theme to which Iris Murdoch returns in *The Unicorn*), the owner of a chain of newspapers will perform evil deeds in spite of himself.[9] Mischa's peculiar mentality, however, prompts him to recruit another for the practical execution of his will. What critics have overlooked is that without his employer Blick is powerless and nugatory; he is significant only because of Mischa's sanction and approval. The five-hundred-pound lens, which seems to symbolize Blick's uncanny knowledge of other people's private lives, is undoubtedly paid for by Mischa. Despite his wit and his theatrical ingenuity, Blick is merely a retainer; Iris Murdoch conveys his submissive fealty to Mischa in the symbolic terms of Mischa's obsession:

> Calvin poured himself out a cupful of warm milk and drank it solemnly, mouthing the liquid roundly, his tongue darting into it like a fish.
>
>   *   *   *
>
>   "I cannot think," [Rosa] said, "why Mischa has not killed you years ago."

"Mischa did kill me years ago," said Calvin in a soft voice.

O'Connor has accurately stated the central idea of *The Flight from the Enchanter*: "That no one, out of love or weakness, should submit to the will of another is the theme."[10] Iris Murdoch describes through the character of Mischa the danger of surrendering personal freedom to someone else. There is no clue to Mischa's megalomania in his social behavior; psychic disorders like his do not usually manifest themselves in polite repartee. The author uses the character of Peter Saward, the vocation-ridden scholar whom Mischa probably supports, to emphasize the self-defeating nature of Mischa's distorted psyche. Peter Saward's failure to stay abreast of his scholarly endeavors serves as an ironic comment on Mischa's attempts to classify and control people. If Peter Saward fails to execute his research in the relatively secure and static region of Eastern antiquity, Mischa's efforts to label and docket something as formless as contemporary society are doomed from the start.

With Fielding, Iris Murdoch believes that the world contains unpredictable elements of good and bad luck. For every Annette who perchance eludes her tormenter, a Nina will succumb to despair and suicide. Once we relinquish control of our private lives, our well-being is out of our hands; at this point we can no longer create our own opportunities but must rely upon dumb chance to extricate us from our problems. The novelist's endorsement of Guild Socialism's friendly attitude to private opinion springs from the lack of respect for personal dignity in our rigidly organized bureaucratic society. Having repudiated our autonomy as operating minds, the carefully synchronized schemes of a Mischa Fox can reduce us to parcels of matter. *The Flight from the Enchanter* is the only novel in which Iris Murdoch develops the socialism she advocates in "A House of Theory." It is not accidental that many of the characters in the book are mocked or morally embarrassed by machines. Rosa Keepe endows "Kitty," her machine at the paint-applicator factory, with a face and a mode of speech; the Poles' aptitude with machinery is parodied by their mechanical physical conquest of Rosa; the most attractive feature of Agnes Casement, according to Rainborough, is her new car: "What had really happened in that moment was that he had become engaged to Miss Casement's red M.G." By their power to dominate us, machines diminish our personal standing to the level of confused, whimpering animals; such is Hunter Keepe's condition after Calvin Blick shows him the photograph of Rosa embracing the Lusiewicz brothers. Iris Murdoch employs a mechanical figure of speech to report Hunter's defenselessness and Blick's ruthless efficiency in this scene:

> Like a flash and with the precision of a machine Calvin put out his foot, and as Hunter tripped he took his arm in a crushing grip and forced him to the floor.

It is nonetheless Hunter and his sister who manage to thwart the designs of Mischa Fox. Fraser complains that "there is nobody sane and ordinary in the book." None of Iris Murdoch's characters, he objects, can oppose Mischa's diabolism with morality in the familiar sense:

> What is wrong with the book, in the crowd of very strange characters who revolve around the sinister Mischa Fox, is, perhaps, precisely the lack of some representative of solid, conventional standards, some symbol of everyday acceptance or discontent. All the characters are surprisers; and a succession of surprises becomes numbing.[11]

Mrs. Meidner, likewise, calls Rosa and Hunter wicked and cowardly.[12] What she and Fraser fail to grasp is Iris Murdoch's prevailing view of the human estate as ambiguous and contradictory. Hunter Keepe *is* vain and ludicrous, but in spite of his faults he answers to responsibility. Mischa had endeavored to destroy Rosa's heart through the Lusiewicz brothers and the *Artemis;* that Hunter can somehow maintain the editorship of the journal until he is aided by an unwatched source, that is, the original founders, shows that Mischa can be resisted. Mischa's thwarted ambitions to own the *Artemis* have more significance as a human drama than as a business transaction. The only means we have to defend ourselves from oppression of any kind are equivocacy and ambiguity. Although he is humiliated by his oppressors, Hunter does acquit himself. Moral questions and relative areas of power are not so closely defined in Iris Murdoch's fictional world as Fraser and Mrs. Meidner would like. The two critics have also overlooked a consistency of method and attitude bodied forth in the novel. Often, as in the case of Annette, Rainborough, or Peter Saward, the antagonist can be the self. It is the absence of a material antagonist that erodes Nina's mind. Iris Murdoch has insisted in her fiction as well as in her polemical writings that our imperfection and psychical isolation engender a morality that can only be discontinuous and imperfect; as Descartes indicated in the Third Meditation, an effect cannot have more formal reality than its cause. If a source is corrupt, its products must also be corrupt.

Iris Murdoch's major exemplar and the character who most ably guards against the threat of her life chilling into nihilism is Rosa Keepe. O'Sullivan sees Rosa as "the intelligent sympathetic and rather bereft woman who exemplifies, perhaps, the fine point of the novel's moral consciousness, who is most deeply and awarely entangled by its complex action."[13] Her first name implies the revolutionary spirit inherited from her namesake, Rosa Luxemburg, another journalistic editor interested in the cause of the proletariat. Rosa's own social conscience produces effects nearly as damaging as those wrought on her German predecessor, who, in 1919, was murdered by soldiers for instigating street riots in Berlin. Rosa's job as a machine operator negates any ideals she may have had about the scouring purity of manual labor:

> She had come to the factory in a mood of self-conscious asceticism. Work had become for her something nauseating and contaminated, stained by surreptitious ambitions, frustrated wishes, and the competition and opinions of other people. She had wanted now at last to make of it something simple, hygienic, stream-lined, unpretentious and dull. She had succeeded to the point of almost boring herself to death.

Rosa's sojourn at the factory, moreover, makes her accessible to the Lusiewicz brothers, sours her temperament, and produces the sort of mechanical response to life most vulnerable to the wiles of Mischa Fox. Rosa occupies the medial point in the pecking order that is unconsciously but inevitably established by her predatory society. While she is the victim of the Poles and Mischa Fox, she is herself capable of great cruelty to Annette, Hunter, and Peter Saward. These three figures all confront her with emotional needs that Rosa willfully ignores. Her refusal to entertain Nina's pleas on the three occasions when the dressmaker visits Campden Hill Square calls to mind Peter's three-time denial of Christ (Mark 14: 66–72). As Calvin Blick points out, Rosa's friendly counsel could have prevented Nina's suicide.

It is understandable that readers may find Rosa an unattractive and, perhaps, totally unsympathetic character. She is, nonetheless, the "fierce Maenad" of Shelley's "Ode to the West Wind," whose long black hair becomes disheveled as she flees the enchanter. The stout middle-class tenacity implied by her surname gives both Hunter and her the ability to withstand Mischa better than some of the other people in the novel. Although Rosa is indifferent to the laments of Nina and Hunter, she does not allow herself to be dominated by Camilla Wingfield, Mischa, or the Poles. As do Jake Donaghue's, Rosa's instincts and intuition serve her well. Terrified at the prospect of framing conscious decisions, she sends Stefan from her home with a sharp slap and acts wisely by leaving Mischa's Italian villa at a moment when he is apparently about to renew his marriage proposal of a decade before. She is contradictory, impulsive, and usually reluctant to act. At the end of the novel, however, we feel that she has progressed morally. Her departure from Mischa convinces her that her decision to break with him ten years before was indisputably right. In itself this revelation is not impressive, especially when we recall the grief and vexation she has gratuitously undergone. But Rosa emerges armed with the knowledge that she is practically immune from any assaults Mischa might plan in the future. Her proposal of marriage to Peter Saward is impractical, but it is nonetheless a conscious resolve to legislate for herself.

If the Keepes have been abetted by luck to resist the fury of Mischa's sadism, they themselves instigated a good deal of it. Rosa contrives to assemble the founders of the *Artemis* at the annual editorial meeting in which Hunter plans to sell the magazine to Mischa. O'Connor has expressed the tensions resonating from this carefully constructed episode:

> Mischa Fox lives in an aura of mystery and grandeur, a symbol of knowingness and power. But the *Artemis* episode, with the old ladies gathering their forces to prevent the sale of the magazine, seems designed to show that his power can readily be resisted.[14]

The meeting is the most jocular scene in the novel. Iris Murdoch conveys hilariously the idea that unruly, disorderly life, in the persons of the now eccentric and infirm founders, can upset rigid mechanical efficiency. She uses stychomythia, a defective hearing aid, and champagne for "elevens" to help create confusion out of the elderly ladies' disjointed statements and questions. That the former suffragettes defeat Mischa without even being conscious of his motives suffuses the episode with a rich irony.

By refusing to secure all of her loose narrative strands in a neat packet of moral doctrine, Iris Murdoch shows that brawling, ambiguous life can defend itself; it is, in fact, the only armor available to us. Just as Rosa and Hunter are jeered and pilloried by Mischa's self-aggrandizing maneuvers, their fractious, impulsive behavior can thwart and injure him deeply. It is rumored that Mischa's parties are elaborately constructed machines (another example of the blighting machine image) designed to culminate in the social degradation of one of the invited guests. At a moment when Hunter thinks Calvin Blick about to publicize Rosa's relationship with the Lusiewicz brothers, he shouts to her to create a diversion. By chance, the paperweight she spontaneously throws across the room breaks Mischa's fish bowl and kills his obsessively cherished fish. Iris Murdoch dissipates Mischa's torment and loss into a description of the event that is both funny in itself and an assertion of our unavoidably comic expressions of personal freedom:

> The water spread in a great circle upon the floor, and within it the fragments of the paperweight were scattered like innumerable pieces of sugar cake. Suddenly fish seemed to be everywhere, gasping upon the carpet, clinging to the lampshades, sliding across polished tables, and wriggling upon chairs and settees. Helplessly, people began to pick them up and run about the room looking for somewhere to put them. Flowers were tossed away, and fishes snatched from cushions or plucked from under stampeding feet were hurled into the vases. One was dropped by mistake into a decanter of gin. Hands reached out and every hand clutched its coloured fish. Under the tables and chairs they scrambled to gather them up, and the room was full of cries.

Mrs. Meidner is not impressed with *The Flight from the Enchanter*. She calls it "a brilliant failure," "too complex," and "too elliptical." Her primary objection to the novel is its apparent disjunctures, between symbol and surface presentation and between character and event.[15] Her complaints about the novel's complexity are plausible but perhaps shortsighted. Any novel of social criticism that contains a large number of characters extracted from various social levels faces the danger of a loose, and sometimes fatally disjointed, plot. Iris Murdoch is more skillful than, say, Wain at filling in the contours of her minor characters; of the twenty-six people who appear in *The Flight from the Enchanter* nearly half qualify as major figures. By trying to render intimately the inner selves of so many of her characters, Iris Murdoch adds a refinement to the novel of social criticism. She subtly defines human contingency as an unfixed, erratic state. Ineluctably, the human qualities most susceptible to the will of others are precisely the ones we must mobilize to defend ourselves; we are the sum of our frailties. Each of Mischa Fox's intended victims conveys vividly the scope and depth of Mischa's frustration. That the private reactions of characters like Nina, Annette, Rainborough, and the Keepes can assume a genuineness that transcends the exigencies of plotting betokens artistic success rather than failure. We can imagine without difficulty these characters existing beyond the confines of the novel. It is because each person in *The Flight from the Enchanter* is so closely observed and faithfully rendered that we tend to forget narrative construction.

Iris Murdoch seems also to have resolved mythically the alleged discontinuity between symbol and surface action. Hunter, whose name is a synonym for Diana the sister of Apollo, is a suitable editor for the outmoded *Artemis*. The ideals of Hunter's mythical ancestor are as obsolete as the goal of female suffrage, upon which the magazine was founded. The goddess of wild animals and vegetation is ineffectual in an age in which man has pre-empted all living forms for his own selfish use; as the descendant of the goddess of chastity, the most Hunter can do, now that chastity is no longer a virtue, is to protect his sister's reputation. The person, incidentally, who saves the *Artemis* with her wealth is Camilla Wingfield, Camilla having been Diana's favorite huntress. Hunter, Rosa, and several of the other characters in the novel dramatize mythologically an observation that Iris Murdoch made in her review of Canetti's *Crowds and Power*:

> He [Canetti] has . . . shown, in ways which seem to me entirely fresh, the interaction of the "mythical" with the ordinary stuff of human life. The mythical is not something "extra"; we live in myth and symbol all the time.[16]

The mythological themes associated with Rosa serve as comments upon her brother, herself, and the contemporary world at large. Her ironic representation as Apollo, the many-faceted Olympian god, underscores, first of all, Hunter's uncertain masculinity. More centrally, the modern counterpart of the god of political life and agriculture quickly becomes politically cynical and conducts an illicit sexual life without bearing actual harvest. And although her hair cascades down her back in the same way as Apollo's, she directs her warlike qualities to the activities of savaging Annette and sadistically torturing Peter Saward. Furthermore, the present-day spirit of healing seems indifferent to her brother's suffering and, as the oracular voice, is reluctant to address Nina, whom her advice could have saved. The contradictory demands of today prevent the unified response to life that allowed our mythical precursors to attain the status of omnipotent virtue.

Mischa Fox's brown eye and blue eye suggest, of course, affinities with Janus. Nothing seems to escape the ken of this modern spirit of doorways and arches; his parties, furthermore, recall the legends about the gates of Janus being opened only in times of war. Mischa's social power is matched by several fables that posit Janus as the first of gods. And, finally, the disputed fact that Janus is related to Diana alludes suggestively to Mischa's fanatical compulsions both to own the *Artemis* and to dominate Rosa's life.[17] The action of *The Flight from the Enchanter* flows in the same eddies as the mythological undercurrents that nourish it. Iris Murdoch departs significantly from mythical tradition only to illuminate specific areas of contemporary life; even then, like Joyce, she retains the original mythical constituents and their narrative congruity in order to reverse their direction in a recognizably satirical way. Her ability to ally herself with the inherited wisdom of antiquity and at the same time to use it in a fresh, exciting way constitutes a creative gift that her commentators have not yet fully acknowledged.

Shelley, in his "Ode to the West Wind," and Iris Murdoch, in *The Flight from the Enchanter,* both prophesy in different ways the ascendancy of unawakened man; both are imaginatively able to convert destruction into immanent creativity. Iris Murdoch, however, is a less sanguine spokesman for the improvement of human society. She does not regard the resurgence of liberty as inevitable, as did her romantic predecessor. Tyranny is less readily identifiable today than it was in the early nineteenth century; the inception of a new millennium transcends questions of economic disparity and parliamentary reform. As in the case of Annette Cockeyne and, in some measure, those of Rosa and Hunter Keepe, a successful flight from oppression requires plain luck. The enchanter we must flee dwells very often within ourselves in the form of mistaken notions about personal responsibility and social equity. Unless we define our moral obligations, we face the prospect of a corrupt social creed that can only be aggravated by the romantic ideas of power and isolation we desperately introduce to ease guilt and doubt. Iris Murdoch retains the terms of this argument in *The Sandcastle,* a novel that further examines, on a deliberately reduced social canvas, man's limitations as a phenomenological entity.

Notes to Chapter Four

1. Edwin Muir, "Novels of Action and Character," *The Structure of the Novel* (London, 1957), 24-26.

2. O'Connor, 61.

3. Gindin, 180.

4. Hangen, 105-6.

5. *Ibid.,* 129.

6. Olga McDonald Meidner, "Reviewer's Bane: A Study of Iris Murdoch's *The Flight from the Enchanter,*" *Essays in Criticism,* 11 (1961), 444.

7. Kenneth Allsop, *The Angry Decade: A Survey of the Cultural Revolt of the Nineteen-Fifties* (London, 1958), 90.

8. R. J. Kaufmann, "The Progress of Iris Murdoch," *The Nation,* 188 (21 March 1959), 255-56.

9. Meidner, 445.

10. O'Connor, 70.

11. Fraser, 41, 40.

12. Meidner, 445.

13. O'Sullivan, 29.

14. O'Connor, 62.

15. Meidner, 435, 446, 439, 440.

16. Murdoch, "Mass, Might and Myth," 339.

17. Sir James George Frazer, *The Golden Bough,* 3d ed., II (New York, 1935), 376-87.

Five

THE SANDCASTLE

Acquiescence as Action

Iris Murdoch's artistic development marks a different kind of advance in the period from *The Flight from the Enchanter* to *The Sandcastle* than in the interval between her first two novels. *The Sandcastle* offers an enlargement and a clarification of moral vision that is suggested but not defined in either of the first two novels. *The Flight from the Enchanter* outstrips its predecessor because of its psychological depth and the unity Iris Murdoch is able to sustain within its startling diversity. *The Sandcastle,* omitting the symbolic and mythical furnishings that may have impressed some of her earlier readers as too consciously contrived, is a much less self-conscious effort than her first two. Standing firmly without hidden narrative supports, *The Sandcastle* can claim to be the first major statement of what Raymond calls the author's "rich ambiguity of moral vision exercised through charity."[1]

Iris Murdoch has said that her fiction coalesces with her philosophical interests "in a general sort of way—in considering, for example, what morality is and what goes into making decisions."[2] Implied in this modestly stated comment is the logical necessity of establishing some kind of objective awareness of reality before framing judgments and making claims. She is vigorously opposed to the Sartrean view of choice as an insular act elected in desperation and extremity. Bill Mor's mistaken apprehension of reality, for instance, causes sorrow and destruction. Fundamentally principled and forthright, Mor unintentionally damages his children, his wife, and Rain Carter because of the immaturity of his moral outlook. If they restore their dignity and aspirations by the end of the novel, Mor is less of a constructive aid than an inhibiting force. A man of few pleasures and rigidly circumscribed activities, he is, curiously, accused of selfishness by his wife Nan and by Bledyard, his colleague at St. Bride's School, where the two men teach. On the other hand, Demoyte, the grizzled former headmaster of St. Bride's, indicts him for being spinelessly self-effacing. These widely opposed views generate still another tension that forms the artistic and philosophical substance of the novel. For in *The Sandcastle,* Iris Murdoch attempts to describe the individual as a decision-making organism who is both free and unavoidably committed to other people.

As a narrative, *The Sandcastle* has little of the dazzling wit or the technical brilliance of the two works that preceded it. In her third novel, Iris Murdoch deliberately turned to the more slowly paced conventional novel of English domestic life. Nan and Bill Mor have been married twenty years and have two teen-age children, Donald and Felicity. For about half of their married life, the Mors have been residing at St. Bride's, a public school in bucolic Surrey, where Bill teaches Latin and history. An effective teacher, Mor is a mediocrity both as a husband and as a father. Don and the golden-freckled Felicity, we soon learn, have constructed a rather elaborate set of private rituals to compensate for their parents' failure to supply moral leadership and family security. And if Nan and Bill have been unable to generate any intimacy or guidance toward their children, their own relationship as husband and wife is even less vital. Narrow, haughty, and domineering, Nan expresses little interest in any activity other than ridiculing her husband's shortcomings. Bill, as a result, has become haunted with a Kafkaesque sense of unspecified guilt that blocks nearly all his acts and resolves. Although he understands objectively that his life is void of drama, excitement, or originality, his behavior has remained blandly conventional.

Such is the domestic atmosphere invaded by Rain Carter, a promising young artist who has drawn the honorific and lucrative assignment of painting Demoyte, St. Bride's retired headmaster. Shortly after they meet at Brayling's Close, Demoyte's handsomely sculptured estate, Rain and Mor fall in love. Iris Murdoch narrates their romantic adventure largely through Mor's point of view, thereby conveying his predicament as an actual experience. His choices are complicated by the unsettled state of his family affairs, by his desire to run for Parliament, and by the choric presence of his teaching associates. While Bledyard voices the Apollonian virtues of family responsibility and social stability, Demoyte proclaims loudly the Dionysian ethic of self-realization. Both interpretations prove ultimately to be but a moiety or broken half view of Mor's complex situation, and he is left to work out his situation alone. New complications arise until, in a brilliantly melodramatic scene, Nan announces to a public gathering that her husband has decided to give up his teaching career for a life in politics. Having discovered earlier that Bill had neglected to explain his political interests to Rain, Nan anticipates correctly Rain's reaction to her disclosure. Rain leaves St. Bride's the next morning, and family unity is restored to the Mor household. Iris Murdoch never goes further than suggesting via name-symbolism that Rain is capable of imparting both freshness and renewal to Mor's withered life. But although we are not told whether Mor would have enjoyed a fuller, happier life with Rain, his resisting her wish that they become lovers serves doubly as an indictment of his manhood and as a statement of his incapacity for rebirth of any sort.

The Sandcastle refutes the critics who conveniently bracketed Iris Murdoch with Wain and Amis as three socially critical Oxford graduates who began publishing novels in the mid-1950's. While both Wain and Amis are primarily concerned with fostering personalism and heightened sincerity to express their sub-Marxist resentment of the Establishment, Iris Murdoch's moral vision is directed outward from the perceiving self. Good and evil, she believes, are merely subjective responses to reality. Reflecting our emotions rather than things as they are in themselves, our notions of what is bad and good are not geared to provide true descriptions of reality. She agrees heartily with Russell's idea, stated in "Mysticism and Logic," that the philosopher's first duty is to describe the world as a free event; Russell pointed out wryly in 1914 that our convictions and desires can be purified and much more easily satisfied if we first overcome our metaphysical prejudices:

> Ethical considerations can only legitimately appear when the truth has been ascertained: they can and should appear as determining our feeling toward the truth, and our manner of ordering our lives

in view of the truth, but not as themselves dictating what the truth is to be.

*   *   *

It is a commonplace that happiness is not best achieved by those who seek it directly; and it would seem that the same is true of the good. In thought, at any rate, those who forget good and evil and seek only to know the facts are more likely to achieve good than those who view the world through the distorting medium of their own desires.[3]

Russell's urge to define reality prompted him to invent a mathematical language to serve as a paradigm of any possibly existing world. Iris Murdoch also uses an objective descriptive method to discover the nature of the world, but, as a novelist, she uses the material and psychological content that the world supplies. Lawrence's rejection of Christianity and of Freud and Iris Murdoch's existential skepticism lead the two writers to the same basic tenets—an awareness of the alienation of man and the primacy of the irrational. Iris Murdoch, however, scorns Lawrence's faith in spontaneity, which, she feels, deprives man of his powers of reflection. Shorn of his ability to conceptualize, man reduces his conduct to acts of unenlightened self-interest and survival.

In her study of Sartre, she anticipated the birth of a new kind of literature, a literature governed and reinforced by an unsentimental, underived apprehension of life: "False certainties must be seen through before true ones can be framed; as moral literature destroys itself, metaphysical literature imposes itself."[4] Her own novels ask the awkward questions and aim at the detached objectivity conducive to this new mode of literary art. She does not pretend, for instance, that Nan ever tried to understand her husband sympathetically or that she ever considered his wishes before her own; in a very real sense, Nan does not deserve to keep Mor. Iris Murdoch's refusal to comment editorially upon Nan, Rain, or Mor and their deeply felt private experiences emphasizes their responsibility to judge for themselves. To exist is to be conscious. Awareness means both choice and an objective understanding of the conflict between one's needs and the impediments the world puts in one's way. Once we acknowledge the nondeducible character of the world we must return to personal consciousness as an underived and acausal phenomenon if we want to explain meaning.

Life, then, can be lived, but it cannot be compressed into a thought process. Jerome K. Jerome's *Three Men in a Boat* (1889), which seems to be the favorite book of Mor's elder child Don, bodies forth comically the world's indifference to our ambitions and self-conceptions. The plans of the three nineteenth-century Londoners to journey to Kingston and back on the Thames are delayed, interrupted, and finally abandoned without regrets. Jerome, himself unshaken by man's inability to fulfill his designs, ends the adolescent sport with a series of disjointed ghost stories that are neither ghostly nor related to the misbegotten Thames voyage. Nan and Bill Mor, like Jerome's benighted optimists, must learn that reality flows on, heedless of their personal convenience.

Most of *The Sandcastle* takes place at St. Bride's School, which is located about twenty miles from London. The neighboring shopping center, the housing estate, and the road to London, which are visible from the school grounds, convey the idea that the school is not insulated from the maddening demands of common secular life. Standards of conduct are as obscure within the confines of St. Bride's gardens and neo-Gothic towers as in the London of *The Flight from the Enchanter*. Hunter Keepe, we recall, flinched from invoking the law concerning foreigners born east of the FPE line to destroy Stefan Lusiewicz. Yet, at the same time, Hunter was willing to go to any extreme to remove Stefan from Campden Hill Square. Mor is also obliged to evaluate conflicting moral criteria as soon as drama and emotion enter his life. The issues that Iris Murdoch forces him to act on are extremely difficult: Is honesty a virtue if it blocks self-realization? Are there degrees of falsehood? Is Mor's falling in love with Rain Carter a worse deception than remaining silent about Demoyte's promise to pay Felicity Mor's college tuition? Does Mor's failure to explain his political ambitions to Rain count as the most contemptible deceit of all?

Withholding judgment herself on these difficult questions, Iris Murdoch is primarily interested in conveying the idea that our encounters with messy, contingent life render absolute morality flaccid and implausible. Mor's love for Rain drives him to the point at which he harbors no compunctions about lying to Nan, to whom he has been married for twenty years. On the other hand, the oversights he commits in his relationship with Rain Carter persuade her to leave him. Finite consciousness can find no simple answer to the problem of virtue in the existing world of matter and conflicting volitions. Although she had treated the theme before, *The Sandcastle* is Iris Murdoch's first sustained presentation of the inconstancy of values. Mor's cherished ideal of standing as candidate for Parliament vanishes shortly after he meets Rain; Nan, who had for years regarded her husband with mocking self-righteousness, finds that she must struggle to keep him. The uncertainty of both human values and personal security is reflected by the radical shifts in mood within many of the chapters in the novel. This motif is most obvious in Chapter XVI, which begins with Bledyard's hysterically received art lecture (perhaps influenced by Jim Dixon's "Merrie England" address in *Lucky Jim*) and concludes with the disappearance of Mor's son after he had nearly been killed trying to climb the school tower with Jimmy Carde. At the lecture, Mor reacts gleefully to the students' joyful havoc and is intensely aware of Rain; his euphoria, however, soon chills to single-minded terror at the prospect of Don's death. In the following excerpt Iris Murdoch attempts to show how a practice that has been developed and fortified by habit over several years can be suddenly reversed:

> It was true that Nan had often said to him in the past—why do we
> go on? And he had always brushed this cry aside. But he had
> believed that Nan was not serious. Then it had suited him to believe
> that Nan was not serious. Now it suited him to believe that she was
> serious. Where was the truth?

Iris Murdoch advises us to expect the unexpected once we form relationships with other people. Nan has fortuitously escaped awkward moments in her twenty-year marriage with Mor, but as soon as she learns that human relations entail more than mere mechanical routine, she is bombarded by demands. Her plight, when she discovers him asleep on the living-room couch with Rain Carter at six o'clock in the morning, is not that the world has exploded into meaningless fragments, but that it has remained solid and relentlessly indifferent to her extremity. And the moment she acknowledges the insecurity of her marriage, a fresh complication enters her life in the form of Tim Burke's amorous advances. Iris Murdoch is no determinist, but firmly believes that our most innocent social encounters can involve us deeply in other people's lives. Mor's seemingly harmless acceptance of Rain's offer to drive him home, for instance, soon involves him in the accident to her car and to his finding himself in an awkward moral position:

If he was to take refuge in the truth, and indeed that was his only possible refuge, it had better be the whole truth. Of course, he would call on Tim Burke on the way home, and that would make at least part of his story true. Or would this be deceitful? Perhaps he had only decided to see Tim Burke as a sort of device to allow himself to spend a longer time with Miss Carter? He wasn't sure. It occurred to him after tonight he had better see to it that he did not meet Miss Carter again except in so far as this was inevitable. Not that it mattered specially.

*   *   *

It was only a few hours ago that he had risen from Evvy's lunch table. What world had he entered in between? Whatever the region was, Mor thought, in which he had been wandering, one thing was certain, that he would never visit it again.

With Beckett, Iris Murdoch feels that a universe of meanings is impossible. Rain's car's heeling over into the ford and Nan's melo-dramatic discovery of Rain and Bill, which depended ultimately on the scheduling of trains between Dorset and Surrey, constitute unfore-seeable yet vitally significant events in the lives of the novel's three main characters. Impersonal reality will always intrude to overthrow our mentalized world. Man is basically neither a "social animal" nor a "reasoning animal" who can rely completely upon his mental resources. He is indeterminate and in the last analysis must attune his mode of being to the accidents and indeterminacy of external reality.[5]

The Sandcastle is about man's ability to choose, to understand the implications of his choices, and to behave in accord with them. Iris Murdoch doubts radically man's ability to act as a free psychic entity; Mor's decisions always wish themselves unmade, in a sense, and not merely because of the irrational forces that operate on him. Con-versely, he fails to see that the choices he does *not* make constitute real choices in themselves; any negative act transforms itself into a positive one when viewed from the opposite perspective. Iris Murdoch does not believe that life furnishes us with convenient intervals during which we can pause to balance our emotional accounts. Any inven-tories must be performed in the midst of rapidly shifting values. Mor's comic flaw is that he insists on postponing decisions until an immediate problem is solved as in Don's chemistry examination and Felicity's dilemma either to attend college or take a secretarial course. Given the protean character of human reality, any problem is as likely to expand to new dimensions as it is to reach a solution, and, as Mor comes to learn, there is no guarantee that a new crisis will not emerge at an unexpected moment.

Man's choices are frequently hindered by unforeseen demands, but just as often he is granted unlooked-for reprieves. In the final reckoning, after good and bad fortune have roughly neutralized one another, he is the product of his own unaided responses. *The Sandcastle* insists that the activity of being human is a highly complex challenge under which most of us, weaker than Henley's *homo invictus,* can easily collapse. Surrounded by bureaucrats and administrators, modern man is not the aggressive, self-possessed forger of his personal destiny that authors in earlier, less mechanized periods represented him to be. Although he is ultimately definable by his acts, he frequently legislates for himself by omission or by passive complicity. William Mor conveys with relentless accuracy the elusiveness of our opportunities and the ease with which we slide into self-elected bondage. Although a universe of absolute values is not conceivable, reality allows for more stamina and initiative than Mor exercises. At the end of the novel he coincides with Fromm's formula of alienated man as an individual who is not the creative center of his own experiences:

> By alienation is meant a mode of experience in which the person experiences himself as an alien. He has become, one might say, estranged from himself. He does not experience himself as the center of his world, as the creator of his own acts. . . . The alienated person is out of touch with himself as he is out of touch with any other person.[6]

Mor appears to be sufficiently armed with ethical principles to acquit himself from any embarrassment. His early religious training has given him a profound respect for the truth as the foundation of all virtue; he conducts his Latin and history classes with a stern hand and with an uncompromising respect for the subject matter being studied. His failure consists chiefly in being unable to translate his convictions to acts. Throughout the novel he frequently allows himself to do things against his better judgment, like driving Rain's Riley, lying to Nan about this first outing with Rain, and accepting a pair of expensive earrings from Tim Burke. The conversion of abstract principles to concrete action involves, in the opinion of many, a contradiction in terms. But even so, it is not unreasonable to expect a closer alignment between Mor's conduct and his professed ethics. Without conscious knowledge, he soon repudiates his principles and begins practicing deceit for purely selfish reasons. He bolts the door of his house to prevent Nan from intruding upon Rain and himself and, shortly thereafter, lies to Rain about giving money to the gypsy woodcutter, who had awakened them by inadvertently pressing the doorbell while sheltering on Mor's front porch from a storm. Thus Mor reaches the point at which he harbors no guilt in deceiving the person for whose benefit he is deceiving his wife. His personal weakness of character and the absence of a basis for his ethical code in everyday reality causes his conduct to degenerate into furtive gestures of immediate self-interest.

Mor is the inevitable product of his prior experiences. For most of his adult life, he has been the victim of Nan's domination. By resigning his will to Nan's, he has forfeited both self-knowledge and a creative understanding of reality. When he finds himself in a position of responsibility and power, he is unable to act. He lies and distorts for the purpose of temporary expediency, and he cannot develop his relationship with Rain to a conclusion, either negative or positive, precisely because of his moral inexperience.

The Sandcastle can be read as a record of Mor's failures, most of which are caused by his self-inflicted ignorance. The novel divides roughly in half: the first ten chapters consider Mor's shortcomings as a parent, a husband, and a prospective political leader; the final ten chapters focus upon his ineptitude as a lover. Mor interests Iris Murdoch not chiefly for himself, but for the effects that his lack of decisiveness has on others. His earlier betrayal of Tim Burke is balanced structurally by his later betrayal of Rain. Each half of the novel evokes from Mor the same response to pressing issues: he begs Tim and then Rain for an indeterminate delay before committing himself to decisive action. Mor manifests his failure as a parent by forcing Don to take the Cambridge College entrance test against his will and by remaining uninquisitive about Felicity's psychic gifts. Both children lie to their parents without remorse and have clearly rejected the standards of adult society. Don turns to Tim Burke's relaxed Irish generosity and his craftsmanship, and Felicity gravitates toward magic and the dimly apprehended truths of her own mystical system.

Iris Murdoch accepts the psychic ramifications of the kinetic principle that any action provokes a reaction. Mor inevitably recoils from Nan's mockery and bullying. Accordingly, he is forced to endure the reprisals of Rain, Felicity, Don, and, possibly, Tim Burke, before the novel ends. Tim owns a jewelry shop in nearby Marsington; he is an artist who values gems and metal work by standards other than their market price. Although a merchant, he expresses little interest in money and property. His greatest pleasure aside from politics lies in giving trinkets and baubles, especially the ones he makes himself, to his friends. Nan's strange conduct toward him in the closing scene suggests that she may be reviving the love affair that Tim himself had tried to instigate four years before:

> Nan went into the kitchen. She nodded to Tim Burke to come with her. She put the kettle on the stove, and a saucepan to boil the egg. She lit the gas. Then she looked toward Tim Burke. He was sitting beside the table in an attitude of dejection. He would not meet her eye.

Donald attempts his suicidal climb of the school tower to punish Mor for his alleged infidelity. Felicity, the inventor of occult rites like the Power Game and tears of blood, directs her black art against her errant father. Iris Murdoch seems to view Felicity's mysticism as hospitably as she does rationalism as an explanation of the universe. The author is probably being merely playful at the expense of traditional Western metaphysics, but Felicity does draw the curtain on the novel's final page, and, directly following her black magic ritual at the seaside, Mor feels himself to be mesmerized:

> He felt as if he were under an intolerable physical strain, as if his body were likely at any moment to fly to pieces. Other strange physical symptoms came to trouble him. An unpleasant odor lingered in his nostrils, as if he could literally smell the sulphur of the pit; and he had from time to time the curious illusion that his flesh was turning black.

But necromancy is as unsatisfactory as rationalism or determinism to account for Mor's lost opportunities. Iris Murdoch prepares for his final betrayal of Rain Carter in a way that makes this act the inevitable product of his own consciousness. The obstacles to his prospective candidacy for Parliament are the unknown financial obligations, the possibly negative reactions of St. Bride's administration, and, chiefly, Nan's personal opposition. Election to office, ironically, is no problem, as Marsington has been a safe Labour seat for many years. Iris Murdoch's belief that the path to vocational fulfillment is less formidable than the one leading to personal freedom and integrity is reflected by the host of obstacles standing between Mor and Rain: Nan's natural objections, Don's disappearance, Mor's indecisiveness about his political ambitions, Felicity's mysticism, Rain's money and property, and her heightened sense of vocation. If Mor's will buckles before Nan's obduracy in the matter of a political career, he is nearly certain to fail in his more significant gesture toward freedom.

Almost all of Mor's responses can be described as prudent, timorous, or downright insipid. He persuades Rain to wait before making her his mistress. When Don is trapped on the parapet of the school tower, Mor is practically helpless. The true hero of Don's rescue is Rigden, the inconspicuous student whose admiration Mor always took for granted; it is Rigden who devises and helps execute all of the strategy that saves Jimmy Carde, as well as Don, from death. Similarly to Rigden's practicality and selflessness in the tower incident, Hensman's conduct at the Board of Governors dinner exposes Mor's ineffectualness. (That Rigden and Hensman both lack first names conveys Iris Murdoch's belief that self-effacement is an ingredient of heroism.) As a junior faculty member, the intrepid Hensman is not invited to the dinner, but he nonetheless assumes the unglamorous task of moving the furniture and decorating the dining room for the event. Mor's immobility when he hears Nan announce his political ambitions to the guests, in a desperate act to divide him from Rain, is in no way commensurate with Hensman's efforts, or with Nan's for that matter:

> Mor told himself that what he ought to do now, now this very minute, was to get up from his seat and lead Rain out of the room. Nan had attempted to corner him by a public gesture. She should be answered in the same way. To rise now and go out with Rain would set the seal on all his intentions. At last Nan had raised the storm. It was for him to ride it. But Rain had turned away her eyes—and although Mor struggled in his seat he could not bring himself to get up. A lifetime of conformity was too much for him. He stayed where he was.

Mor reveals in this scene that, contrary to Freud, he is enclosed within the social rather than the narrowly sexual limits of his previous existence. It is here that the reader is convinced that Mor was probably attracted to Nan in the first place, twenty-odd years earlier, because he saw in her decisiveness, however gross, an unlimited reprieve from the responsibility of choice.

Anticipating the accusation that she weights the scales too heavily against Mor, Iris Murdoch keeps his behavior toward Rain consistent. Although the treatment is subtly modulated, we can almost predict Mor's failure to refute Nan openly at the Board of Governors dinner. He had deserted Rain twice before in moments of extremity—the first time, when he remained at the squash courts to hear Bledyard's reproofs, and later, when he searched for Nan in the rain at six o'clock in the morning. Mor does face a harder decision at the end of the novel, when he leaves Nan while their son is still missing, than he did when he rebuffed Tim Burke's entreaties to enroll himself as a Labour candidate. We must also remember, however, that he has a great deal more to gain. Furthermore, Nan's public announcement gives Mor an opportunity that he could never create himself. Her own ingeniousness and temerity spare him the need of waging a painful scrimmage. He need only leave the dining room without bothering about the amenities of making arrangements or offering explanations.

Yet Iris Murdoch seems convinced that this melodramatic episode does not demolish Mor in Rain's judgment. He might have been able to regain Rain's esteem by staying with her in the faculty dining room after she comes back at midnight to finish the portrait of Demoyte. Iris Murdoch's fiction contains no clearer example of existentialism than the last two chapters of *The Sandcastle*. Kierkegaard stated in the *Concluding Unscientific Postscript* that only the direct confrontation of an objective uncertainty can evoke a heightened subjective reaction in the perceiver; meaning, for Kierkegaard, is the knowledge that the pursuit of an intuited truth does not grant the individual a moment's delay. It is solely through subjectivity and incomplete understanding that we can apprehend reality. Mor's downfall is not caused by Nan's vulgar melodramatic public gesture. His crucial mistake is leaving Rain to finish the painting after their unspectacular private confrontation. His presence in the faculty dining room would have been a concrete gesture to recover lost ground. But the impending loss of Rain's love does not revive Mor's blunted personality. He lacks the stamina and moral perception to convince her of the wrongness of her choice:

> Mor hesitated. He had a terrible feeling that if he left her now

he might never see her again. They would speak tomorrow. He would force her to agree with him. It could not be otherwise.

"We are both overwrought," he said. "We will speak of this again tomorrow."

"Yes, yes," said Rain, "please go. I must work now. Please go."

Mor got as far as the door. He stood watching her. She had begun to paint again, dashing the tears from her eyes.

"Rain," he said.

She did not answer.

"Tomorrow," he said.

"Yes," said Rain, "yes."

She went on painting. Mor stayed for a minute or two watching her, and then he went out and closed the door behind him.

Iris Murdoch concurs in part with Kierkegaard's dictum that only by immersing the self in a situation that imperils our most cherished values can we gain the self-knowledge and self-control required to perform significant acts. Mor has neglected to understand fully that marrying Rain obviates an immediate future in politics. Ironically, the man who had no hopeful prospects in his domestic or professional life now wants the best that both offer without legislating actively in the interest of either.

After waiting for a suitable hour to call upon Rain the following morning, Mor explains that his blasted romance was inevitable. Demoyte replies, "Coward and fool . . . ! Nothing was inevitable here. You have made your own future." Mor's failure to respond to the exigencies of his relationship with Rain destroys its logical and emotional structure. In the course of the action, Mor is frequently aided by the generosity and the initiative of others; Tim Burke constantly gives keepsakes and curios to Nan and Don and, more significantly, personally offers Mor the chance of becoming an M.P. Demoyte, besides agreeing to finance Felicity's college career, encourages Mor's relationship with Rain. When Rain decrees that she and Mor will live together, Mor is as elated by the decision itself as he is by the prospect of a new life.

Rain's indirect proposal of marriage, however, does not release Mor entirely from the responsibility of choice. The contingencies of the context still demand that he explain his intentions to Nan and that he behave toward Rain in a manner befitting their engagement. Urged to choice until the end by Mor's indecisiveness and naïve selfishness, Rain finally leaves St. Bride's. Mor's privations teach him that the blessings and the privileges of life do not form a consistent pattern; he finds his occupation by forfeiting his love; furthermore, his political candidacy is finally Nan's choice, not his own. If the Mors are to live in London as a family, it is because Nan wants to shun the embarrassment of remaining in a place where her neighbors and associates know that she nearly lost her husband to another woman.

The closing pages of the novel, after Mor's disenchanted exit from Demoyte's estate, reveal the remorseless indifference with which life continues. As soon as Mor leaves Brayling's Close, he is assaulted by a new set of obligations entirely divorced from Rain. While he is bicycling home, Felicity rushes to tell him of Don's return; this new event changes the coloring of Mor's entire personal existence. When the door of Don's bedroom closes behind father and son and the narrative goes on for another half page, there is no doubt that Mor's romantic adventure has ended. Iris Murdoch's deliberate change in point of view from Mor to Felicity indicates a complete shift in values, relations, and duties. Don will assist Tim Burke in the jewelry shop, Felicity will go to college, Mor will stand as a candidate, and, possibly, Nan and Tim will become lovers. This dispensation excludes Mor's residual affection for Rain Carter. If Mor hopes to adjust to his new demands as a father, a husband, and a public citizen—and he had better, for he has nothing else that is substantial—he will be forced to acknowledge that his romance with Rain Carter has ended and that he can do nothing to restore the promise with which she briefly graced his life.

The Sandcastle is organized to express Mor's predicament with boldness and clarity. We have already discussed the novel's two-part structure and the author's modulated presentation of Mor's tendency to desert Rain at critical moments. Another supporting motif is furnished by the actions and opinions of some of the minor characters. The novel's chief spokesman for immediate tangible values and Mor's main advocate in his pursuit of Rain Carter is Demoyte. The roaring ex-headmaster of St. Bride's, whose portrait Rain has been commissioned to paint, exemplifies the principle of *carpe diem*, which underscores Mor's indecisiveness and which appears formally in the novel in a passage from Propertius's elegies:

> Tu modo, dum lucet, fructum ne desere vitae.
> Omnia si dederis oscula, pauca dabis.

> Ac veluti folia arentes liquere corollas,
>   Quae passim calathis strata natare vides,
> Sic nobis, qui nunc magnum speramus amantes,
>   Forsitan includet crastina fata dies.

Jimmy Carde translates the selection thus:

> While the light remains . . . only do not forsake the joy of life.
> If you shall have given all your kisses, you will give too few. And
> as leaves fall from withered wreaths which you may see spread
> upon the cups and floating there, so for us, who now as lovers hope
> for so much, perhaps tomorrow's day will close the doom.

Demoyte's fierce secularism is expressed by his stern educational theories and by his emphatic endorsement of an aggressive life. This "chorus of plain truth,"[7] as Kaufmann calls him, sees nothing amiss in Mor's deceiving Nan about the source of Felicity's tuition money. He is, similarly, just as eager to abet Mor's hopes for a full, rich life with Rain Carter. As a practitioner of his own lawless existentialism, however, Demoyte is a puzzle. We are never informed of the nature of his relationship with Miss Handforth, his housekeeper, but the unorthodoxy of a middle-aged schoolteacher working voluntarily as a domestic hardly escapes notice. A romantic arrangement with "Handy," however, shows only that Demoyte is unafraid of flouting convention. He lives an orderly bachelor life, as far as we can tell, with his finely bound books, his elegant furniture, and his rich Oriental carpets. Never having applied his bold moral theories to his own personal life, Demoyte addresses the reader from the spectators' gallery, not from the arena. His professional foil is the Reverend Mr. Giles Evarard, his successor as headmaster of St. Bride's. Under the awesome leadership of Demoyte, St. Bride's academic standing reached an unprecedented stature; "Evvy's" lisping piety and gentleness, however, threaten to reinstate the mediocrity that characterized the school before Demoyte's long incumbency. And, ironically, while Mor loves the corrosive and sarcastic Demoyte, Evvy's mildness inspires no affection. Iris Murdoch nevertheless takes care to show that academic excellence and personal appeal are not legitimate substitutes for a rich, active existence. In that Demoyte cannot claim to have applied his *carpe diem* theories with success to his intimate private life, Mor, as well as the reader, is right to withhold his approval of them as a sustaining conduct of life.

In his Sunday sermon to the students, Evvy preaches that our personal needs will be satisfied at a distant point determined by divine veracity. Along with Evvy's patent Hegelianism, the spare, lean orthodoxy of Bledyard the art instructor constitutes the Apollonian influence at St. Bride's School. And, once again, Iris Murdoch introduces an ambiguity between the man and his moral doctrine for the purpose of warning the reader against accepting absolutes as guides to personal behavior. Bledyard's colorless, sparsely furnished room on the upper landing of a Quonset parallels his theories on art and ethics. He would like to restore Byzantine techniques in portraiture because artists, he believes, cannot view other people with enough reverence to represent them faithfully. Our abstract conceptions of human traits distort our copies of them as they occur in specific variants—individuals. At the same time he maintains that the individual as such is not a suitable subject for serious art; an artist should direct his vision to man's godlike attributes and to those qualities that best reflect his relation to God.

Bledyard is not able to apply his aesthetic of willed self-effacement to morality with total success. He tries, in their melodramatic colloquy on the squash courts, to convince Mor that the unity of his family is more important than any relationship he can have with Rain Carter. Bledyard, however, may be discouraging Mor for selfish reasons; he does not deny Mor's rejoinder that he is in love with Rain himself, and his actions on several occasions seem to suggest that he is. His theories on art, which, incidentally, cancel the validity of practically all forms of portrait painting, have extinguished his own artistic impulses. At one time a promising artist, Bledyard has deliberately given up painting. His theistic morality, furthermore, which may be hypocritical, seems to have outfitted him poorly for human intercourse. Bledyard is a bachelor, and although he has the respect of his colleagues at St. Bride's if not that of the students, he does not have their affection. Seen by Felicity sitting alone in a field, he is, to all appearances, a lonely, unhappy man who testifies, as does Demoyte, that a person cannot encase himself in a body of theory or doctrine.

Another important ambiguity in the novel is Iris Murdoch's characterization of Rain Carter. It is by no means clear that Mor would have enjoyed a happy life with her had he decided to desert his family. Rain's exuberance and impulsiveness are certainly a bright change from Nan's dreary pomposity. But, like Nan, Rain is a stronger character than Mor, and, also like Nan, she is not averse to

exercising her will. Her aggressiveness is less obvious than Nan's only
because it is more refined. Iris Murdoch suggests more than faintly
that Rain's energy and zeal could crush Mor's self-dignity as rapidly
as Nan's obtuseness.

Miss Balakian's opinion that Iris Murdoch's governing theme is
"a search for the meaning of love and its frequent elusiveness"[8] is
lucidly justified by *The Sandcastle,* particularly by Rain Carter. She
and Mor discover love in an unexpected place as they accidentally
spy water on the parched Surrey landscape. Similarly to Nan and
Tim Burke later in the novel, they become acutely aware of one
another by sharing a crisis, or what Sartre would call a "limit
situation." And although Rain emerges from the afternoon's outing
scratched, spattered with mud, and deprived of her car, the reader
feels that she has subtly contrived to gain Mor's esteem. If O'Connor
is correct in his opinion that Rain sees in Mor "the strength and
character of her recently dead father,"[9] she perceives these qualities
and determines to act long before Mor has assessed the situation.

Rain's motives are never openly stated. We know little of her
past aside from her great love and admiration for her father and the
fact that he ended her romance with a painter she had fallen in love
with in Paris when she was nineteen. Rain also mentions, perhaps
significantly, that she had cut her hair short while living in Paris, but
she does not explain whether she did this in despair (as Georgie Hands
in *A Severed Head*), in spite, or in obedience to her father. It is
even possible that her broken romance and the shearing of her long
hair had nothing to do with each other. But the fact that she has
kept her hair short for the past five years and has had no love
interests in that time suggests, possibly, an extremely strong paternal
link about which she prefers to remain silent. Except for one brief
scene, *The Sandcastle* is never reported from her point of view; Mor's
muddled, untested mind provides, in addition, no critical access to
Rain's motives. The only clear truth about her is that, from the
start, she controls the direction and the emotional velocity of her
relationship with Mor.

Rain, under the guise of impulsiveness, creates her own opportunities: she reaches for Mor's hand when they are picking flowers in
Demoyte's moonlit garden; she attempts incursions on Mor's confidence by asking him to help her investigate Demoyte's character for
the painting; and she seems to maneuver Mor into situations in which

they will share private secrets. Without apparent provocation she
drives him to school and then to the environs of Marsington from
Brayling's Close; she invites him to drive her car; and she asks him
to accompany Demoyte and herself to dinner while Nan is away.
After her stop at Mor's house allegedly to leave an explanatory note,
she scarcely resists his attempts to force her inside. Once she is in
the house, she is easily persuaded to hang up her coat and take a
drink. In this scene, as in the rest of the novel, Rain and not Mor
urges their relationship to some kind of conclusion. Although he is
satisfied at this point with having shared a mutual declaration of love,
Rain's greater practicality calls up the question of their prospects of
a future together. Finally, only a mind as innocent as Mor's could
misinterpret the transparency of Rain's plight when she states her
embarrassment over having no place to sleep:

> Rain sat up and made a rueful face. "I've been very silly," she
> said. "I told Mr. Demoyte that I was going up to London and
> would spend the night there. I had to say that so as to get away
> from him—otherwise he would have kept me the whole evening.
> And I did intend when I'd delivered the note to get into my car
> and drive up to London. It's parked in the school grounds. But
> what shall I do now?"

As has been stated, Iris Murdoch does not speculate overtly about
what kind of wife Rain would be to Mor. His inability to read the
signs may very well have proved his earthly salvation, as he may not
have been able to deal with Rain's strength of character and secular
élan on a daily basis. According to the logic of their relation, however,
Mor behaves immorally. Rain tells him not to follow Nan after Nan
discovers them asleep on the couch; later, she begs him to explain to
Nan their intentions of going away together. If Rain, as the intruder
who is trying to destroy Mor's marriage for her own profit, should
not say these things, she should not *have* to say them. Her doing so
indicates that she understands Mor and his duties in a way that he
does not.

Iris Murdoch is convinced that love is no simple matter; its
demands are unfair and remorselessly uncompromising. What Mor
cannot see is that the morality generated by his commitment to Rain
requires his leaving Nan and the children at the earliest possible
moment. As soon as he encouraged Rain to fall in love with him, he
became responsible for her welfare and happiness. The cruelty with

which he is obliged to treat Nan is only a detail to be executed with cold detachment in the interest of his ultimate goal. Within his created situation Mor's only duties are those directly concerned with Rain.

This challenge, of course, is one that braver and more resolute spirits than Bill Mor's would prefer to avoid. Before he can take a mental inventory, he sees that he must forsake his job, his wife, and his children with stark ruthlessness. His hesitation, although natural, violates his commitment to Rain. Logically, it is she who ends the relationship, just as she had instigated it by grasping Mor's hand in the rose garden. Discussing her childhood in the south of France, Rain introduces a theme that is to figure largely in her sojourn at St. Bride's:

> I can recall, as a child, seeing pictures in English children's books of boys and girls playing on the sand and making sandcastles—and I tried to play on my sand. But a Mediterranean beach is not a place for playing on. It is dirty and very dry. The tides never wash the sand or make it firm. When I tried to make a sandcastle, the sand would just run away between my fingers. It was too dry to hold together. And even if I poured sea water over it, the sun would dry it up at once.

Rain learns as a child a truth that Mor remains ignorant of until his middle age: the ingredients of our lives never coalesce to form a balanced composition of emotion, duty, and rational understanding; our transient values, the motives of others, and the world's inscrutability prevent a clear alignment of finite claims. Iris Murdoch follows Kierkegaard by implying strongly that at an indeterminate point we must plunge into the abyss of dread and doubt. Gindin relates this problem to the novel's title and to the dramatic implications of Rain's childhood reminiscences:

> From the schoolteacher's point of view, Rain provides too much energy, too much vitality, for him to cope with in his circumscribed world, as a deluge of rain can wash away a sandcastle. And, significantly, there is a torrential rain on the day when the school teacher [sic] displays his inability to deal with all the complications of the affair. The elements of the affair—the grains of sand and the moisture—exist, but the sand is either too dry or too wet.[10]

Demoyte had said of Rain, "Her sense of vocation is like a steam hammer." Mor, on the other hand, allows his book on political concepts to remain unfinished, and he responds with the same flac-

cidity to his chance of becoming an M.P. His life lacks both form
and direction; unlike Rain, he is unable to see that love is a responsibility requiring both adaptability and grit. She will not settle for a
stale husk; her ability to respond to her painting in a time of crisis
shows her the folly of taking Mor from his family and his teaching—
the most vital objectifications of his personality. She realizes that she
would not be able to continue living without the creative outlet of
painting. Accordingly, depriving Mor of his sustaining purpose would
wreck the moral constituents of his relation with the external world.
Her realism and moral toughness enable her to assess her future
with him. He lacks the clarity to reverse the habits and practices of
a lifetime. Although her feelings are deeply engaged, she does not
allow them to prevail over what she is driven to understand as lucid
fact: " 'I love you,' said Rain, 'I do love you, I do. But what does
that mean?' " She refutes Mor's claim that he will complete his book
by pointing out that had he the urge to create, nothing could have kept
the work unfinished. She has learned that he does not have the
manhood she had endowed him with; yet, she remains silent about
her misjudgment. Either emotional confusion, self-disgust, or a patro-
nizing desire to be gentle with him prompts her to say a moment later,
"Perhaps, after all, it has been because of—father." Without denying
the possible validity of Rain's remark, we must recognize that her
prime concern at the moment is to be rid of Mor. As supporting
evidence for this theory Rain lies openly to him for the first time when
she agrees to continue the discussion the next morning.

The three major figures in *The Sandcastle* conform remarkably to
Aristotle's dictum that characters must act according to necessity and
probability. As Mor, Nan finds love in an unlikely quarter—the tatty
jewelry shop of Tim Burke. Yet her complacent self-dogmatism, her
suspicion of new experiences, and her intolerance of people whose
mode of being differs from her own screen her from anything as
disorderly and unpredictable as romance. If she seems to favor an
intrigue with Tim Burke later, it is with the fierce pride of a conqueror
and possibly with the motive of blocking Mor's candidacy. Iris
Murdoch's portrayal of Nan as a selfish, insensitive wife is both
brilliant in itself and useful as a commentary upon Mor. Her captious
self-righteousness is conveyed in a few short lines of dialogue at the
very beginning of the novel:

   "Five hundred guineas!" said Mor's wife. "Well I never!"

"It's the market price," said Mor.

"You could articulate more distinctly," said Nan, "if you took that rather damp-looking cigarette out of your mouth."

The author explains through her characterization of Nan that smugness and inflexibility are not feasible in our world of instrumental values. In the next exchange of dialogue, Nan objects to the school's installation of floodlighting in its quadrangle; ironically, the floodlights later figure vitally in the saving of her son's life. She also calls Don and Mor "a pair of social cowards." Yet it is she who proves to be the social coward before the end of the first chapter by opposing her husband's political aspirations: "My dear, I know, it's attractive, London and so on, but in real life terms it means a small salary and colossal expenses and absolutely no security." Like the big eaters in the fiction of Katherine Mansfield, Huxley, and Waugh, Nan is too vulgar and obtuse to perceive inconsistency in herself. Characteristically, she finds flowers unsanitary and during her amorous encounter with Tim Burke plucks all the leaves from his sycamore tree. Her objections to Mor's romance with Rain Carter are stated in collective, impersonal terms: Rain's French background and her search for a father-substitute. Nan's obstinate unreason would never allow her to admit that another woman could turn Mor's head.

Yet, Nan is flexible and purposeful enough to succeed where Mor fails. Her instinct for self-preservation proves to be stronger than his sense of vocation *or* his love for Rain Carter. In short, Nan is able to devise a strategy and to execute it. After her return from Dorset she behaves reasonably and affectionately, placating Mor in a way she had never found necessary before. She makes herself physically attractive, as Sir Leopold's reactions to her at the Board of Governors dinner bear witness. In keeping with her ruthless self-assurance, she reads the rough drafts of the unposted letters that Mor had written to Tim Burke and herself, and she acts in accord with their contents. Naturally, Nan omits telling Mor of her discovery of the hidden letters and, as a palpable sign of her contempt for him, does not bother to return them to their hiding place. The humanistic issues confronting the Mor family seem to be greater than those indicated by Fraser's summary of the novel:

> The affair is broken off—family and work, as in "real life", are obviously more important than "romance"—and the private will fulfills itself, though costingly, through its engagement to the social spirit. There is a sense, here, of the solidity of the normal.[11]

A part of the novel that refutes Fraser concerns the gypsy wood-cutter who materializes near the ford where Rain's car is moored, later on Mor's porch, and finally at the side of the road, leaving the vicinity of St. Bride's on the same morning that Rain escapes to France. Gindin has interpreted this obscure figure in accordance with the undercurrent of irrationalism and loss that pervades the novel:

> The wandering, formless creature . . . appears in *The Sandcastle* in the form of a gypsy present at crucial moments in the relationship between Rain and Mor. The gypsy becomes a vague image of the way things are going, of the impending disastrous end to the affair. Mor, after he has passed the gypsy at several different times, tries to find him, control him, and make him part of the understandable universe. But the gypsy is deaf, and . . . represents something beyond human communication or control, some inanimate force not subject to human construction or illusion.[12]

The gypsy, then, represents the elusive forces that man's carefully designed schemes cannot explain or subordinate. His appearance on Mor's porch is no more logical or consciously deliberate than Nan's half an hour later. The coincidence of his exit from Mor's life with Rain's stands as a mockery to Mor of a chance missed that is never to be offered again. The immediacy with which the woodlander confronts Mor and his enigmatic presence at St. Bride's convey the importance of the unspecifiable element in human affairs.

The artistic congruity and inevitable thematic movement of the novel make it an impressive work of social criticism. Mor is a competent teacher but a failure as a parent. Unable to legislate for himself, he aspires to become a political leader, one who legislates for others. He oscillates helplessly between two strong women without clearly understanding the nature of his attachment to either of them; his affair with Rain, in fact, begins and ends without his knowledge. Philosophy intersects with social criticism in Mor's existential failure to cultivate objectivity. Although he lectures convincingly on the subject of freedom, he does not grant enough reality to the needs of others to dignify his choices. His habit of surrendering the initiative has kept him too closely locked within a set of private values that have not been deepened or refreshed by the indifferent material world. The presiding irony of *The Sandcastle* is that social values and institutions, like education, party politics, and marriage, are somehow able to preserve themselves. Mor will probably serve society as ably as a politician as he had as a schoolmaster, in spite of the discontinuity between his public and private lives. Periodic family crises and Nan's selfish obduracy will also hold together the Mors' marriage, at least nominally. The inception and the preservation of values, both social and religious, continue to interest Iris Murdoch in *The Bell.* (The social influence of Mor's early Methodist training is never stated outright in *The Sandcastle;* nonetheless, his sympathy for stern authority actuates both his adult choice of professions and his preference for strong-willed women.)

As her moral vision matures, we shall see Iris Murdoch growing more restive and critical of man's ability to create a just ontology for himself. While the characters in *The Sandcastle* may not satisfy their immediate aims, they manage, often by luck or in spite of themselves, to fuse their efforts and values with those of society at large. The characters in *The Bell* forsake their ideals and possessions without compensations. Mor has the chance to substitute for one sort of life another that may be less personally satisfying but is at least socially significant; the only characters who are not morally and vocationally marooned at the end of *The Bell* are Nick Fawley, who is dead, and Dora Greenfield and Toby Gashe, whose immaturity prevents them from glimpsing more than a small part of the waste and sorrow that lie behind them at Imber Court.

Notes to Chapter Five

1. John Raymond, "The Unclassifiable Image," *New Statesman,* 56 (15 November 1958), 698.

2. Mehta, 54.

3. Bertrand Russell, "Mysticism and Logic," *Mysticism and Logic* (Garden City, New York, 1957), 6, 29.

4. Murdoch, *Sartre: Romantic Rationalist,* 42.

5. Vivien Mercier, "Arrival of the Anti-Novel," *The Commonweal,* 70 (8 May 1959), 149-51.

6. Erich Fromm, "Alienation Under Capitalism," in Eric and Mary Josephson, eds., *Man Alone: Alienation in Modern Society* (New York, 1962), 56.

7. Kaufmann, 256.

8. Balakian, 268.

9. O'Connor, 63.

10. Gindin, 179.

11. Fraser, 42.

12. Gindin, 183.

Six

THE BELL

The Unheard Voice of Love

THE BELL marks Iris Murdoch's return to a mythological setting for the purpose of blending philosophy and social criticism. Most of the novel's action takes place in Gloucestershire at Imber Court, residence of a lay brotherhood attached to the Benedictine convent, Imber Abbey. As a work bearing mythical significance, *The Bell* is more successful than *Under the Net* or *The Flight from the Enchanter*: the novel's physical setting links the daily activities of the Imber brotherhood with a spiritual tradition that serves both as a standard of judgment and an entity to be judged. Writing about the theater in 1946, Sartre denounced what he called "the literature of characters" in favor of "the literature of situations," particularly extreme situations. If the theater is essentially "a collective religious phenomenon," it will stress man's recurring efforts to discover beauty, truth, and knowledge, that is, teleological myth, rather than realism:

> As a rule, an audience is made up of the most diverse elements: a big business man sits beside a traveling salesman or a professor, a man next to a woman, and each is subject to his own particular preoccupations. Yet the situation is a challenge to the playwright: he must create his public, he must fuse all the disparate elements in the auditorium into a single unity by awakening in the recesses of their spirits the things which all men of a given epoch and community care about.[1]

The religious and political conservatism of the late 1950's supplied

113

the novelist with a physical and moral setting that would be both topical and of immediate interest to her readers. To exploit her theme, Iris Murdoch, again following Sartre,[2] probes more deeply into her characters' minds and private histories than she had in prior novels. She immerses herself in the minds of her characters with such aplomb and intelligent awareness that even the most contradictory attitudes appear rich and convincing at the time they are presented. The Christian setting, aside from providing a familiar standard of judgment, permits her to dramatize more fully the individual psyches of her characters. We are given, for instance, ampler background material concerning figures like Dora Greenfield and Michael Meade than we were in the case of William Mor. While Mor disclosed his being through his actions and decisions, the people in *The Bell* reveal themselves to us through their historical thought processes as well. Although Mor's past figures centrally in his abortive romance with Rain Carter, this information is sketched in somewhat casually to accommodate the existentialist theme. In *The Bell,* Iris Murdoch, working within larger blocs of personal and collective experience, spells out vividly the prior actions of her major characters; the result is not a slackening of dramatic intensity but a vision of human life as an organic continuum in which the same kind of problem, often personified by the same individual, can return without reason or justice to challenge our moral standing. One of the novel's mythical themes, in fact, impinges on the idea that those who fail to understand the past are condemned to relive it.

As has been suggested, the more layers of human reality the novelist discloses, the more suspicious she grows of man's capability to act in his own interest. René Micha's estimate of *The Sandcastle* and *The Bell* is unjustifiably cheerful: "Dans le cas de *The Sandcastle* ou de *The Bell* . . . une lumière heureuse baigne tous les accidents de la fable. . . ."[3] Ironically, one of the major philosophical influences on *The Bell* is the atheistic doctrine of Eternal Recurrence promulgated by Nietzsche in *Thus Spake Zarathustra* and *Ecce Homo.* Nietzsche insists that different states of the universe repeat themselves, that at both the psychological and the social level we keep reliving our lives in eternally recurring patterns. While time is unlimited, the number of positions, alterations, and developments of force is bounded. Consequently, our actions and mental states, if not in fact rigidly determined, must eventually be repeated. This cyclical interpretation of reality, Nietzsche claims, will give hope and encouragement to the strong; accordingly, the weak and unhappy will be crestfallen to learn that they must repeat similar events again and again. Iris Murdoch revises Nietzsche's credo only from the standpoint of human volition. A regular, uniform pattern or format does choke the creative will, but the individual's own acts, not an externally derived historical process, trap him within the stifling necessity of cause and effect. The characters in *The Bell,* curiously, never see themselves as enclosed within the cyclical patterns that they themselves have constructed. Unlike Jake Donaghue and Rosa and Hunter Keepe of *The Flight from the Enchanter,* most of them lack the self-knowledge to free themselves from their behavioral patterns. In a setting that fosters the idea of timelessness and spiritual freedom, Iris Murdoch's characters are unable to develop the moral clarity to deal with challenges that proved insuperable in the past, when, theoretically, the characters were less well armed.

Imber Court has been activated by the brotherhood to serve as a transitional zone between the cloistered Abbey and the secular world. In one of her rare authorial intrusions Iris Murdoch remarks: "Those who hope, by retiring from the world, to earn a holiday from human frailty, in themselves and others, are usually disappointed." Like Peter Saward of *The Flight from the Enchanter* and Bledyard of *The Sandcastle,* the lay members of the Imber community are not morally impelled to pursue their ideals in a world of compromise and confusion. Characters like the Straffords, Catherine Fawley, Michael Meade, and Peter Topglass have not been attracted to Imber because of their spiritual dedication. They are, simply and frankly, unable to adapt to the tensions and strains of ordinary life. The Straffords, for instance, join the brotherhood in order to distract themselves from their unhappy marriage. Perhaps the wisest character in the book, the enigmatic Abbess, explains the practical utility that a brotherhood like Imber can provide in today's fragmented society. It is noteworthy that she is not immediately concerned with the reconstruction or modification of Scripture to suit public needs; this is a problem that can be met later. Her realistic, unsentimental outlook recognizes the need to create a gentler milieu in which the socially deracinated can study and learn their basic human obligations:

> With an ease which at first surprised him and which later seemed
> part of an inevitable pattern, the Abbess imparted to Michael the

idea of making the Court the home of a permanent lay community
attached to the Abbey. . . . There were many people, she said, and
Michael was but too ready to credit her, since he felt himself to
be one of them, who can live neither in the world nor out of it.
They are a kind of sick people, whose desire for God makes them
unsatisfactory citizens of an ordinary life, but whose strength or
temperament fails them to surrender the world completely; and
present-day society, with its hurried pace and its mechanical and
technical structure, offers no home to these unhappy souls. . . . Our
duty, the Abbess said, is not necessarily to seek the highest, regardless of the realities of our spiritual life as it in fact is, but to seek
that place, that task, those people, which will make our spiritual
life most constantly grow and flourish; and in this search, said the
Abbess, we must make use of divine cunning. "As wise as serpents,
as harmless as doves."

The hopes of the community, however, are blasted by the persistence
of human infirmity and by the constant intrusion of finite demands.
Although they maintain a lucrative garden in which they cultivate
lettuce, carrots, apples, and pears for the market, the brothers cannot
engender spiritual or human understanding. Premonitions of the
streamlined, competitive modern world are continually present at
Imber in the jet planes that perform aerial maneuvers above the
convent and in Nick Fawley's newspapers, which litter its grounds.
At the first sign of outside pressure, the community collapses, scattering its disturbed, bewildered members to different parts of the
British Isles.

Although the brotherhood seek to enrich their lives with vocational
dignity and spiritual purity, they succeed only in making themselves
vapid and dreary. Our first glimpse of Imber is through the secular
eyes of Dora Greenfield. Although Dora herself does not perceive
the discrepancy, we are immediately struck by the way the feigned
earnestness of the brotherhood has stripped the locale of its beauties.
The contrast between the baroque chapel and the religious service
taking place there is our first indication that the community has
drained piety of its joyful aspects: "Dora's gaze wandered for a
while among pale egg-and-dart friezes and pink scrolls and stucco
garlands until it found its way back to the sober scene below." When
Dora returns to the chapel she is impressed by "an annihilating
silence," and the entire spectacle has a tawdriness she is unable to
reconcile with her husband's profound reverence for the brotherhood:
"In the bright daylight the room looked, Dora thought, even more

derelict, like an aftermath of amateur theatricals." Paul's own room, Dora notices, has also fallen victim to the same misguided spirit of privation and chastisement that forms the general mentality of Imber:

> It had been a grand bedroom in its time, with green panelling and a great mirror set in the wall. It was furnished now with two iron beds, two upright chairs. . . . Two new but cheap mats were on the floor, which otherwise was bare. The room echoed as they spoke.

The community's stoical interpretation of the Christian life has undermined more than beauty, art, and joy. By surrendering "worldliness," the brothers have forfeited their understanding of the principles by which the operating world is sustained. Dan Jacobson has observed the advantage that the cloistered Abbey holds in this respect over the Court: "The Abbey in the bell [sic] is a central image of power, at once human and impersonal."[4] From what we are allowed to see, the unworldly nuns are more sensible and good-natured about the benefits of practicality and cheer than the brotherhood. The Abbess and the Bishop both recommend brightening the occasion of the installation of the new bell with publicity and merriment; Mother Clare leaps into the lake to rescue Dora and Catherine Fawley from drowning; Sister Ursula, the liaison officer between the Abbey and the Court, votes for the purchase of a mechanical cultivator to expedite the Court's garden project in spite of the prevailing animus that only the most primitive tools should be used in the execution of this God-appointed task. The very fact that matters like the purchase of a cultivator and the shooting of predatory animals must be brought to a vote reveals that the community's ideal of harmonious action in the service of God is impractical and self-defeating.

Differences of opinion soon reach the state at which subcommittees must be appointed to study problems connected with the management of the Court. Another unforeseen consequence prompted by the juxtaposition of discordant wills is the question of power. As she demonstrated with SELIB in *The Flight from the Enchanter* and with St. Bride's School in *The Sandcastle*, Iris Murdoch is chary of the idea that progress in organizations automatically takes place with the passage of time. Growth and development can be ensured only by conscious efforts to refine and build upon the programs of the past. Michael Meade's failure as the leader of the Imber brotherhood is his disregard of cross-purposes and of relative values in corporate situations. As unavoidable as factions and hot tempers in any group

adjustment to the competitive demands of his society: "He arrogates to himself acts that are above his spiritual level."[8] Like William Mor in this aspect, Michael demonstrates that without self-knowledge a person forfeits any positive goal, either personal or vocational. About fourteen years before the time of the novel, Michael had lost his job as a schoolmaster because of his homosexual friendship with Nick Fawley. Although Nick, who was only fourteen or fifteen at the time, reciprocated Michael's advances in full measure, an evangelist sermon shamed him into explaining their situation to the school authorities. Curiously, this shattering of his rarefied idealistic love by earthy fundamentalist doctrine teaches Michael nothing. Despite the vague sense of *déjà vu* he experiences at several critical stages in his similar attachment to Toby Gashe, Michael's self-ignorance allows him to make the same kind of mistake he had made fourteen years before. At the age of twenty-five, Michael was convinced that he had mastered his homosexual tendencies and could turn immediately to the priesthood. His failures at this point and at Imber Court spring from his inability to acknowledge the vital presence of his uncensored instincts. This shortcoming betrayed him into conciliating his affection for Nick with his spiritual fervor. And again, years later, at the first moment of excitement he shares with Toby—their suddenly noticing the low-flying jet planes performing aerial maneuvers— Michael unconsciously clutches Toby's arm. Instead of trying to evaluate the meaning of his involuntary gesture, Michael collapses into his habitual practice of converting his sexual energy into a category of reason:

> He felt within him an infinite power to protect Toby from harm. Quietly he conjured up the vision of Toby the undergraduate, Toby the young man. Somehow it might be possible to go on knowing him, it might be possible to watch over him and help him. . . . He was conscious of such a fund of love and good will for the young creature beside him. It could not be that God intended such a spring of love to be quenched utterly. There must, there must be a way in which it could be made a power for good. Michael did not in that instant feel that it would be difficult to make it so.

Instead of acknowledging the discordancies in his personality and acting on his observations, Michael expects the meaning of his life to unfurl before him in a prefabricated network of benign motives and positive achievements: "He expected the emergence in his life of patterns and signs. He had always felt himself to be a man with a definite destiny, a man waiting for a call." Ironically, the significance of his life does manifest itself to Michael, but in a way he had never anticipated. The repetition of prior experiences forces him to face the same challenges that confronted him as a much younger man. Jung, in the essay "On Synchronicity," states that the *sentiment du déjà-vu* is a meaningful coincidence so improbable that it must depend upon some unknown property of the psychophysical world. The *déjà vu* is based, Jung continues, on a foreknowledge that can occur in dreams or in the waking state. "In such cases mere chance becomes improbable because the coincidence is known in advance."[9] Michael has the advantage of foreknowledge in both his waking activities and his dreams. He experiences on several occasions the recurring dream that the nuns from the Abbey have drowned him and are hauling his corpse from the lake. To underscore the centricity of this recurring pattern, Iris Murdoch begins Chapters VI and XVIII with the same words:

> Michael Meade was awakened by a strange hollow booming sound which seemed to come from the direction of the lake. He lay rigid for a moment listening anxiously to the silence which [Chapter XVIII here substitutes *that*] had succeeded the sound, and then got out of bed and went to the open window.

On the second occasion, however, the booming sound is real. Dora Greenfield is wildly ringing the medieval bell that she and Toby Gashe had wrested from the lake. Thus Michael's vaguely apprehended self-concepts have inverted themselves and materialized to fuse with his hidden psychic being. The sounding of the bell, among other things, is the sensory expression of Michael's self-delusion and of his failure to balance the coincidences in his life. His emergence as a person demands his deliverance from the recurring patterns that have dominated his life. As the action develops, we see that Michael, the leader of the brotherhood, is more of an initiate into life than Dora, Toby, or either of the Fawleys.

The inscription upon the medieval bell reads, "Vox ego sum Amoris. Gabriel vocor." By refusing to understand his homosexuality, Michael forfeits both human and divine love. His self-delusion makes him a haunted creature who tries in vain to divide himself from the source of his energy and impulses. But nature refuses to permit

internal monologue. Any reader would agree that dullness cannot be justified or glorified so long as it provokes tedium. Probably certain sections in *The Sandcastle* and *The Bell* can be read less attentively than others; but before we censure Iris Murdoch, we must first acknowledge the originality and the difficulty of her moral objective. Description in *The Sandcastle* and *The Bell* serves a greater purpose than lyrical self-indulgence or garnish. As has been stated, the region of material things claims a potentially great importance in our lives; aside from creating solid physical settings, Iris Murdoch's descriptions exploit the texture and density of an inert, baffling realm that resides more closely to our plans and enterprises than we might normally imagine. The inescapable presence of material reality even extends to the supernatural: Before Toby can hoist the legendary bell from the bottom of the lake, he must account for various weights, balances, and frictions and for the tensile strength of his makeshift block-and-pulley mechanism. Because of the insistent reality of the physical world, Iris Murdoch implies, sometimes our most idealistic schemes involve as much engineering skill and mechanical dexterity as they do inspiration or psychological insight.

A character equally guilty as Michael Meade of neglecting both the complex plenitude of the world and the true state of her own personality is Catherine Fawley, Nick's twin sister. Like Michael, she is disturbed by recurring dreams about drowning. Frequently associated with water, which she characteristically fears, Catherine dwells constantly upon the idea of her guilt and spiritual unworthiness. When the new bell capsizes into the lake she blames herself, in keeping with the medieval legend concerning the lascivious nun. Catherine's speech, as she makes ready to drown herself, is childish and melodramatic. Her language reflects accurately an undeveloped, misdirected spirit locked within its own arbitrary limitations: "God has reached out His hand. A white garment cannot conceal a wicked heart. There is no passing through that gate. Goodbye." Souvage has evaluated the forces behind Catherine's distorted mentality at this point in the action:

> As we know, Catherine has transferred to Michael her former passionate devotion to Nick. Although she is to enter the Abbey as a novice (at the moment of the bell's installation), she is in love. In a person as unbalanced as Catherine such love will breed guilt . . . she comes increasingly to identify herself with the guilty nun who drowned herself in the lake.[12]

Thus, as in the case of Michael, myth, reality, the past, and the present all coalesce to mock Catherine's self-imposed bondage. Both Fraser and Stephen Wall believe that Michael and Catherine will marry after she recovers from the shock of the attempted suicide. Wall calls her "the final legacy left him [Michael], ironically, by his love for Nick."[13] Catherine and Michael are both unable to transmute their fragmented piety into a realistic self-appraisal or a satisfying human relationship. It is, ironically, Nick the wastrel, alcoholic, and homosexual, who refines his love for Catherine and Michael, thus freeing them to encounter each other with a fresh maturity of vision. Voicing what is perhaps the central moral impulse of the novel, the Abbess advises Michael that emotional attachments are not to be shunned or overlooked; although our sorrows all derive from unsatisfactory finite love, only by loving can we gain a true other-directed understanding of reality:

> Remember that all our failures are ultimately failures in love. Imperfect love must not be condemned and rejected, but made perfect. The way is always forward, never back.

Nick, rather than the spiritually inclined Michael or Catherine, renounces his flawed love in the interest of a nobler goal. The transfiguration of his residual homosexual affection for Michael and his incestuous love of Catherine ("Nick told Michael of his twin sister whom he loved, he swore, with a Byronic passion.") is the only immediately discernible result at Imber of the miraculous restoration of the medieval bell. Nick's confrontation of Toby, when he persuades Toby to confess his relationship with Michael to James Tayper Pace, is a grotesque inversion of the Mass ceremony. Suitably, Toby's confession to James—which follows Nick's coercive "sermon" —undermines the sham structure of the brotherhood and liberates Michael from further temptation, just as Nick's suicide does. Accordingly, Nick's sabotage of the new bell unsettles Catherine's emotional poise and provokes her ensuing declaration of love to Michael. The Zarathustran ideal of destruction as positive creation is the transvaluation of values that Imber so drastically requires. But Michael misinterprets Nick's magnanimous act as vengeance, and none of the brotherhood ever regards Nick as any more than Catherine's dissolute twin.

Dora Greenfield and Toby Gashe, the young engineering student

who spends several weeks at Imber before beginning his studies at
Oxford, form a deliberate contrast to the brooding, self-doubting
pair of Catherine and Michael. Dora and Toby are the youngest
inhabitants of the Court, and they are both Londoners. But whereas
Toby has a youthfully romantic attitude toward the hardy simplicity
of rural life, Dora is a thoroughgoing child of the pavements. She is
suspicious of the green, sculptured country landscape, instinctively
preferring the bustling conviviality of the metropolis. When Dora
returns to London from Imber, she feels immediately at home amid
the city's crowds and noise:

> She stood for a while and let the crowds course round her, delight-
> ing in the rush and jostling, the din of voices and trains, the smells
> of oil and steam and dirt, the grimy hurly-burly and kind, healing
> anonymity of London. Already she felt more herself.

Although their attitudes toward the brotherhood change radically,
Dora approaches Imber peevishly, while Toby adjusts painlessly to
its routine of prayer and gardening. Both Dora and Toby are fresh
and supple, and both refrain, out of good will and unpretentious
heartiness, from making moral judgments about others. Their common practice of wading and of trailing their hands in the water as
they paddle across the lake suggests symbolically their natural zest
for life. As students (Dora has just given up her art studies in
London), they are at Imber, theoretically, to learn from the brotherhood. Surprisingly, by resurrecting the sunken bell, it is they, the two
newcomers, who supply the needed lesson in divine and human love;
but the significance of their act is never really grasped by themselves
or by the others.

Chapters XIII and XIV form the thematic and quantitative middle
of the novel. By rejecting the fake piety of the community, Dora
and Toby acquire in these sections the knowledge that permits them
to execute their "miracle" later in the novel. Toby's unauthorized
visit to the cloistered cemetery and Dora's journey to London show
them that, for the living, there is no escape from life. Having grown
restive after his shocked confrontation of Michael in the Land-Rover,
Toby decides to explore the forbidden area inside the convent walls.
He is met by absurdity and death, the unavoidable facts of human
life anywhere. The cemetery is bordered by a column of cypress
trees, symbolic of death, and greeting Toby's arrival is a gracious
invitation to sit on the swing that hangs from one of the trees.

Accordingly, Dora's trip to London cures her of the isolation and moral solipsism that haunts her at Imber: "It was as if her consciousness had eaten up its surroundings. Everything was now subjective." In London, Dora regains her moral balance and her vision of the measureless extensions of finite reality. Her ritualistic modern jazz dance with Noel Spens prepares her emotionally for her visit to the National Gallery, where the solid human reality described in the paintings destroys her solipsism. Once she is convinced of the real existence of objects removed from her consciousness and control, the world regains its vividness and depth. Although she never again attains the moral focus she experiences at the National Gallery, her illumination reveals to her that the substance of her life resides in facing her marital problems rather than in trying to escape them.

As Souvage points out, Toby Gashe is a secondary character in *The Bell*.[14] Toby is, nevertheless, worthy of critical consideration because of the clarity with which he dramatizes several of his author's major philosophical beliefs. Preparing to enter Oxford, Toby is an initiate into the responsibilities of manhood. The suitability of his visit to the religious community of Imber at this stage of his development is suggested by Jung's "The Archetypes of the Collective Unconscious":

> It [the Church] is a striving that can be found in the most varied forms among all primitive people who are in any way developed and have not yet become degenerate: I mean the institution or rite of initiation into manhood. When he has reached puberty the young man is conducted into the "men's house," or some other place of consecration, where he is systematically alienated from his family. At the same time he is initiated into the religious mysteries, and in this way is ushered not only into a wholly new set of relationships, but, as a renewed and changed personality, into a new world. . . . The initiation is often attended by all kinds of tortures. . . . These practices are undoubtedly very old. They have almost become instinctive mechanisms, with the result that they continue to repeat themselves without external compulsion. . . . They are engraved in the unconscious as a primordial image.[15]

Ironically, Toby discovers that, as a religious institution, Imber is a different kind of "men's house" than he had supposed; he is also forced to acknowledge surprising traits in his own personality. During his first weeks at Imber, his life with the brotherhood drenches him with a sense of godliness, worthiness, and gratitude. His amorous encounter with Michael Meade, however, makes him conscious of himself and of others in a way he had never anticipated. His first disgusted reaction soon turns to compassion, and he finds himself unable to perform his daily chores with the same single-mindedness as before. As soon as he and Michael signify their love to each other, Toby becomes curious and adventurous, violating, as has been stated, the cloistered area behind the convent walls. His stay at Imber discloses to him elements of human life from which he had thought himself immune. But, as has been suggested above, in spite of his doubts and frustrations, he is better prepared emotionally for college life than if he had never visited Imber.

Progress in human knowledge, Iris Murdoch believes, demands emotional involvement and baring ourselves to the complexities of others. Toby benefits, ironically, from his impassioned association with Michael even before he understands his predicament. After he leaves Imber, Toby's acquired vigilance for life's hidden possibilities will make him at once more understanding and better equipped to meet emotional challenges creatively: "What Michael had done was to Toby a tremendous revelation. His whole conception of human existence was become in a moment immensely more complex and even in a brief space had made progress."

Iris Murdoch, then, justifies dramatically Dora's and Toby's discovery of the legendary bell. Their vigorous engagements with dense, abounding life and their basic honesty and tolerance have made them the likeliest candidates in the novel to participate in an awesome act. Iris Murdoch shows, however, that the bell incident is not merely the product of the combined insouciance of Dora's and Toby's wills. Dora's motive for removing the bell from the lake is to jar the orthodox complacency with which the community judges her. Toby, in turn, also demonstrates the obscurity of human motives by using Dora as proof that he can love a woman. Nonetheless, transcending the entire question of motive-seeking is the material fact that Dora and Toby cause the bell to ring by falling into it as they embrace: Gabriel, the voice of love, peals forth at the expression of heterosexual physical love, however confused or impure it may be.

Love, for Iris Murdoch, is legitimate whether it is sacred or profane. But, as the contradictory texts of the two sermons show, absolute love of God is a difficult mental operation; our finite imperfections have not yet reached the refined state in which we can sustain a satisfactory, all-encompassing spiritual belief. Catherine and Michael prove that unwatched elements of our personalities always intrude to deprive the rigidly devout soul of his emotional stability and spiritual security. Berkeley censured Locke for trying to fuse subordinate and superordinate elements; Iris Murdoch demonstrates, through Toby, Dora, and Nick Fawley, the least reverent and scripturally doctrinaire persons at Imber, that more tangible progress can be made by directing our spiritual energy to the reality of other people than to a supernatural force.

Nietzsche remarks somewhere in *Zarathustra* that we must learn to crawl before we can walk and that we must learn to run before we can fly. As Iris Murdoch's novels testify, human knowledge and human relationships are difficult goals in themselves; Nick Fawley has to commit suicide to provide merely the first stage for a possible *rapprochement* between his sister and Michael Meade. Iris Murdoch seems to stand behind the Abbess's statement to Michael about refining imperfect human love. Only by loving others can we gain the selfless apprehension of reality that will allow love of God to be more than a screen between ourselves and the challenge of everyday reality. As clumsy and impure as their act is, the voice of love answers the embrace of Dora and Toby. James Tayper Pace and Dora's husband Paul may suspect that Dora had committed adultery with Toby; ultimately, their dour, uncharitable views reflect more unkindly upon them than upon her. By participating in a joyful expression of human love, she and Toby unconsciously achieve a goal that eludes their judges. The two young visitors to the Court succeed without premeditation in establishing the human-centered morality in which religious convictions can best flourish and proliferate into a secure metaphysics.

Souvage and Marvin Felheim argue convincingly that, contrary to Mrs. Meidner's belief, Dora rather than Michael is the main character of *The Bell*. Souvage mentions that Dora initiates most of the action in the novel and that she "responds to the challenge of the bell in a more positive way than that of the other characters." Dora's personal story, Souvage continues, frames the entire novel: she is the first character we meet and the last we see in the final chapter.[16] With the possible exceptions of Toby Gashe and Nick Fawley, she makes more moral progress than any of the other figures in *The Bell*. At the beginning of the book she feels guilty, frightened, and curiously old—"Dora was still very young, though she vaguely thought of herself as past her prime." But by the time the action is finished, she feels rejuvenated. Seen first as an art student, she prepares at the end to go to Bath, where she has a job waiting for her as a teacher. Within an hour after her arrival at the train station in nearby Pendelcote, she loses her shoes and is rebuked for leaving her suitcase on the train and for omitting to cover her head in chapel. At the close Dora's ingenuous spontaneity triumphs over the methodical righteousness of the others. Her most important self-discovery is that her marriage is a failure. Although this revelation is divisive in spirit rather than gloriously uplifting, as one might expect in a novel with a religious setting, it marks a definite advance on her part. The general temper at Imber is so misguided that the destruction rather than the expansion of existing values is what the brotherhood requires. All of the characters in *The Bell* entertain in some way erroneous assumptions about themselves and about social reality. By destroying a spurious value, Dora performs a creative act. Felheim regards her moral progress in roughly these same Nietzschean terms— moral rectitude is often so isolated that it can manifest itself only as loneliness and endurance:

> She is the last to arrive at, and the last to leave, Imber. One of her first acts there is to lose her shoes by the lake; she is somewhat afraid of the water, as she cannot swim. Her final action is to row upon the lake in a kind of lonely triumph (she has meanwhile taught herself to swim so "the depths below affrighted her no longer") with the feeling that "it belonged to her." The religious community has failed, the members have scattered, but Dora, who had no vocation, has found herself.[17]

It is consistent with Iris Murdoch's moral vision that her two major characters in *The Bell* remain ignorant of each other. Michael Meade finds women coarse and vaguely repulsive and therefore avoids relationships with them. He and Dora had seen Toby wading naked in the water in Chapter V. Curiously, Dora thinks that this experience has somehow linked her emotionally with Michael, and she never revises this erroneous view. She is uninquisitive, careless, and erratic, but there is an elusive quality about her that endears her to men. At the stormiest moments of their marriage, Paul never doubts his love for her; Toby selects her in preference to Catherine Fawley as a female partner with whom he can affirm his heterosexuality; Noel Spens, the London reporter who follows her to Imber, admits

in his characteristically guarded way that Dora is the kind of woman
whom men love in spite of their better judgment: "You're unreliable
and untidy and ignorant and totally exasperating but somehow I'd
like to have you around the place again."

Dora's unsoundness is expressed by her choice of a husband. Of all
the men she could have married, Paul Greenfield is probably the
one least suited to her spritelike personality. The possible scion of
German-Jewish heritage, Paul labors diligently to achieve professional,
social, and religious eminence. He transfers his self-conscious per-
fectionism to others, expecting from them the same exactness that he
practices himself in his studies of medieval woodcuts and manuscripts.
In spite of Mrs. Meidner's disclaimer,[18] Paul is a brilliant portrait of
a devoted scholar who has lost himself in trite details; the nature of
his job has betrayed him into forsaking the human for the mechanical
and the derived. He knows the train schedules between Paddington
and Pendelcote; he can estimate accurately a taxi-driver's tip for any
given distance; he presumes correctly that Dora will go to Noel
Spens's house when she leaves Imber to spend the day in London.
The predominance of his practicality and rational judgment over his
heart is comically conveyed by his giving Dora one of his dirty shirts
to wear as pajamas. Lacking human values, Paul can understand
Dora only as an adjunct of his sound, reliable principles of honest
effort and conservative personal habits. In short, he fails to respect
Dora as a distinct person with her own legitimately held values and
personal history. This is why their marriage is unhappy: "It seemed
to her that Paul was urging her to grow up, and yet had left her no
space to grow up into. He wanted to teach her everything himself,
but lacked the time and the patience to do so."

Both Paul and Noel Spens try to organize Dora, but despite her
superficiality and lack of inner order she manages to resist both of
them. Iris Murdoch believes that all people crave frankness and
candor in their personal relationships. She returns to this theme with
perhaps greater intensity in *An Unofficial Rose* and *The Unicorn,*
but Dora is like Randall Peronett and Hannah Crean-Smith in that
her unsatisfied urge to plain dealing results in a form of violence.
Her resentment toward the brotherhood prompts her to coax Toby
to remove the bell from the lake. After her unannounced return from
London she discovers the other Imber residents listening placidly to a
recorded Bach concert:

They had a secure complacent look about them: the spiritual
ruling class; and she wished suddenly that she might grow as large
and fierce as a gorilla and shake the flimsy doors off their hinges,
drowning the repulsive music in a savage carnivorous yell.

*   *   *

In this holy community she would play the witch.

By a process never quite adequately explained, Dora soon elevates
her resentment and spite into love. Her first reaction, when she
overhears Nick Fawley and Noel Spens discussing the medieval bell,
is to protect the community from the unkind judgments of the
outside world. Although she is confused and alone, Dora's sense of
purpose at the barn where the bell is hidden transcends immediate
selfish concerns: "She felt herself to be a priestess, dedicated now to a
rite which made mere personal relations unimportant." Thus raw
impulse asserts once more its integrity at the expense of trained
reason. Wall states that while Dora is an inferior painter, she is
nevertheless a true artist.[19] She has no religious or historical sense,
but the ones who do are all haunted by uncertainty and insecurity.
During her first train ride to Imber, Dora is distracted by a red
butterfly that she rescues from being trampled by the unknowing
passengers; forgetting her luggage, she departs from the train with
the butterfly cupped in her hand. Paul's acerb remark that Dora's
neglect of the suitcase typifies her rings truer than he realizes. The
delicate, fluttering beauty of a butterfly—which, appropriately represents resurrection in Christian symbolism[20]—has much more natural
appeal to Dora than the heavy, dull brown suitcase.

Strictly speaking, Dora is an adulteress and a thoroughgoing
sensualist; but Iris Murdoch, warmly humane and sensitive to the
complexities of daily life, does not invoke the letter against her. Dora's
erotic vagrancy is somehow less damaging than Paul's implacable
righteousness, Mrs. Mark's callous interference, or Michael's obdurate
blindness to his homosexual instincts. This romantic motif is, of
course, undercut by the frequently obscured network of character
interrelationships in the novel. Dora, nevertheless, succeeds because
her mind is not freighted with learned theories about Christianity
and the necessary ingredients of the Christian life. Her revelation at
the National Gallery solidly refutes the doctrines preached by James
Tayper Pace and Michael Meade. Truth does not dwell in un-
questioning devotion to abstract rules or in self-exploration. Dora's

mystical experience, as the roses grown by the Peronetts in *An Unofficial Rose,* shows that reality is compatible with perfection and that perfection must be sought outside the perceiving self.

This view coincides in part with Platonic and Cartesian theory: Our own personal imperfection provokes us to seek the good and the beautiful elsewhere. These qualities, Iris Murdoch insists, are available in finite reality. Our ability to improve our understanding does not merely demonstrate our inescapable imperfection as mortals; it also proves that we can partake actively of the perfection we see in the external world. Iris Murdoch reveals herself ultimately to be as much of a romantic rationalist as Sartre: dumb Dora's theoretical ignorance gives her the spontaneity that fosters a free interchange and helps destroy academic barriers between people.

The remoteness of this goal gains expression in the bell incident. It is not accidental that while Dora furiously rings the traditional bell, Nick Fawley is explaining the bell's recovery to Noel Spens as a potential news item and Toby Gashe is confessing to James Tayper Pace his relationship with Michael. James had said earlier that, above all, the community needs a miracle. Ironically, when the wished-for miracle occurs, none of the regular members of the brotherhood understand its significance. Gabriel, after whom the bell is named, appears in Daniel 8 and 9 as the angel of comfort who announces the advent of the Messiah; in like manner, Iris Murdoch conveys stylistically an actual myth unfolding at Imber (italics are mine):

> The clamour arose, distinctive, piercing, amazing, audible at the Court, at the Abbey, in the village, and along the road, *so the story was told later,* for many miles in either direction.
>
> *   *   *
>
> Then someone pushed very roughly past her. *Dora said later* that if it had not been for that violent shove she would not have paid attention and not have started to wonder.
>
> *   *   *
>
> There was no response from the barn. Paul must have left it; *as it turned out later* he had gone back by the concrete road to the Court to telephone a London colleague.

Gabriel Pearson develops a good argument that the symbolic references of the traditional bell defy logical explanation by virtue of their nearly magical inexhaustibility.[21] It is true that the demands of human and divine love, as Iris Murdoch presents them, are indefinitely extended in their ramifications and possibilities. The potential perfection of reality is attainable only through selfless apprehension of one's human and nonhuman environment. Love is a mental and emotional exercise directed outward from the perceiver to the prereflective world. Thus love demands the logical priority of objective knowledge disengaged from personal need or acquired prejudice. Our prevailing concepts will continue to distort our ethical principles unless we learn to view ourselves objectively. Dora, as an unformed personality, does not have this barrier to overcome. Accordingly, Toby Gashe can scale the convent walls more easily than he can domesticate the impulses awakened in him by Michael Meade. The subjective apparatus is not only irrelevant but also our most nettlesome obstacle in the search for objective truth. Wall shows with some accuracy how the shifting symbolic value of the bell satirizes the erroneous, self-derived moralities of several of the characters in the novel:

> Catherine sees the bell as a sign of divine displeasure, Nick, presumably, as an instrument of vengeance, Dora as firstly a means of redressing the inferior balance of her own position at Imber and secondly as an artifact with a mysterious attraction and authority,— not to mention the attitudes of less important characters such as Paul Greenfield who is interested in the bell as a piece of art history, and Mrs. Mark who regards it as a fit subject for decoration in a spirit of craft revivalism—it surely becomes difficult to postulate for the bell a static or fixed symbolic meaning. In fact, its significance alters, according to the perspective in which it is viewed. The author nowhere gives any indication that any one of these attitudes, or some superior insight given to the reader alone and not shared by any of the characters, is to be regarded as authoritative.[22]

The miraculous restoration of the bell brings about the collapse of the Court. Rather than inspiring the brotherhood spiritually, the bell incident destroys an important zone of transition between secularity and scriptural doctrine. Even though the religious attitudes informing the Christian life as it is led at Imber are not worth preserving, Iris Murdoch's ultimate message in *The Bell* is probably the total isolation of religion in contemporary England. Dora Greenfield learns to swim and develops efficiency in matters of business and housekeeping. But these advances are meager in comparison to what has been lost by the absorption of the Court into the Abbey. Dora, the last lay survivor at Imber, will tell her experiences over a glass of West Country cider to her friend Sally in Bath. Meanwhile, the Anglican faith has lost a body of worshippers potentially able to accommodate religious doctrine to public need and to the moral demands of everyday living. The bell arouses in Paul only his antiquarian interests;[23] characteristically, he abandons his domestic cares to discuss it as an artifact with the experts at the British Museum. Catherine is restored to the indifference of common secular reality: "The doctors were not unhopeful of a complete recovery. The insulin was making her fat." Michael fails to rise to the intensity of Catherine's dramatic expression of love; he is relieved at her departure and recoils from her love as if it were an indecent and unnatural human reaction: "That Catherine had been in love with him, was in love with him, was something in every way outside the order of nature."

Michael's failure to accept a human truth, that is, heterosexual love, is equalled by the narrowness of his religious vision; his mentality at the end of the novel attests once more to Iris Murdoch's belief in the interdependence of human and spiritual love. Michael's chief worry at the end is that Nick despaired when Michael renounced him for a younger man. Michael is chagrined that Nick committed suicide without leaving a tangible sign of their mutual affection. Instead of examining his belongings and the charred remains in his fireplace, Michael had only to recognize Nick's undermining of the bell and his suicide as the sacrificial acts of love that they were. Catherine had previously urged Michael to permit Nick to come to Imber, thinking he could profit from the inspiring presence of the Abbey, "that great storehouse of spiritual energy across the lake." Ironically, Nick responds to the spiritual energy radiating from the Abbey with a force beyond the comprehension of either Catherine or Michael. Not only does the Imber brotherhood collapse under the supernatural weight of the miracle, but all of the members leave on different trains or at least in different coaches. Oblivious to the manifestations of human and divine love, Michael gives up his aspirations to the priesthood and finds his belief in God destroyed. The discovery of the bell, instead of inspiring his spiritual fervor, exposes his shallow awareness of the natural and the supernatural worlds. The revelations supplied by the bell and by Nick's suicide are utterly wasted on Michael. He is relieved at Dora's departure, and, whereas Nick responds immediately to the awe and wonder generated by the reclamation of the bell, Michael deliberates and feels uncomfortable. As the titular head of the brotherhood, Michael is content to ignore the deeper significance of the events at Imber in favor of practical matters of business (italics are mine):

> Since the events of the previous morning, Michael *had been occupied.* He *had summoned* the doctor to Catherine and *interviewed* him. . . . He *had spent* some *time,* with Margaret Strafford, by Catherine's bedside. He *had had speech* with the Bishop and *seen* him *off* with such dignity as was possible in the circumstances. With Peter, he *had investigated* the wooden section of the causeway and discovered that two of the piers had been sawed through just below the water level. He *had made arrangements* by telephone with a firm of contractors. . . . He *had interviewed* the foreman who had arrived with tiresome promptness. He *had answered* some twenty telephone calls from representatives of the press, and *talked* to half a dozen reporters and photographers who appeared on the spot. He *had visited* Dora. He *had made decisions* about Catherine.

Syntax and word choice express Michael's boredom with the entire proceedings. One of the most remarkable features of *The Bell* is its consistency of moral vision; Iris Murdoch resists smuggling into the novel any religious or skeptical doctrine that does not derive naturally from her basic humanistic assumptions. Her essay "A House of Theory," originally published in the same year as *The Bell*,[24] stressed the necessity of refreshing the arcane concepts of science by creating a transition area between the laboratory and the market place. Her similar recommendations in *The Bell* show that she respects organized religion as a force equal to science or politics for the erection of moral values. The failure of religion to date is traceable to its followers. Any conduct of life that fails to regard the self as an organism containing primary instincts or impulses will eventually undermine itself. All of our efforts will either pale to colorlessness or explode into violence if we try to gainsay the potency of our irrational drives. We participate in reality, Iris Murdoch believes, with more than our disembodied minds; the worship of God, as an act of love, demands a broader and more liberal understanding of the ways in which His creations reveal themselves to us in finite experience. As an organic synthetic development, love of God is the final ratification of disciplined human sentience.

Iris Murdoch considers this same problem in reverse in *A Severed Head*. In that novel, it is not the life-denying repudiation of the first movers of our consciousness that she investigates, but the wanton parading of animal instinct without the controlling faculties of restraint or reason.

Notes to Chapter Six

1. Jean-Paul Sartre, "Forgers of Myth: The Young Playwrights of France," *Theatre Arts,* 30 (June, 1946), 330.

2. Murdoch, *Sartre: Romantic Rationalist,* 45-46.

3. Micha, 301.

4. Dan Jacobson, "Farce, Totem and Taboo," *New Statesman,* 61 (16 June 1961), 957.

5. Barrows, 498.

6. O[lga]. M[cDonald]. Meidner, "The Progress of Iris Murdoch," *English Studies in Africa,* 4 (March, 1961), 26.

7. Jean-Paul Sartre, *Being and Nothingness,* trans. by Hazel E. Barnes (New York, 1956), 568.

8. Jacques Souvage, "Symbol as Narrative Device: An Interpretation of Iris Murdoch's *The Bell,*" *English Studies,* 43 (April, 1962), 91.

9. Carl G[ustav]. Jung, *The Structure and Dynamics of the Psyche,* 522.

10. Marjorie Grene, *Introduction to Existentialism* (Chicago, 1960), 46-47.

11. Meidner, "The Progress of Iris Murdoch," 27-28.

12. Souvage, "Symbol as Narrative Device," 94-95.

13. Fraser, 44-45; Stephen Wall, "The Bell in *The Bell,*" *Essays in Criticism,* 13 (July, 1963), 272.

14. Souvage, "Symbol as Narrative Device," 94.

15. Carl G[ustav]. Jung, *Two Essays on Analytical Psychology,* trans. by R. F. C. Hull (New York, 1956), 115-16.

16. Souvage, "Symbol as Narrative Device," 83-84.

17. Marvin Felheim, "Symbolic Characterization in the Novels of Iris Murdoch," *Texas Studies in Literature and Language,* 2 (Summer, 1960), 195.

18. Meidner, "The Progress of Iris Murdoch," 25.

19. Wall, 269.

20. Hangen, 59.

21. Gabriel Pearson, "Iris Murdoch and the Romantic Novel," *New Left Review* (January–April, 1962), 141.

22. Wall, 271; see also Micha, 298.

23. Gindin, 179.

24. Iris Murdoch, "A House of Theory," 218-33.

Seven

A SEVERED HEAD

The Moral of the Minuet

Except for *The Italian Girl, A Severed Head* is the shortest, the "flattest" in character portrayal, and the sprightliest in tone of Iris Murdoch's novels to date. On the other hand, it bears the mark of a professional artist who continues to address her readers in a veiled manner. *A Severed Head* examines different kinds of personal power, their sources, and their effects upon other people. Iris Murdoch does not agree with Comte that the large corporate society will attain the perfection in which private volition and civic policy blend to guarantee material prosperity to all. *A Severed Head* discusses personal drives to power that can arise only in a specialized society like ours, in which scientific technology, the arts, and political organizations transcend national boundaries. The professional types in the novel—the scholar, the artist, the businessman, and the psychoanalyst—and the obscure points of convergence in their lives dramatize our inescapable moral interdependence as social beings. Iris Murdoch believes us to be more vitally interrelated than our public administrators have understood. The ways in which persons gain power over others today show the damage that may occur when human relations are organized and defined by social fiat rather than by private conviction.

The various drives to power portrayed in *A Severed Head* are the natural products of our unnaturally specialized age and the exalted position occupied by psychoanalysis. Instead of enduring discomfort and pain silently, it has become fashionable to discuss our most intimate problems, especially on the psychoanalyst's couch. The first surprise in the novel is Antonia's confession to her husband Martin Lynch-Gibbon that she is having a serious love affair with his friend Palmer Anderson, a popular American analyst practicing in London. By virtue of the faith accorded him by his mangled society, Palmer is frequently referred to as a modern magician. His gracious manner and his sleek, groomed appearance are conveyed most vividly to Martin, who is the narrator of the novel, by the epithet *silver*:

> He has that tall lanky "rangy" loose-jointed graceful close-cropped formidably clean American look. He has silver-grey hair which grows soft, furry and inch-long all over his round rather smallish head, and a smooth face which looks uncannily younger than his years.

Complementing Palmer Anderson's silvery glow is the golden penumbra cast by Antonia. Their love affair, instead of revolting Martin, elevates Anderson and Antonia in his judgment to the privileged status of parents; curiously, he grows fonder and more respectful of the tarnished pair because of their deception. They, however, are much less comfortable than Martin about their moral emancipation. Although they have framed a rational explanation for their conduct that impresses Martin, the two have not convinced themselves that their affair falls within the moral purview of rational civilized action. The natural misgivings of Antonia and Anderson undermine both their illicit relation and the ascendancy they have gained over Martin. Once again, we must turn to Nietzsche to appreciate the full significance of this unorthodox love triangle. As has been suggested, much more psychic and social depth is generated by our social relations than the organizers of modern society have observed. Iris Murdoch forces us to examine our intimate personal values in the light of both social developments and the psychological criticism of history by previous writers in order to understand her attitude.

Nietzsche claims that although they were small in number, the Jews came out of the desert as a master warrior race; they exercised their strength by wrathfully conquering weaker nations who resisted their predatory claims. Being small, however, they were eventually crushed and enslaved; their prophets, at this dire time, performed what Nietzsche calls "the miracle of the inversion of values." Jehovah was no longer seen as dour and scornful, but as a benign deity ready to forgive His people should they repent and obey His mandates. This redirection of spiritual values proclaimed the ethic of meekness and love of neighbor in place of the earlier virtues of valor, self-discipline, and power. The apogee of this movement, says Nietzsche, occurs in the Christians, a sect of the Jews. The slave morality engendered by Christianity exalted the teaching of humility, loving-kindness, and sympathy; even the Christian God is willing to dispense with the letter of justice in order to sacrifice Himself to others. Lawrence borrows Nietzsche's basic precepts in his *Fantasia of the Unconscious* and directs them to the question of what he believes to be the inversion of roles in modern marriage and contemporary society:

> Instead of being assertive and rather insentient, he [modern man] becomes wavering and sensitive. He begins to have as many feelings—nay, more than a woman. His heroism is all altruistic endurance. He worships pity and tenderness and weakness, even in himself. In short, he takes on very largely the original role of woman. Woman meanwhile becomes the fearless, inwardly relentless, determined positive party.[1]

Iris Murdoch is too much the theoretical moralist to concur with Nietzsche or Lawrence that man can transcend himself through obedience to instinct. In an age whose values have become unspecified and transitory, it is difficult to align an instinctive drive with a corresponding specific value. The golden Antonia and the smooth, silver-crested Anderson need Martin's compliance to justify themselves. Life requires structure, discipline, and organization; unable to supply these ingredients themselves, Antonia and Anderson look to the acquiescence of Martin. They become offended upon learning that he has transcended their rules and their needs by having secretly conducted for eighteen months an illicit affair with Georgie Hands, a young instructor at the London School of Economics. Antonia and Anderson want to help and understand him in order to assuage their own guilt. Lacking principles that derive from her own inner convictions, Antonia is positively revivified by Martin's disclosure of his irregularities: "To have me presented as so easy, so defenceless, a quarry to a mingled power of censure and of love excited her, gave her a sort of sexual thrill."

Our age of specialization and technical analysis has distorted both human values and the sovereignty of our private undertakings. The psychoanalyst, who has been empowered by society to restore confidence and moral wholeness, is as deluded and confused as the general public. Palmer Anderson is evidently the target of Iris Murdoch's sustained satire of Freudianism in the novel. In Freudian terminology, the impulses deriving from the brute authority of Anderson's id clash with his moral code; hence, the superego assumes control. In satisfying his own psychorational needs, however, Anderson violates Martin's freedom. Underlying Anderson's smug psychological principles is a satirical, but somewhat accurate, version of Freud's evolutionary mechanism. Conspicuously absent from Anderson's program of study are the accidental, the contingent, and an awareness of the human personality as an organic continuum: "The psyche is a strange thing. . . . It is almost entirely a matter of mechanics, and mechanical modes are the best to understand it with." Anderson overlooks the equal validity of other points of view and the countless ways in which people confront the world; consequently, he cannot understand Martin's deviation from the emotional needs of his own unsteady relation with Antonia.

Ironically, Martin is disinclined for some time to resist this interference. It is here that Iris Murdoch amplifies and augments the social criticism of Nietzsche and Lawrence discussed above: the imputed "slave morality" that these two prophetic writers despised is not a simple case of resignation and submission in *A Severed Head*. By divorcing their values from those of the human community at large, Antonia and Anderson come to require Martin's approval as a constituent of their attachment. Thus, the oppressor becomes his victim's victim, the anvil destroying the hammer, as it were. By default, Martin can claim real power even though he remains ignorant of this truth.

Contingency goes still further to correct the excesses caused by willful human inconsistency. The balance of discordant public and private interests in our lives is, contrary to Freud, often so delicate that a sudden shift or dislodgment in one area can upset our entire moral stability. Rather than functioning as the mechanical constituents of a depersonalized social network, we are vitally involved in each other's lives; everyone in the novel is in some way unsettled by the decision of Antonia and Anderson to live together. Martin eventually thrashes both Anderson and his sister for interfering in his life.

Accordingly, Georgie Hands responds violently to the harm wrought upon her in publicizing her illicit relationship with Martin, by engaging herself to Martin's brother Alexander, and by attempting suicide. There is nothing in the world of facts and experience to controvert human equality and the need for plain dealing in social relations. Injustice, either social or political, provokes its own dialectic; whether we are neglected or maligned, human nature recoils from intimidation. It is this aspect of modern life, our interpenetrability as social beings, that the administrators and specialists have overlooked. Iris Murdoch does not sanction Martin's affair with Georgie. But this relationship contains none of the destructive guilt of Antonia's intrigue with Anderson. In addition to deceiving Martin openly, they try to make him approve of their conduct and allow his life to be governed by it. Georgie, accordingly, recoils when she discovers the unfairness of Martin's commitment to her.

Iris Murdoch abides faithfully within the limits of human contingency in her investigation of moral issues. As diligently as her characters try, they cannot escape accident, incompleteness, and their own susceptibility. When Martin discovers Antonia and Anderson in bed, the adulterous couple are borne up by graceful, voluptuous images:

> An enormous double bed faced the door, its white headboard festooned with trails of gilded roses. The snow-white sheets were parted. A pair of lamps, mounted on tall carved ecclesiastical candlesticks, also gilt, shed a soft radiance from either side. There was a scattering of rosy Persian rugs upon the white carpet.

Palmer, likewise, drapes himself in richly embroidered dressing gowns. On the two occasions when Martin discovers him thus splendidly attired, he sees that Palmer is wearing nothing underneath. Iris Murdoch's satirical intention seems to be the same as Byron's in *Don Juan*: despite our efforts to the contrary, the naked flesh and human imperfection always peer insistently through the finery and the veneer. Seeing his tormenters lounging in their sumptuously appointed bed, Martin calls them Ares and Aphrodite. The epithets are more apt than the three characters realize, for Martin is soon to assume the role of Hephaestus with great force and cunning. Vulcan, or Hephaestus, was the most ill-favored of the gods in classical mythology. Born lame, he was cast out of heaven because of his mother's displeasure upon seeing him. Zeus, however, later gave him as his bride Aphrodite, or Venus, in exchange for forging thunderbolts. When Hephaestus finds his wife making love to Ares, or Mars, the god of war, he casts an invisible net over them and summons all the other Olympian deities to mock them in their open shame. Significantly, Martin, as Iris Murdoch's neo-Hephaestus, injures his foot after descending the staircase to Anderson's cellar, where he performs his first act of reprisal—the savage beating of Honor Klein.

Complementing the pseudo rationality encouraged professionally and practiced privately by Palmer Anderson are the sculpture and the personal ethic of Alexander Lynch-Gibbon, Martin's celebrated elder brother. Alexander is drawn to images of disembodied heads in both clay and bronze, a predilection that Martin recoils from as obscene and indecent. (As we shall see, Martin's creative act of writing *A Severed Head* is to liberate him from the evolutionary cycle of clay, bronze, silver, and gold.) Alexander's passing allusion to Freud's remark about Medusa—Alexander is a prodigious quoter, ranging from *A Midsummer Night's Dream* to Service's "The Cremation of Sam McGee"—suggests the futility of shaping our personal lives according to purely rational criteria. As we have observed, the search for rational justification damages both the allegedly bold and confident romance of Antonia and Anderson and their personal standing as individuals: certain features of human behavior cannot be tidily compressed into a thought process. Freud's reference to Medusa as the mythological figure the sight of whom turns men to stone has a direct bearing upon the satire developed in *A Severed Head*. According to Freud, Medusa is a classic embodiment of the castrated and castrating woman who robs men of their masculinity.[2] Of all the characters in the novel, only the compliant, tractable Martin escapes the formal, intellectualized sexual patterns of his cerebral society and ratifies his manliness in a dark sexual alliance.

The lesson he painfully absorbs is the disorderly, anarchic multiplicity of the human and the material world. At the beginning of the novel he is smugly satisfied with the doubleness of his private life. Between them, Antonia his wife and Georgie Hands his mistress gratify all of Martin's aesthetic and psychosexual needs:

> In almost every marriage there is a selfish and an unselfish partner. A pattern is set up and soon becomes inflexible, of one person always making the demands and one person always giving way. In my own marriage I early established myself as the one who took rather than gave.

*   *   *

I adored Georgie . . . for her dryness, her toughness, her independence, her lack of intensity, her wit, and altogether for her being such a contrast, such a complement, to the softer and more moist attractions, the more dewy radiance of my lovely wife. I needed both of them, and having both I possessed the world.

This tidy predictable world bursts to pieces when Antonia blithely announces that she and Alexander have been lovers for years and are now getting married. While she is imparting this humiliating news, Martin's stricken glance settles upon the magnolia tree in his garden. Suitably, the magnolia tree—associated symbolically in the Western world with virtue, youth, and feminine beauty[3]—appears lifeless. For reasons already suggested, Martin married a woman five years his elder whose family enjoyed great prominence in London society. (At the time of the novel, Martin is forty-one, Antonia forty-five, and they have been married for about eleven years.) Antonia, it seems, increases in beauty as she grows older, that is, as she grows physically into Martin's conception of his long-deceased mother. Alexander, too, bears a striking resemblance to their mother. When Antonia and Alexander abscond—to Rome, fittingly—Martin's fixed psychological world erodes:

> That he [Alexander] in whom, more than any other my mother lived again should so quietly and so relentlessly have defrauded me cast a shadow that was like a scar upon the innocence of the past which I had believed to be impregnable. . . . But my reaction to Alexander was something much more automatic than a judgment, and much more relentless. It was odd that the pain of it felt so like loneliness. Through him so much of my past had been peopled, which was now a stricken solitude.

This complication reveals once more Iris Murdoch's talent for dramatizing psychic reality in the light of intellectual history. Martin's mother-fixation proves itself to have had no equivalent or archetype beyond his imagination; the past, then, is not only an unreliable guide to the present but is as unfixed and ambiguous as the present or the future. The mysteries in our lives extend indeterminately in all directions, and the meaning of any given phase must always be reconstructed in accordance with new developments. Martin's understanding cannot keep pace with the rapid changes in his life; hence he misjudges the nature of his governing impulses. Our task as phenomenal beings is to examine more critically the principles that regulate our lives and especially their human counterparts. Our misjudgments and ungrounded concepts can involve others as well as ourselves in damaging relationships.

As the novel proves, a decision does not affect only the person who makes it. Georgie Hands is loving, tactful, sensible, and uncomplaining. Yet Martin's fixations impose a psychological limit on his feelings for her. His bogus mother-complex, which he is later forced to discard, prevents him from seeing Georgie clearly and from according her her true objective worth as an individual. Modern man's fear of rejecting his false principles, even after they have been unmasked, is labeled rational, civilized behavior by Antonia and Alexander. Of the few critics who have discussed *A Severed Head,* Gindin explains most persuasively how rationality serves in the novel as a weak substitute for honest vexation toward what is known to be injustice and violence:

> Like Miss Murdoch's other novels, *A Severed Head* mocks the spurious kind of rationality man invents for himself. When Martin is first told of his wife's affair with Palmer Anderson, he is asked to be rational and understanding, specifically to remain friendly with the pair, to dine with them often and join them for drinks in their bedroom. Rationality, in this society, is close to sterility, a form of gentle behavior that refuses to make any distinctions between human entanglements. . . . But the rationality itself . . . is always false, always an enchanting abstraction by means of which the human being, either deliberately or accidentally, deludes both others and himself.[4]

As novels that describe our self-consciously fraudulent behavior, *The Bell* and *A Severed Head* mark a peak for Iris Murdoch in her treatment of the effect of outside awareness upon private undertakings. The infidelities in *A Severed Head* are executed so cheerfully that we would expect modesty and remorse to be marginal. Antonia and Anderson parade their sexual intemperance publicly and even urge Martin to endorse it. Contrary to Anderson's belief, rationality is the flimsiest explanation that we can advance for human conduct; as limited beings, our knowledge of other people (and often of ourselves) is too fragmentary to form the basis of accurate judgments; furthermore, there is a universal tendency to interpret experience in line with our personal needs. But individuals cannot be conveniently shelved or immobilized; they continue to develop, substituting and reshuffling personal values regardless of our schemes. The uncertainty and irrationality of human attachments gain expression by the ease with which personal values can be dislodged. Jake Donaghue's publication of *The Silencer* in *Under the Net* kills his friendship with Hugo Belfounder; as soon as the popular press reports its version of the events leading to Nick Fawley's sabotage of the new bell, the spiritual undergirding of the Imber brotherhood collapses. Martin Lynch-Gibbon cites a truth that pertains directly to the evanescence and irrationality of our subjective values:

> Knowledge, other people's knowledge, does inevitably modify what it touches. Remember the legend of Psyche, whose child, if she told about her pregnancy, would be mortal, whereas if she kept silent it would be a god.

Let us compare Martin's remark with the following extract from *The Silencer*:

> For most of us, for almost all of us, truth can be attained, if at all, only in silence. It is in silence that the human spirit touches the divine. This was something which the ancients understood. Psyche was told that if she spoke about her pregnancy her child would be a mortal; if she kept silent it would be a god.

Although he refuses to face the fact, an essential component of Martin's love affair with Georgie Hands is its secretness. His bringing Georgie to his home in Hereford Square as a way of "breaking down the doubleness" conveys the shallowness of his principles. As soon as he thinks he hears Antonia at the front door, Martin forcibly ejects Georgie from the house in the manner of a high corporation executive trying to conceal an indiscretion with one of his secretaries. At the end of the novel, Anderson leaves London because he cannot rationalize away Martin's knowledge about the intimacies of his private life. Curiously, other people's knowledge of our immoderate acts rather than the acts themselves touches us more deeply, a truth that undermines the efficacy of psychoanalysis. As inhabitants of a world regulated by scientific analysis, we are ashamed to have our inconsistency exposed to the attention of others. Yet, in the opinion of Iris Murdoch, we cannot change the fact that we are imperfect combinations of rational and irrational elements. The attempts of Antonia, Anderson, and Martin to prove otherwise culminate in self-ridicule. Unless we acknowledge the presence in our personalities of obscure forces that are not amenable to the dictates of reason, we shall never affirm the potential dignity of our estate as human beings. Although Anderson makes his living discussing the thoughts and deeds of others, the weakness of his tie with Antonia and his retreat to the United States reflect his inability to apply scientific method to his own private life. Even a modern magician like Anderson cannot change the human psyche. Iris Murdoch does not recommend as a moralist that we conceal or parade our irrational drives. What she objects to is the practice of Michael Meade, Anderson, Antonia, and, to some extent, Alexander Lynch-Gibbon, of justifying our lawless impulses by explaining them with an arbitrary term. For in each of these cases, the arbitrary term, although convenient, fails to explain or justify the impulse.

Misses Seelhaft and Hernshaw, Martin's two secretaries, mysteriously learn of his marital problems before he explains them. After Georgie Hands recovers from her overdose of sleeping pills, there is a festive gathering around her hospital bed, comprised of Antonia, Honor Klein, Martin, Alexander, and Anderson, who has appointed himself Georgie's attending physician. When the dignity of our private ordeals is lost, so is moral seriousness. The general inclination to avoid objective appraisals of our discordant impulses leads only to shame and further dishonesty. True freedom, Iris Murdoch insists, is neither the ability to rule our lives by rational criteria nor the desperate consecration of our moral isolation. The only way we can protect ourselves from the judgments of others is to nourish our principles with the objective knowledge that personal dignity cannot be achieved by a fragmented person. The characters in *A Severed Head* behave furtively and are so easily mortified because they lack conviction: they cannot reconcile their privately elected acts with a set of moral principles derived from a disinterested, balanced understanding of social reality.

The scourge in the novel, the Nietzschean destroyer of her society's sham rationality, is the redoubtable Honor Klein, Palmer Anderson's half sister and an anthropology don at Cambridge. The vigor with which she repudiates the social morality of her time mirrors the depth of her author's concern with social values in the Western world today. The importance of Honor Klein in *A Severed Head* and in Iris Murdoch's thought in general shatters the mood of insularity and the good-natured trial-and-error attitude toward moral values that James Hall (who excludes Iris Murdoch from his study of modern fiction, *The Tragic Comedians*) posits as the presiding spirit in the British novel today:

> The British comic tradition is one expression of confidence that
> horrors can be handled. . . . The importance of their contemporary
> comedy is its ability to absorb with some cheer the shocks that else-
> where have produced a sophisticated hell-fire-and-salvation brand
> of existentialism. In recent years they [British novelists] have spoken
> for a precarious sanity that can face horrors and retain some self-
> command; they speak for the human element which does not quite
> accept the logic of the terrors it has proved.[5]

Although she may be unrepresentative of the comic spirit in modern
British fiction, Iris Murdoch is searching for bigger game than Hall
understands. With the entire tradition of Western thought in her
philosophical armory, she is aiming at a humanistic reconstruction
of inherited values, including our basic concepts of human existence.
The collisions resulting from this dialectic are reflected in the comic
structure of *A Severed Head,* particularly in its numerous farcical
and melodramatic scenes. In a situation where there is no presiding
morality to reconcile conflicting values, their opposition will be grat-
ing and jarring. Thus, Honor Klein and Martin battle furiously
in Anderson's cellar, Martin intrudes upon Honor and Palmer Anderson while they are in bed together, and various intimate conversa-
tions are interrupted and broken off by untimely entrances. Jacobson has tried to establish the link between fictional technique in *A
Severed Head* and the novel's social satire:

> Miss Murdoch is trying, among other things, to shock us out of
> our received notions of sexual morality (of morality in general,
> one can say), and it is for this reason that the surprises are pressed
> upon us with such intensity, and that they are of such a horrendous
> nature. It is for this reason, too, that in the midst of perversion,
> violence and talk of madness, the farcical aspects of the situation
> are muted, but are, if anything, made as emphatic as possible.[6]

Honor Klein, as has been suggested, personifies the Dionysian
aspect of this dialectic. She has little regard for values like democracy,
Christian charity, or scientific rationalism. Her dissonant morality
alters both the novel's formal comic pattern and the diagrammatic
sexuality of most of the characters. The most apt analogy to Honor's
rather savage mystique is Nietzsche's representation of the warlike,
disciplined nomadic Jews before their enslavement by Christianity.
The pair of Chinese incense holders in Georgie Hands's room that
appears on the opening page of the novel foreshadows Honor's bar-
baric Eastern primitivism and the unusual atmospheric phenomena

associated with her throughout the novel. She is continually equated
with fogs, mists, and sulphurous fumes. Martin can scarcely see
through the thick London fog as he drives her from the Liverpool
Street Station to her half brother's home in Pelham Crescent; when
Martin discovers that he is in love with the strangely charismatic
Honor, while walking alone on the Victoria Embankment, the day
is heavily overcast. Likewise, their strenuous battle takes place in the
cold, dank cellar of Pelham Crescent, "the bleak musty cavern that
was Palmer's cellar." Also, Honor refrains from boarding the air-
plane to New York at the end of the novel. Eventually the sun does
pierce the sulphurous mists, as Martin finally wins her, but he must
first endure arduous ordeals reminiscent of the ones accompanying
knightly quests in medieval legends: the night journey (from the
Liverpool Street Station to Pelham Crescent), the test of physical
strength (in Palmer's cellar), the subtler but more deeply felt psychological afflictions (Martin's staggering disclosure of his wife's infidelities and Honor's love affair with Palmer Anderson), and the
humiliating loss of his earthly kingdoms (his wife, his best friend, his
mistress, and his brother).

The graceless Honor has no counterpart in the modern British
novel. Instead of falling victim to psychoanalysis—society's newest
instrument for domesticating our dark primal impulses—the troll-like
Honor has no trouble routing her adversaries: Alexander takes Antonia to Rome, and Anderson, the new man of science, departs for
America, the new world, with Georgie Hands. The sun's final penetration of the London mists recalls the end of *Zarathustra,* where
Nietzsche's inspired prophet-poet boldly advances to proclaim the
master morality. The enemy of her society's values, Honor is a master
swordsman, executing a drill display that rivals Sergeant Troy's in
Far from the Madding Crowd. Iris Murdoch compresses a great deal
into this frightening scene. While Honor is dazzling Martin with her
swordsmanship (she holds her samurai sword "in a two-handed grip"),
the clamoring London church bells are distantly celebrating the New
Year and Antonia and Anderson are witnessing a performance of
Götterdämmerung. Honor, the wrecker of the *status quo,* approached
her half brother and Antonia for the first time as a primitive Oriental
warrior returning to her aristocratic rulers after a great military vic-
tory. Iris Murdoch uses this confrontation to adumbrate the eventual

overthrow of the presiding morality by the Nietzschean virtues of hardiness, raw power, and malevolence:

> Palmer had his arm around my wife. . . . They seemed in that momentary vision . . . like deities upon an Indian frieze, enthroned, inhumanly beautiful, a pair of sovereigns, distant and serene. They turned towards us. . . . I came up beside Honor Klein.
> Something strange happened in that instant. As I turned to look at her she seemed transfigured. Divested of her shapeless coat she seemed taller and more dignified. But it was her expression that struck me. She stood there in the doorway, her gaze fixed upon the golden pair by the fire, her head thrown back, her face exceedingly pale; and she appeared to me for a second like some insolent and powerful captain, returning booted and spurred from a field of triumph, the dust of battle yet upon him, confronting the sovereign powers whom he was now ready if need be to bend to his will.

Water imagery contributes to Iris Murdoch's portrait of Honor as an indomitable sea hag who successfully effects a transvaluation of prevailing values in accord with her own primeval wisdom. She is often seen wearing a very old dark green coat; her face and short black hair frequently glisten with moisture as she enters lighted rooms from a darkened background. Her movements, her gestures, and her mode of conducting her personal relations suggests an ancient godlike wisdom both cruel and terrible to witness. Georgie Hands finds herself compelled to explain her affair with Martin when Honor questions her; Martin, accordingly, is unable to keep himself from falling in love with her. After their savage fight, he finds that he cannot recall her name or her face. This memory lapse may be too obviously staged by the author, but her point is that Honor imparts an awesome power even in defeat; like the ancient Hebrew god of wrath, she is not to be named or encountered directly.

Gindin is mistaken when he interprets Honor as the id.[7] First of all, Iris Murdoch is emphatically not a Freudian; secondly, Honor does not act in derision of moral law. Her code of conduct is authentic, even if it is not Western or Christian in origin. Her fierce secularity prompts her to undermine both her half brother's self-conscious attachment to Antonia and Martin's liaison with Georgie Hands. Honor admires the samurai sword—an aristocratic symbol, as in Yeats—because it is forged with great skill and reverence. As a Jew, she conforms to the Semitic ideal articulated by Arnold in "Hebraism and Hellenism": Whatever awe or wonder she evinces originates in her profound respect for discipline and for the cultivation of wisdom and control. Honor is exposed to sin and participates in it, yet she transcends her incestuous bond by adhering to her precepts of obedience and self-control ("All I say is that only lies and evil come from letting people off." "With me people pay as they earn.").

Rather than seeking affinities with Freud, we can gain a richer understanding of both Honor Klein and Martin by tracing the concept of sexual power as it is presented by Nietzsche, Jung, and Rider Haggard. Jung's doctrine of the collective unconscious, which claims that deposits of universal experiences manifest themselves unconsciously as archetypes of recurring mental activities, is an obvious legacy of Nietzsche's concept of eternal recurrence. Jung differs from Nietzsche, however, in that he believes that the individual must liberate himself from deterministic behavioral patterns before he can realize his creative freedom: "Possession by an archetype turns a man into a flat collective figure, a mask behind which he can no longer develop as a human being, but becomes increasingly stunted."[8] The only immutable elements in Jung's account of personal realization are the stages in the developmental process. The individual can indeed prevent his growth from being arrested and thus ensure his emergence as a developed personality. The first stage in Jung's three-part evolutionary program suggests several important truths that Martin learns from his association with Honor Klein, for example, that there are inexpressible, antisocial traits within his own personality and within the world at large that influence his acts and decisions:

> The first figure of the unconscious is the shadow—the personification ... of all those tendencies that the individual rejects on moral or aesthetic grounds, and keeps in suppression because they are contrary to his conscious principles. It also contains qualities that the individual has not developed in his conscious life—in some cases capacity for thinking, in others capacity for relationships, and so forth. ... In order to develop an objective attitude to his own personality, or in order to *be* a fully developed personality, the individual must accept the existence of those trends within himself which are least approved and those which have not yet been lived.[9]

The next stage also involves an active merging of opposites; here the individual encounters his soul-image or anima, the sum of his hidden feminine characteristics.[10] Honor Klein, rather than the image of his deceased mother in the person of either Antonia or Alexander, proves to be Martin's unconscious female ideal. As the demonic female principle, the demiurge, Honor forms the counterpart in Martin's mind of the chief or the medicine man, personified by her half brother, the psychoanalyst, as modern magician. Her mighty will, her menacing stare, and the novel's title suggest the same creative influence that operated upon Rider Haggard's characterization of Ayesha, the ageless white African queen in *She,* who can be approached only after one endures many hardships and mysterious trials.[11]

The final phase of personal development in Jung's program is individuation; the individual here achieves a balance between his ancestral memories and his own finite consciousness. Iris Murdoch never permits the reader to view firsthand the working out of this stage in Martin's personality. It is even possible that Honor has completely captivated him and made him her eternal vassal. According to Jung's archetype, the father protects his son from physical dangers, while the mother shields him from the threats of the imagination.[12] Martin may have transferred the tutorial role, that of the mother-image, to Antonia and Alexander and at the end of the novel bestows it, perhaps, upon Honor. Unfortunately, this explanation has many weaknesses. It fails, first of all, to account for the numerous accidents and reversals in ordinary experience. Secondly, we cannot forget that Honor Klein is also a human being, in other words fragmentary, contingent, and vulnerable. Referring to Mrs. Tinckham and Hugo Belfounder in *Under the Net,* Peter Saward in *The Flight from the Enchanter,* Demoyte and Tim Burke in *The Sandcastle,* and Michael Meade and (somewhat incorrectly) the Abbess in *The Bell,* Gindin points out that frequently in Iris Murdoch's fiction characters fail to live up to the trust and infallibility granted them by their associates:

> All the novels include one or more God-images, characters of wisdom and insight to whom the other characters turn for advice. . . . But the God-figure never really works in the structure of the novel. The advice either turns out wrong or the God-figure never meant at all what the character thought he meant or the God-figure himself is equally perplexed.[13]

In spite of her will to secular power, Honor Klein is incomplete, a characteristic that is deliberately, and perhaps fatally, underplayed until the novel's final sentence. The love of Martin is essential to both her emotional gratification and her fulfillment as an individual. She comes to Martin's room in Lowndes Square, in the final chapter, not because he wants her, as she claims, but because she sees in him a person worthy of her love. Martin's rejection of the minuetlike sexual pairings, separations, and reshufflings in his private circle is creative. Stripped of moral preconceptions and emotional ties, the often ludicrous neo-Hephaestus can finally encounter Honor Klein as an equal. Pearson's interpretation of Martin's moral development is both artistically persuasive and verifiable by specific references: "Martin achieves his Honour, after passing through the false relationships of child love (to Antonia) [,] brother-love (to Alexander), homosexual love (to Palmer) and father love (to Georgie)."[14]

As the narrator of the novel, Martin possesses the combination of native intelligence and bewilderment James regarded as essential in the first-person narrative.[15] Jacobson has explained Martin's name as "the implication of a fine eighteenth-century rationalism coming to a bloody end."[16] We might also add the idea of Martin as a martyr who sacrifices his rationality to Honor's atavistic pay-as-you-earn *Realpolitik*. He possesses clear affinities with British neoclassicism: at different points in the novel he compares himself to Hume, Garrick, and Dr. Johnson. But the broad range of suggestiveness supplied by Martin's last name disallows any simple explanation of his character or his fortune. The "Gibbon" part of Martin's surname implies, along with the ugly sound of its antecedent "Lynch," a subhuman mode of life that finds expression both in Martin's willing service as toady to his wife and her lover and in his cool acceptance of Honor's incestuousness. (Iris Murdoch perhaps blunders when she expects the reader to view Martin's moral acquiescence merely as a sign of his creative rejection of society's values.) In addition to the polarities of rationalism and beastliness, "Gibbon" suggests stateliness, grandeur, scholarship, and history. (Martin is a military historian, which explains his affinity with the author of *Decline and Fall of the Roman Empire*, his subliminal attraction to violence, and his remorse about his unfinished study.) And, as a final point of comparison, Martin's alliance with Honor reflects his predecessor's scorn for the barbarities of Christian society and morality. Rationalism, or the ethic of proportion and moderation, has been inverted and distorted to the degree at which it must be discarded.

We have already suggested, along with Honor's ambivalence,

Martin's humiliation as a necessary prelude to his offering of himself as a suitable mate to her. While he waits at the airport to steal a last glimpse of Honor and Palmer Anderson before their flight to New York, he remarks to himself: "I felt as if I were about to be present at a murder, though as the victim or the assassin was not quite clear." Iris Murdoch remains, thus, mute to the end about the moral ambiguities she develops in *A Severed Head*. Martin, who seems to gain in perceptiveness and strength as he becomes more intimidated, says that his love for Honor is "monstrous . . . devoid of tenderness and humor, a love practically devoid of personality." The terrifying naked objectivity with which he sees her indicates, perhaps, a revitalized self-understanding and moral solidity.

The stylistic irony of *A Severed Head* centers about Martin's failure to recognize that he is recording the events leading to his own moral development. The man of reason, armed with wit, a sense of moral proportion, and his personal sorrows, is also Honor's antitype or animus and is, therefore, as essential to her psychological growth as she is to his. Their depersonalized, unapologetic love, as a clash of opposing forces, may foreshadow the new social order so drastically needed to replace our pseudoscientific telly-admass morality. In Nietzsche, who is probably the main philosophical influence on the novel, beauty and order are begotten only by violent, self-destructive collisions. The Joycean allusion to John the Baptist or the Precursor in the novel's title certainly signals a new order rising out of the ashes of its corrupt predecessor.

The progress made in the novel toward the overthrow of false social values is authentic. Although Honor remains relatively static in her perceptions and values throughout the novel, she and Martin do free themselves from the inward-turning, self-reflecting sexual patterns of their circle. Martin's ethical progress is discernible, apart from his objective acts and deeds. He is, at first, mild and retiring, but secretly sybaritic and unorthodox. Perhaps his greatest private sorrow at this stage is his vague feeling of emptiness and dissipated energy: Martin suspects that he would have enjoyed a richer, more edifying life as a scholar rather than as the merchant he has become; the inheritance of a flourishing wine business and a sensitive palate prevail, however, over his speculative impulses. Georgie Hands is right when she refers to his passion for servility: "If people interfere with you it's because you like it. . . . You're dying to be interfered

with. You're sort of a vacuum into which interference rushes." As
a means of sustaining his inferiority Martin marries a woman five
years his senior and presents his mistress with vulgar gifts that titillate
his masochistic impulses:

> I loved to give Georgie outrageous things, absurd garments and
> gewgaws which I could not possibly have given Antonia, barbarous
> necklaces and velvet pants and purple underwear and black
> openwork tights which drove me mad.

For his first forty-one years, Martin is unable to conduct a candid
personal relation. All of his intimate associates pander in some way
to his tenacious self-mortification. His reaction to Antonia's infidelity
shows no profound sense of loss or moral asperity: "Since when? and
how many times?" "If I broke your neck now I'd probably get off
with three years. . . . What have I done to deserve this?" His sour,
yet disarmingly ironic response to the news of Antonia's long-standing
affair with Alexander, much later in the novel, suggests both greater
emotional control and a new moral maturity. Reflecting his author's
approval of Russell's argument in "Mysticism and Logic," Martin
attains dignity by pursuing an extremely indirect route. Alone and
without prospects, he is willing to suffer silently in his gloomy
Lowndes Square flat.

Shortly before this episode he had reversed his good-natured compliance toward Antonia's relation with Palmer Anderson by blacken-
ing Anderson's eye. Honor Klein had earlier called Martin with
terrifying accuracy a violent man. Martin does more than convert
a theoretical interest in warfare by thrashing Honor and Anderson;
he exploits an untapped fund of creative energy that leads to his
writing a compelling novelistic memoir. His projected book on
military strategy incomplete, Martin nevertheless outstrips William
Mor of *The Sandcastle* by writing a detailed, full-length account of
the events leading to his union with Honor Klein. It is material that
Martin writes *A Severed Head* shortly after the conclusion of the
seven-week period (from 24 December to 11 February—from
Christmas Eve until the start of Lent) which it records: he tells
the reader that Georgie Hands "is now twenty-six" (presumably at
the time of his writing about her), and he later attributes this same
age to her in a conversation with Antonia and Anderson. We have
no way of determining the honesty or factual accuracy of Martin's
memoir. At one point he drafts three letters to Honor concerning the

same event—their brawl in Anderson's cellar—and each version differs sharply from the next. Of greater importance is Martin's impulsive decision to compose *A Severed Head*; he is obviously willing to sacrifice the mature perspective of leisurely retrospect in favor of the immediate discharge of creative energy. Honor Klein is the driving force behind the composition of *A Severed Head,* and Martin responds to her inspiration with more resoluteness than he had demonstrated in eleven years living with Antonia and in his unfinished military history. Honor, then, is not the last step in Martin's development. As the severed head, she is the precursor of a new order introduced by the flow of creative energy that went into Martin's novelistic memoir. The bewildered narrator, the playful tone, the use of melodrama and broad farce tend to underplay everything in the book. It is, perhaps, a sign of Iris Murdoch's restraint and caution that she couches her boldest social criticism in her most oblique novelistic manner to date. Martin, who may be her spokesman, develops more than any of the other characters: not only does he loose himself from his circle's patterned sexuality, but, by recording his revolt, he shows that he is trying to understand its full significance.

Most readers would share some of Walter Allen's chagrin over *A Severed Head*: "One is . . . left at a loss to disengage a meaning that satisfies."[17] The flaw in this otherwise remarkable novel is the hurried mythical resolution at the end. Standing in Martin's flat, Honor refers to Herodotus's account[18] of Gyges and Candaules, two kings of Sardis:

> "Do you recall the story of Gyges and Candaules?"
> I thought a moment and said, "Yes, I think so. Candaules was proud of the beauty of his wife and he wanted his friend Gyges to see her naked. He concealed Gyges in the bedroom—but Candaules' wife realized that he was there. Then later, because he had seen her, she approached him and forced him to kill Candaules and become king himself.

Martin, as Gyges, has distinction or honor thrust upon him by the excesses of others, but the fact that Gyges' reign as the ruler of Sardis was mediocre may be just as important to the conclusion of *A Severed Head*. More germane, however, is Martin's displacement of the Jungian chief or medicine man as Honor's consort. His emotional endorsement of Honor's liaison with her half brother is designed to suggest Martin's creative rejection of his society's values and the force of his love for Honor. But this mythical parallel is effected at the expense of compositional unity. Until the final page, Iris Murdoch had dramatized closely the insecurity and the blinding pace of modern life. On the novel's last page, however, she arbitrarily collapses her comic-historic theme into a neat bundle of myth.

The humorous cartoon below depicts the formal, Restoration-like sexual alliances and inclinations traced in *A Severed Head*.[19] Iris Murdoch's next novel, *An Unofficial Rose*, shows a continued interest in the horror, the raw comedy, and the far-reaching emotional complications that can reside within neat, formalized social patterns.

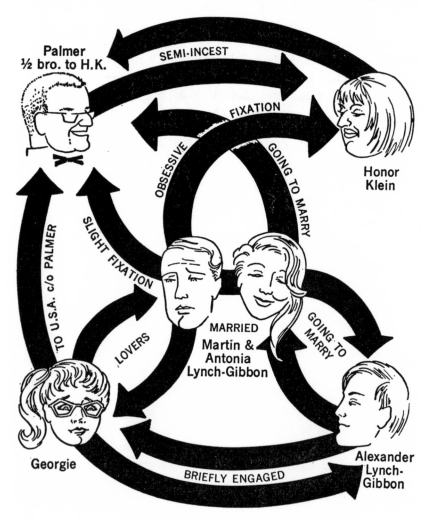

Although *An Unofficial Rose* is as stylized and dancelike in its thematic interconnections, it is a more balanced work. In spite of the first-person narrator in *A Severed Head,* the reader feels at the end that the two main characters are being led into a blurred relationship that bears withhheld mythological significance. In *An Unofficial Rose* the actions and emotions depicted are frankly social, one fact that accounts for its excellence. Iris Murdoch marred *A Severed Head* by adding a new term and a new set of relations chosen to lend the novel mythological depth. The result is that we see Honor and Martin as the constituents of an ambiguously related myth instead of as people.

Notes to Chapter Seven

1. D. H. Lawrence, *Psychoanalysis of the Unconscious* and *Fantasia of the Unconscious,* Philip Rieff, ed. (New York, 1960), 134.

2. Philip Rieff, *Freud: The Mind of the Moralist* (New York, 1959), 179.

3. Hangen, 163.

4. Gindin, 190-91.

5. James Hall, *The Tragic Comedians: Seven Modern British Novelists* (Bloomington, Indiana, 1963), 5.

6. Jacobson, 956.

7. Gindin, 192.

8. Jung, *Two Essays on Analytical Psychology,* 246.

9. Avis Dry, *The Psychology of Jung: A Critical Interpretation* (London and New York, 1961), 95.

10. Carl G[ustav]. Jung, *The Integration of the Personality,* trans. by Stanley M. Dell (New York, 1939), 24, 78-80.

11. Morton Cohen, *Rider Haggard: His Life and His Works* (London, 1960), 110.

12. Jung, *Two Essays on Analytical Psychology,* 208.

13. Gindin, 188.

14. Pearson, 143.

15. Henry James, "Preface to *The Princess Casamassima,*" in Richard P.

Blackmur, ed., *The Art of the Novel: Critical Prefaces by Henry James* (New York and London, 1934), 66-68.

16. Jacobson, 956.

17. Walter Allen, *The Modern Novel in Britain and the United States* (New York, 1964), 283.

18. Herodotus, *The Histories,* trans. and ed. by Aubrey de Selincourt (Baltimore, 1954), 16-18.

19. Raymond Queneau, "A World of Fantasy," trans. by David Pryce-Jones, *Time and Tide,* 42 (6 July 1961), 1119.

Eight

AN UNOFFICIAL ROSE

Some Uses of Beauty

A NOVELIST must grasp his subject emotionally as well as intellectually, writes Robert Liddell in *A Treatise on the Novel.*[1] Iris Murdoch flawed the conclusion of *A Severed Head* because she tried to extend her artistic vision beyond her personal values. She herself has called the work's major fault a "giving in to the myth" at the expense of personally felt social values.[2] *An Unofficial Rose,* another venture in the novel of incident and plot, evades this trap by virtue of both its artistic unity and its narrative control. Iris Murdoch's most Jamesian work uses very few characters and settings to describe in depth the rich psychical and material possibilities created by intersecting motives; action in the novel, then, is secondary to reaction, the way characters feel about what is happening to themselves and their families.

Technically as well, *An Unofficial Rose* evolves from the tradition of the highly dramatized point-of-view novel associated with James and Lubbock. In a work centering so decisively around the idea of personal choice, Iris Murdoch brings the reader as close as she can to the naked moral issues facing her characters. Authorial comment—either as smuggled-in myth or as summary statement—would dilute the intensity and immediacy of her characters' problems as actual personal events. As a moralist, Iris Murdoch feels that her duty is to present moral problems, but not to resolve them; if the novel aspires to the level of realistic moral criticism, the author must

efface himself. In daily experience we have no infallible moral code
or oracular voice to consult in times of duress. People must depend
exclusively upon their own resources. By omitting moral judgments,
Iris Murdoch describes personal consciousness with maximum faith-
fulness and immediacy. Existentialism excludes determinism of any
kind; Iris Murdoch's intrepid detachment, furthermore, conveys the
open-endedness and the kinetic force of personally elected acts. By
showing that our decisions lead to new, more complex choices, she
achieves both her moral purpose and a sense of the amplitude and
the awesome difficulty of human problems in the empirical world.

The most noteworthy English influences upon *An Unofficial Rose*
are its setting and its character types. Several of the character types—
the professional soldier, the retired civil servant, the lord of the
country estate, and the aesthete—are common to British fiction.
While preserving many of their traditional marks, Iris Murdoch
shrinks from explaining them as products of their social class. Most of
them live either at Grayhallock or Seton Blaise, a pair of stately
Kentish mansions situated about two hours from London by car.
The relative isolation of the two estates from the nearest community,
the easy, long-standing friendship between the neighboring families,
and the presence of the rose nurseries and three generations of
Peronetts at Grayhallock suggest the formalized neatness and conscious
gentility of what Beach, in *The Twentieth Century Novel,* calls "the
well-made novel." But the raw power of the book's main interest—
sexual love—creates an emotional resonance that shatters the social
amenities and drives practically all the characters from their ancestral
estates. Thus Iris Murdoch fuses setting and structure into a solid
psychological milieu that explains character interaction without limiting character movement.

Rupert Brooke's "Grantchester," from which the novel's title is
taken, contrasts the disciplined, regimented life in Germany in 1912
("Here tulips bloom as they are told") with the natural freedom of
England ("Unkempt about these hedges blows/An English unofficial
rose"). Iris Murdoch, however, scorns the smug insularity that
Brooke lightly satirizes later in the poem. Grantchester, Grayhallock,
and Seton Blaise, like St. Bride's of *The Sandcastle* and the Imber
Community of *The Bell,* are all susceptible to external pressures and
inner disorders. The exodus from Dungeness at the end of *An
Unofficial Rose* signals the death of those social elements that Brooke

playfully mocked before the First World War destroyed traditional assumptions about class and conduct:

> But Grantchester! ah, Grantchester!
> There's peace and holy quiet there,
> Great clouds along pacific skies
> And men and women with straight eyes,
> Lithe children lovelier than a dream,
> A bosky wood, a slumb'rous stream . . .
> In Grantchester their skins are white;
> They bathe by day, they bathe by night;
> The women there do all they ought;
> The men observe the Rules of Thought;
> They love the Good; they worship Truth;
> They laugh uproariously in youth . . .

In *Aspects of the Novel*, Forster praises Meredith for his masterful use of "contrivances": "Incident springs out of character, and having occurred it alters that character."[3] *An Unofficial Rose* effects the same interpenetration of character and episode that Forster admired in *The Egoist*. In the Murdoch novel character, action, and setting cohere in a rapidly moving process that culminates in social criticism. Life at Grayhallock and Seton Blaise is too arid to nourish changing human values. When Felix Meecham enters Grayhallock's drawing room to propose to Ann Peronett, he is momentarily arrested by an oppressive, deadening quality that contrasts with the fragrant roses in the adjacent nursery: "The room looked desolate as if it had not been occupied for weeks. It smelt musty." Hugh, at an earlier point in the novel, senses the undercurrent of violence lurking beneath Grayhallock's serene exterior; before the end of the novel, all of his worries will externalize themselves suddenly and abrasively:

> Flattering words in high quarters had attended his retirement. Yes, he could pass as a distinguished man, just as he could pass as a good husband, and few would ever know anything to the contrary. But the terror and the glory of life had passed him by.
>
> *   *   *
>
> Hugh reflected that it was a peaceful scene, a scene even of positive innocence. . . .
>
> *   *   *
>
> Yes, it was an innocent little world. It was an innocent little world, except that Steve was dead and Randall was drunk upstairs and Emma Sands was at this moment existing somewhere in London.

Randall's foul-mouthed entrance soon thereafter explodes the sham atmosphere of domesticity bred by the knitting, the dominoes, and the after-dinner pipe. Part One of the novel closes with Randall's violent withdrawal from Grayhallock and the formal beginning of his rift with Ann. By the end of the book only Ann remains to care for the rose nurseries, the monumental chestnut trees, and the enameled gardens of Grayhallock and Seton Blaise. Three generations of Peronett males—Penn Graham, Hugh's Australian grandson, Randall, and Hugh himself—as well as Felix Meecham and his homosexual brother-in-law Humphrey Finch must go elsewhere to satisfy their romantic impulses. Accordingly, Beryl Finch and Sarah Peronett Graham do not marry until they escape the blighting shadow of their parents' homes.

Genteel manorial life, then, proves uncongenial to the unorthodox yearnings of Iris Murdoch's characters. Randall and Hugh find the tenor of life much more bracing at Emma Sands's flat in Notting Hill Gate, where, amid stale tobacco fumes and assorted bric-a-brac, they discover excitement and involvement. *An Unofficial Rose* extends the domain of the psychological novel by introducing attitudes and relations that enlarge the region of social fact shared by reader and writer. F. O. Matthiessen remarks in his Preface to *Henry James: The Major Phase* that aesthetic criticism, by reaching to the milieu that nourishes the creative act, can provide valuable insights into an artist's social views.[4] The sharp edge of Iris Murdoch's shifting-point-of-view technique in *An Unofficial Rose* clarifies the conditions that must be satisfied before a moral generalization can be logically advanced. Borrowing from Hegel's phenomenology, Iris Murdoch suggests that the interlocking needs and values of various individuals accurately convey the collective mentality of society in a given era, that is, in the objective mind. Although her agnostic humanism prevents her from retracing the Dialectic to the point of view of the Absolute, she nonetheless believes that subjectivity develops into philosophy because of the human warmth that private conscience supplies to public morality.

The obscure, irrational ways the characters in *An Unofficial Rose* interact expresses the novelist's belief that philosophy today needs fresh ideas to describe man's social identity. Today's sociological methods and Freudian psychology neglect both individual need and the authentic link between private impulse and social responsibility.

In this respect, Iris Murdoch is clearly working along the same lines as Forster, Arthur Miller, and, to some extent, Angus Wilson. Hugh Peronett voices, shortly after his wife's funeral, his amazement that at the age of sixty-seven he still has a boundless, unpredictable future: "The future. It's rather miraculous to find that, even at my age, one has one!" Iris Murdoch had, of course, argued convincingly in her earlier novels, especially in *The Sandcastle* and *A Severed Head,* that the future is always a challenge replete with unforeseeable surprises and reversals.

Aside from insisting upon Hugh's age, Iris Murdoch sustains in *An Unofficial Rose* the view, first dramatized by Martin Lynch-Gibbon, that social freedom is an involuntary adventure in dissent. At a new level, she reworks the Hegelian idea that difference, irregularity, and aberration vitalize life by fending off the dead hand of uniformity. She believes that antisocial and unorthodox self-expressions form a greater part of our daily comings and goings than most of us imagine. And although her highly stylized character relationships limit sharply the immediate relevance of her observations, she does succeed brilliantly in creating a genuine mood of urgency *and* a living social organism. For instance, Ann discovers herself to be in love with two people at the same time; she and her daughter Miranda both compete for the love of Felix Meecham; Hugh and his son Randall seek sexual adventure at Notting Hill Gate in London. Instances like these, at once so unorthodox and so powerful, prove that our most disturbing challenges cannot be resolved either by foresight or by traditional theorizing. We can realize our freedom only through direct personal encounters whose uniqueness and particularity preclude the usefulness of acquired wisdom. Moral imperatives, as we know them, are irrelevant to emotional involvement. Hugh becomes capable of self-renewal only when he learns that Emma Sands is not reducible to a theory or to a set of prior experiences.

An Unofficial Rose develops boldly and exhaustively the idea, first stated in *A Severed Head,* that the complexity of human events often minimizes the role of immediate motives. Randall acts brutally and decisively by using the money from the sale of his father's Tintoretto to abscond with his mistress. On the other hand, the clarity of his act is "stolen" from him by the gestures of others: without the efforts of Miranda, Emma Sands, Mildred Finch, and his father, Randall would never have been able to legislate so daringly in his own behalf.

Randall's one free act in the novel, his choice of a wife, is his deepest failure.

The novel poses no easy answers to the moral problems it raises, other than insisting that voluntary immersion in contingency and chance provides our only outlet to being. Felix Meecham, unlike Randall, resists making positive arrangements about his personal life: "He would have much preferred whatever happened to happen under its own laws, far away from him, and for him to be able to stroll in when all had been completed." Inactivity, however, soon proves to be not only impractical, but unreasonable. A member of the Establishment and a regular army colonel with a strong sense of private and professional honor, Felix soon finds himself competing furiously to gain Ann's love. Ann herself, the most passive character in the novel, destroys the domestic peace of Clare Swann. She defeats Clare regularly in the annual local flower competition, and she has also unintentionally aroused the romantic fervor of Clare's husband. No less than Randall, Ann foments disorder; furthermore, the disorder is the product of her own acts and of her own being. Regardless of our efforts to the contrary, as soon as we form social relationships, we cannot help influencing or being influenced by others.

It is this unknowable yet inescapable feature of our social lives that both our prevailing morality and our conscientious motive-hunting cannot explain. Part of the moral urgency of *An Unofficial Rose* inheres in the frankness with which Iris Murdoch describes the moments of stress and crisis in her characters' lives. Bizarre, incongruous thoughts race through Hugh Peronett's mind at the funeral of his wife for forty years: while the other mourners are dutifully listening to the graveside sermon, Hugh meditates about Fanny's will, his motives for marrying her, and his illicit relation with Emma Sands twenty-five years earlier. He does grieve over Fanny's death but only after the funeral, when the household has resumed its daily routine:

> Of course he had loved his wife. . . . His marriage, whatever its
> shortcomings, had been a real living thing and not an empty shell.
> He had imagined that now, when it was all over, he might have
> felt, all the same, a sort of relief. But what came to him instead
> was a quite new sorrow, a dreadful sense of her absence. He kept
> missing her, searching for her. But she was nowhere now.

Robert Taubman calls *An Unofficial Rose* "the height of what can be achieved in her [Iris Murdoch's] peculiar style."[5] Style, subject matter, and social comedy do cohere in a way that makes *An Unofficial Rose* the author's most unified work. Always urgently committed to the theme of human love, she treats with relentless honesty the subtle oscillations and convergences between our selfish and our other-regarding impulses. She seems to find most people shamelessly romantic, but in a blatantly selfish way: Hugh sells his prized Tintoretto mainly to render Emma Sands more accessible to his advances; Miranda, who loves Felix Meecham, lies to dissuade her mother from marrying him; Randall disregards his family and pro- fessional obligations to conduct a Continental debauch with Lindsay Rimmer; the three governing passions of Mildred Finch are to be an aunt, a grandmother, and Hugh's mistress. Even the rigidly orthodox behavior of Ann derives, perhaps, from her selfish refusal to gainsay her conventional morality. Disinterested moral precepts and a Kantian respect for the law perform small service in these lives. Hugh gives up his affair with Emma Sands, not from guilt or distaste for conduct alien to his position as a husband, a father, and a civil servant, but simply because of a waning desire. In her search for flexible, civilized values, Iris Murdoch studies the fully engaged mind—the mind impelled to activity and desire by an emotional commitment. Without yielding to our irrational impulses, we can never encounter another person in the kind of situation that tests our most closely held values:

> It had never crossed his [Hugh's] mind, once the first terrible time was over, to try to see Emma again; and this not because of any sense of duty, but because of a steady failure of inclination, a steady diminishing of appetite.

Iris Murdoch does not consider the eroticism pervading the Gray- hallock-Seton Blaise-Notting Hill Gate society as self-defeating. There is a bracing, healthy quality that she recognizes in forceful expressions of will. Her uneasiness springs from the belief, expressed in "A House of Theory," that received Christian-democratic morality, Sartrean existentialism, and trial-and-error empiricism all fail to describe the conflict of reason and emotion. Love, as the profoundest act of human perception, requires decisive self-legislation. The moment and the person never quite correspond to our moral preconceptions or to our notions of personal convenience. From the conventional stand- point, all of the lovers in *An Unofficial Rose* are strangely mated, which explains the novel's title. As John Rainborough does in *The Flight from the Enchanter*, a person can always destroy an emotional relation by subjecting it to rational criteria; yet, any emotion as powerful as love stimulates a great range of mental activity—both rational and irrational. The expectation of love never matches the experience itself. Each step in our private relations moves us in a fresh, unexpected way. Only a vigorous will can deal with the battery of opaque, subtly intertwined motives the lover faces in his free perception of another person. Mental constructs grow dull and abstract before the other's immediacy and solid reality. Ann finds herself driven to a logical and emotional impasse when she attempts to analyze the progress of her veiled, yet disturbingly persistent, romance with Felix Meecham:

> Ann had become aware, even years ago, that Felix was partial to her. She had accepted his exceedingly discreet homage . . . with a warm and amused gratitude, as the sentimental foible of one who was by now a confirmed bachelor. She and Felix were, after all, dreadfully old. But she had liked it; and when, during the last year, Felix had been, when alone with her, the smallest bit more frank, as if taking for granted a hazy and never actually mentioned *something* between them, she had liked that too. Then there was an occasion at Seton Blaise, when they had wandered away from the others along the shore of the lake, and in a moment of silence he had taken her hand. . . . She knew of course that it would be insane of her to fall in love with Felix. But as soon as she got as far on as to say these words to herself her heart began to flutter. She and Felix were, after all, dreadfully young.

One can always dwell on the paradoxes and the contradictions begotten by a deeply felt emotional experience. The absence of a sound moral code based on experience, the existentialists and the positivists agree, makes every problem both surprising and unique:

> "If you don't see them [the objections to selling the Tintoretto painting in order to free Randall for Lindsay] you must be morally blind," said Hugh. Then he asked himself: what are the objections, exactly?
>
>   *   *   *
>
> She must not let him see what she really felt, So there was something which she really felt?

An intelligent appraisal of one's social relationships ideally precedes emotional commitment. Iris Murdoch's point, however, is that mental inventories can never keep pace with the erratic shifts in values that our attachments, as dynamic processes, engender. At an indeterminate point, the individual must decide whether to abandon convenience and sober reflection in exchange for the opacity of another. It is here that Iris Murdoch refreshes and invigorates the Jamesian novel of subtle moral distinctions. The strategic word, which appears several times in the novel, is "authority"; Iris Murdoch seems to grant a measure of creativity to the person who responds emotionally to another:

> This falling in love was, he felt, the best thing he had ever done. It had that absolute authority which seems to put an act beyond the range of right and wrong.

* * *

> She was shapely and complete; and like a kaleidoscope, like a complex rose, her polychrome being fell into an authoritative pattern which proclaimed her free.

* * *

> But now the picture presented itself to him blown up, huge, authoritative; and with its vast and as yet unclarified implications it frightened him.

* * *

> He desired, for its own sake, Randall's will to take what it wanted and damn the consequences. These were mad thoughts, but they rose with authority, and he knew that, quietly, they had been with him a long time.

Ironically, it is Hugh, the grandfather, widower, and retired civil servant of sixty-seven, who makes the boldest transition to the chafing demands of his new situation. The first step toward one's appreciation of the world's inexhaustible multiplicity is finite love. Hugh rises above doubt and self-brooding to pay court to Emma Sands, his paramour of twenty-five years earlier, instead of succumbing to his recent bereavement. In spite of the untimeliness of his act, Hugh leaves Grayhallock at the earliest opportunity after Fanny's funeral to make his intentions known to Emma. Unlike William Mor and Michael Meade, he grasps the immediacy of his emotional situation and behaves accordingly. The theme of freedom and self-discovery as organic adventures conducted in the face of objective uncertainty is sounded in a tape-recorded excerpt from Emma Sands's latest mystery story; the idea closely resembles Jake Donaghue's *Silencer* in its patent existentialist attitude toward decision: "If you're going to do it, it's got to be now. There's no time for theory now, no time for ifs and buts. You're in the dark, and you must go forward in the dark." By selling his Tintoretto and, therefore, creating personal freedom for himself and his son Randall, Hugh elects life over art. The words Iris Murdoch uses to record his self-renewing pursuit of Emma recall the doubt and urgency inferred in the tape-recorded thriller:

> Hugh had been doing nothing lately except think about Emma. . . . He was still, of course, almost totally in the dark. He not only did not know what Emma was thinking, he did not know exactly what he wanted, not *exactly* that is. But he knew relentlessly in which direction he must go, and in that direction he struggled on alone, under a banner on which were inscribed the words *Liberty* and *Starvation*.

Emma, however, proves to be a hollow object for Hugh's sexual passion; after she spurns his advances, Hugh concludes that he must have had good reason for breaking with her when he did. As a writer of diluted thrillers, Emma has grown old and has used herself up by sacrificing life to a debased form of art, a practice reflected in both her physical bearing and in the horrifying way she conducts her personal life. Emma is described as "a wary lizard" and "toad-like"; she calls herself, aptly, "an inquisitive old reptile" and "an old dry object like a stuffed alligator." By beating her female secretary-companions and settling for the illusion of romance with Hugh rather than a forceful, candid relationship, she violates the Kantian ethic of treating people as ends in themselves. Frederick P. W. McDowell's criticism of her involuted ethic sums up her values and aspirations: "Emma is now cynically beyond the need for emotional involvement or finds as much commitment as she needs in the thrillers she writes."[6] Along with Ann's prize-winning floral patterns, Emma's thrillers embody Iris Murdoch's censure of a life dedicated to art instead of to the reality of other people: after turning to detective fiction to assuage the sorrows resulting from Hugh's neglect, Emma loses her gift for normal human relationships. She notes with bittersweet satisfaction that Hugh, the individual who first instigated her progress in inhumanity, should ultimately be the one to feel its sting. Her preference for brutalized personal relations equates her with Heidegger's "liberated individual": Emma's "solitary projection of herself" as the center of her moral values takes her into a lonely, inhuman region of solipsism and willed extinction:

> Heidegger's individual learns to subordinate to their due place the concerns of everyday—and with them the people as much as the

things that he is concerned with. . . . Here no one can follow him; he creates a world and a history out of the very fact of their inevitable cessation—and in that world or that history, as there is room for only one catastrophe, so there is room for only one solitary soliloquizing actor. Others are stage properties, placed perhaps by chance, but manipulated as he will by this strange virtuoso, playing, without author or audience, as his own sense of tragic fitness may direct.[7]

Part of Iris Murdoch's novelistic strategy is the practice of moralizing through either an unsympathetic character or one who seems poorly qualified to speak with such pointedness and authority on a particular moral issue. This practice emphasizes both the difficulty of moral action and the sometimes frightening gulf between abstract knowledge and concrete performance. Closely related to Bledyard's art criticism, Jimmy Carde's translation of Propertius, and Antonia Lynch-Gibbon's statement about marriage being an adventure in development is Emma's remark concerning the abuse of social freedom: "One must not play the god in other people's destiny. In any case one can never do it properly." Of all the characters in the novel, Emma best exemplifies the failure to abide by her own principles. After being cheated of her Prospero-like act of freeing Lindsay for Randall, Emma hires Jocelyn Gaster as her secretary-companion to re-enact the cycle of sadism and Lesbianism she had instituted with Lindsay. Emma's lot at the end of the novel is the unavoidable product of her distorted liberation. By forfeiting the reality of other people, she will never gain the humane wisdom required to compose a first-rate novel. Her subtlety and cleverness have led her only into the cul-de-sac where she changes her will to spite her friends and writes thrillers to accommodate the public's taste for violence.

A much younger version and a chilling parody of Emma Sands is Randall and Ann's daughter, the innocent and destructive Miranda. She and Emma, who are probably fifty years apart in age, have, ironically, either loved or have been loved by practically all the male characters in the novel. A travesty of the mother-daughter rivalry involving Ann, Miranda, and Felix is the fact that Emma, who is old enough to be Miranda's grandmother, was once in love with Felix. They respond identically to the protestations of their sedulous lovers ("Oh *that*"), and, by practicing coyness and deceit to secure their selfish ends, Emma and Miranda stand as the major exemplars of

willed violence in the novel. A legacy of Ivy Compton-Burnett's
satanic juveniles, Miranda is, nonetheless, an obscure, mysterious
figure to Hugh, to her Australian cousin Penn Graham, and to Felix:

> Hugh looked at Miranda. . . . She must surely, he reminded
> himself, be fourteen now. Or was she? It was shocking not to
> know.
>
> *   *   *
>
> He did not even know her age and now did not dare to ask.
>
> *   *   *
>
> But then Miranda was not a girl. Yet she was not a little girl
> either. What was she then?
>
> *   *   *
>
> How much did Miranda understand about the matter? How much
> did she know of the Facts of Life? How old was she, anyway?
>
> *   *   *
>
> He was still rather vague about her age. . . .

Cunning and self-seeking comprise the essence of Miranda's character.
Having been secretly in love with Felix Meecham for years, she
prevents Ann from marrying him by lying about Randall's plans for
the future. Miranda's beautifully timed and deftly improvised falsehood reveals the shocking truth that the fates of Grayhallock and of
Seton Blaise have been shaped by her selfish will.

Content to remain silent about her innermost feelings, she acts
swiftly and efficiently at crucial moments. She is practical, mature,
and self-composed in all her dealings with her parents. By jumping
out of a tree into Felix's arms, she legislates in her own behalf at a
time when Ann threatens to yield to his entreaties. She also heart-
lessly dominates her Australian cousin Penn, whose trip to England
proves to be a more pungent social education than he had ever
expected. As that of Toby Gashe in *The Bell,* Penn's curriculum in
self-knowledge and human values in general transcends his adolescent
prospects; his father's rough secular humor and the robust heartiness
he reads about in Joseph Furphey's *Such Is Life* are poor training for
the sudden changes Miranda awakens in his psychic chemistry:
"Guilt now blackened his vision and complicated his pain. His
desires grew hideously precise. . . . The first Miranda had been a
heavenly vision. The last Miranda was a doll of flesh."

Miranda is less discomposed about the urges Penn arouses in *her*.
Taking advantage of his boyish timidity and his equivocal standing

in Grayhallock as a visitor, she freely indulges her own nascent sexual feelings in a characteristically violent and disguised manner:

> Miranda gave him no peace . . . and began at this time literally to pinch him. She would come suddenly up behind him, seize the skin of his arm or some other part of him between her little pincer-like fingers, and squeeze as hard as she could. Penn became covered with bruises.

Entering Miranda's room late at night, Penn feels that he is like Caliban; she resists his awkward physical advance, by bringing down a paperweight upon his knuckles. The act is not accidental: a neophyte automobile mechanic and cricketer, Penn attaches great significance to manual dexterity. Miranda, Emma Sands's counterpart in violence, damages the source of Penn's vocational and recreational activity with the same gesture she uses to mutilate his sexual urge. Like Felicity Mor, she is drawn to witchcraft and occult rites; Miranda's incantations, however, are more clearly thematic than Felicity's. When Miranda unleashes her volley of scorn against Penn and destroys her dolls, she is inaugurating the formal end of her childhood. In an act analogous to Prospero's drowning of his book, she sinks in the nearby lake the German knife Felix had once given to her dead brother Steve. Mirroring her father's propensity for an ordered, structured life, she will wait patiently for the time when she can destroy Randall's relationship with his mistress Lindsay Rimmer and have him for herself.

Miranda bears obvious affinities with Honor Klein of *A Severed Head* as a legacy of the "She-who-must-be-obeyed" principle bodied forth by Jung and Rider Haggard. In his review of *An Unofficial Rose,* Robert Nye emphasizes the themes of self-understanding and power: "The important thing is that each character *chooses* his ruin, and is baffled by his will."[8] Iris Murdoch subtly justifies Nye's criticism by referring stylistically to Rider Haggard's *She.* The image of Miranda rises imperiously before Penn, we are told, "like a column of flame." Ayesha, the indomitable white goddess in *She,* actually perishes by falling into a pillar of flame. Iris Murdoch's allusion to Ayesha, although heavily veiled, foreshadows the grief Miranda will eventually suffer. *An Unofficial Rose* develops Jung's idea of the mana personality in line with humanistic comedy, whereas *A Severed Head* offered only an undramatized mythical version of the same theme. The schemes Miranda devises are unnatural to a person of any age, and the highly structured future she scrupulously plans violates the reality of the unknown and unknowable future. As Emma Sands, who grows old avoiding rich, dark personal attachments, she herself figures to be the victim of her own life-denying machinations. For all her confidence and purpose, Miranda is, finally, extremely immature and unrealistic. Her disappointed lover Penn Graham suffers from guilt and uncertainty, but his ineptitudes are natural and will gradually disappear. His falling in love with Miranda demonstrates an openness and cordiality that Miranda has little hope of acquiring so long as she remains locked within her inflexible schemes for the future. The happiness and fecundity of Penn's roistering family among the currajongs and coolibahs of Australia attest to a richer mode of being than the meager survival she envisions for herself as her father's consort.

Iris Murdoch conveys the impracticality of Miranda's closely ordered program through narrative structure and, more immediately, through the erratically developing fortune of Mildred Finch. Mildred favors any kind of involvement or excitement over stale inactivity. A tireless instigator and schemer in her own right, she is willing to inconvenience herself to secure her goals: to assist Felix in his pursuit of Ann, she invites Ann and Miranda to stay at Seton Blaise; she also travels to London and even to India in the hope of rousing Hugh's romantic impulses. Mildred's commanding passions in life, as has been mentioned, are to be a grandmother and, somewhat incongruously, to be young again and have an affair with Hugh, whom she has quietly loved for the past twenty-five years. As Hugh's confidante in his intrigue with Emma Sands, Mildred is both powerful and helpless. Her persistence finally yields rewards, but in ways she had never anticipated. Her most significant act, as Hugh's confidante, is to encourage him to sell the Tintoretto. The sale of the painting, she realizes, has a strong bearing on her own chances with Hugh. If he sells the painting, he will give the money to Randall for his escape from Ann and marriage; Emma, therefore, will be alone at Notting Hill Gate and, theoretically at least, more vulnerable to Hugh's advances; at the same time, the departure of Lindsay and Randall will open a clear line of attack for Felix on the bereaved heart of Ann.

Taubman has commented upon the complexity and fragility of the web of intrigue uniting the characters in the novel: "In their situation the result of any action is unpredictable because one factor in the equation cannot be changed without affecting the rest."[9] By advising Hugh to sell the painting, Mildred jogs the labyrinthine social machine into renewed activity. Iris Murdoch never explains whether Mildred's act is selfish or magnanimous; are the consoling long-range prospects of being an aunt to the child of Ann and Felix and thus achieving a sort of immortality more alluring than the immediate satisfaction of becoming Hugh's mistress? Or does Mildred encourage Hugh to do what he has wanted to do all along because she loves him and wants to see him happy? These questions occur, naturally, to Mildred, but instead of allowing herself to be trapped within their intricacies, she decides and then acts with surgical precision. Iris Murdoch may be subordinating Mildred's fate to the novel's theme, which McDowell regards as a serious flaw in *An Unofficial Rose*.[10] Mildred, at any rate, faces bright prospects in the final chapter, perhaps by grace of an arbitrary manipulation of the adage that God helps those who help themselves. Her wishes will probably be gratified, but in a way only remotely connected with her assiduous labors. Her daughter Beryl, whom Mildred had always regarded as a prosaic, unfeminine schoolmistress, will marry and make her a grandmother; Felix will probably wed Marie-Laure, his devoted French mistress in India; and, in the final paragraph of the novel, Hugh turns from the deck rail of the India-bound ship toward Mildred's stateroom and an unexpected, but perhaps refreshing liaison.

Mildred's long-awaited trip to India, then, promises to be a delayed honeymoon of sorts. The idea of life's swarming abundance, which is so hostile to Miranda's fastidious plans, furnishes the novel's main structural principle. In one of those key passages that reveal the discontinuity between a character's professed values and his observable acts, Douglas Swann tells Ann that a rigid code or structure undermines life's contingency and its unpredictable dialectic: "Goodness accepts the contingent. Love accepts the contingent. Nothing is more fatal to love than to want everything to have form."

Contrary to O'Sullivan, *An Unofficial Rose* is anything but "dull" and "uninteresting in subject matter."[11] Iris Murdoch explores the psychic origins and expressions of various love relationships and shows them all to be antisocial. Without being able to say why, the Peronett family in England objects to the marriage of Sarah to

the Australian Jimmie Graham. With Steve dead, Hugh laments
that there is no longer a Peronett grandson to carry on the family
name; the decidedly "unofficial" union of Lindsay and Randall,
however, may very well reverse his sorrow, but again in a way that
is socially unacceptable. Each of the erotic attractions in this heavily
plotted novel reveals the same truth: our most intimate feelings
disregard conventional propriety. Humphrey Finch, Mildred's homosexual husband, is in love with young Penn, who loves Miranda, who
loves Felix; Felix, in turn, is in love with Ann, who cannot decide
whether she is still emotionally drawn to her disreputable husband.
This rhythmic design is further complicated by the fact that in
addition to Ann, Randall is loved by Lindsay Rimmer, Nancy Bowshott, and perhaps even Clare Swann. When we consider, in addition,
the love triangle involving Emma Sands, Hugh, and Mildred, who
is Humphrey's wife and Felix's half sister, we can justify the claim
that Iris Murdoch's social comedy is a rich embroidery interlaced
with keenly felt, renewable values.

Counterpointing the wild human emotions described in *An Unofficial Rose* are Hugh's Tintoretto and the flowers at Grayhallock.
Ronald Bryden states correctly that Randall's rose nursery stands
at the center of the novel.[12] The cultivated symmetry and fragrant
beauty of the roses accentuate man's failure to bring the same
excellences to his own life. The motif gains expression through
Randall, who, as the proprietor of the nursery and an artist in
horticultural techniques, responds to the flowers more acutely than
do any of the other characters:

> He could have knelt before these flowers, wept before them,
> knowing them to be not only the most beautiful things in existence
> but the most beautiful things conceivable. God in his dreams
> did not see anything lovelier. Indeed the roses were God and
> Randall worshipped.

As awesome and beautiful as the roses are, however, they cannot
sustain Randall's active devotion; as does anything else derived,
constructed, or cultivated, they pale before the solidity of another
person. Not only does Randall leave Grayhallock and the nursery,
but, as soon as he embraces the housekeeper Nancy Bowshott, he
forgets the roses he had nostalgically gathered. As Hume said, the
reason must always be the servant of the passions. The irrefutable
immediacy of another person generates a milieu that creates its own

values and morality. The incentive of dynamic human contacts, Iris Murdoch insists, transforms other concerns into remote abstractions.

Hugh's sale of the Tintoretto in Part IV, the middle section of this seven-part novel, reflects the same social humanism, but with an important variation. The expectation, however unpromising, of resuming his love affair with Emma prompts Hugh to sell his painting. And as soon as it leaves the family, rational order collapses: Randall deserts his wife and child, Felix besieges Ann, Miranda confounds Ann and Penn, and Hugh becomes a persistent suitor at Notting Hill Gate.

Perhaps Iris Murdoch is reworking in *An Unofficial Rose* the major argument of "The Sublime and the Good," that morality forms an organic part of aesthetic perception. This idea seems to have informed Dora Greenfield's mystical experience at the National Gallery in *The Bell* and will reappear in a different form in *The Unicorn*. The qualities of individual human beauty and depth, which Tintoretto conveyed in his early version of "Susannah Bathing," can inspire others to search for the same features in normal experience. The ultimate value of the painting is that it allows Randall, Lindsay, Felix, and Hugh to undertake their private goals more expediently than they could have done otherwise. The moral lesson of the great artist has been conveyed—in the form of encouraging shapely, candid relationships—but according to the indefiniteness that the novel develops as the core of human experience. It is not a mistake that Lindsay resembles the figure in the painting. Hugh comes to realize, through her, that his Tintoretto symbolizes a lifetime of suppressed desires as well as beauty and artistic excellence. By selling the painting, he opens himself and others to the radical particularity that Iris Murdoch believes all great art should encourage.

Each of the novel's seven parts contains elements of loss and renunciation and a rallying of the spirit of at least one of the characters in preparation for a new or a renewed attachment to another person. This dialectical movement generates abounding human activity; the novel opens with a funeral and ends just before Hugh is to enter Mildred's cabin on the ship headed for India. Although little may have been accomplished by the characters, the advance is one from stasis to movement. Hugh's casual reminder to himself in the final paragraph that Mildred is expecting him conveys the important truth that new adventures always await us

and that finite man, who is by definition indeterminate and unresolved, cannot logically be completed until his death.

Taubman has noted the curious absence of personal satisfaction
experienced by the characters in the novel: "As the characters join
in a final chorus . . . all they can congratulate themselves on is just
being alive—on having survived."[13] The book does contain a great
fund of unexploited or misdirected natural ability. Lindsay has all
the glowing radiance of the Tintoretto figure; yet, despite her
endowments, she is content to be Randall's mistress and the object
of Emma's satanic Lesbianism. Randall, theoretically at least, is not
deserving of a woman of Lindsay's poise and majesty. His passion
for stuffed dolls, which his daughter outgrows, signifies an immature
mind misplaced in an adult situation. The writer of shoddy plays,
he manifests the same fatuity in his private life that he does in his
art. The great quantities of whiskey he drinks inflate him with
manly power, but he is humbled by practically all of his encounters
with females. Miranda, Lindsay, Emma, and even Ann reduce him
to the level of an awkward adolescent when he tries to assert his
masculinity to them. Emma may be right when she says that Lindsay
only symbolizes an undefined goal Randall is seeking. His lack of
self-control misleads him into overreacting, which he mistakes as a
sign of deep sensitivity. He deserts Ann, an overly submissive woman,
to live with Lindsay, an extremely forceful organizer and planner.
(In the medieval ballad, Lord Randal is killed by his sweetheart.)

While luxuriating with Lindsay in Rome—even the setting contributes to his basic insecurity—Randall refers to her as "the Aphrodite
of the world of sleep." Yet his unconscious being belongs to his
former life. His dreams of Ann and Grayhallock, recurring between
sexual bouts with Lindsay, show that freedom, demanding the content
of human experience, is a greater challenge than he had imagined.
Iris Murdoch believes that our relationships are dynamic, open-ended,
and conducive to surprising developments; Randall's constant proximity to Lindsay awakens new perceptions and judgments that detract
from her luster. Regardless of prudence or daring, our choices
generate a relentless dialectic; Randall habitually dwells on the
alternatives he had previously rejected:

> There was only one thing in the world that he was really good
> at, and that he would never do again. He saw in a vision the

sunny hillside at Grayhallock with its slight haze of green and its
myriad little coloured forms and he sighed. Ann.

Oscillating between the extremes of freedom and bondage—actually,
he had enjoyed more creative freedom at Grayhallock—Randall has
not yet found a congenial mode of being. The life of sensuality he
leads with Lindsay in Rome begets its own contrary rhythm; lavish
spending and debauchery merely whet his ungratified vocational
desires and arouse a disturbing sense of loss regarding Ann. Randall
will be ready to desert Lindsay earlier than Miranda calculates.

Woven into the energetic social comedy of *An Unofficial Rose* is the
idea of heredity. The members of the Peronett family share striking
tendencies and values but direct them to original goals. Hugh and
Randall are both restless at Grayhallock with their sedate, mono-
chromatic wives; father and son both despise and envy one another
for the rebelliousness each manifests so ineptly in his quest for
romance. Miranda and Randall both enjoy playing with dolls, and
each tries to infuse his life with direction and structure. Ann and
Miranda reveal themselves to be capable of jealousy, and the final
acts of both, so different in motive impulse, are arrantly selfish.
Although Miranda, as her name suggests, incorporates several of
the personality traits of her parents, Ann and Randall are the two
most dissimilar characters in the novel. One of the great ironies
of *An Unofficial Rose* is that Iris Murdoch counterparts its surging,
rhythmic prose with a grimly uncompromising moral prognosis. No
two characters personify the book's philosophical spirit better than
the incompatible pair, Ann and Randall. Each reacts in his unique
way to an unsatisfactory marriage, and each dramatizes the nugatory
benefit derived from protracted suffering and discord.

Randall, as we have seen, recoils from Ann to discover his selfhood
and, in the process, alienates himself from the source of his creativity.
Ann stays at Grayhallock to do Randall's job in the nursery as well
as her own prosaic domestic chores. Curiously, the reader and many
of the other characters in the novel feel little affection for her. Like
the Reverend Evvy in *The Sandcastle,* she is the kind of bland
personality that inspires little warmth in others. Unable to seize or
even recognize happiness, she embodies the principle of mindless,
uncritical allegiance to abstract rules of conduct. Ann's dutiful
cultivation of her childhood training robs her of the ability to exercise
a purely self-regarding act and, hence, reduces her to a cipher in

other people's schemes. At the end of the novel, she catches Fanny's runaway cat Hatfield, thus moving symbolically into the vacant niche formerly occupied by her dead mother-in-law. Grayhallock, it seems, will be presided over by a pallid, formless mistress for another loveless cycle. But, like the more stringent reign that Emma Sands hopes to institute with Jocelyn Gaster, the new cycle at Grayhallock will accentuate the misdeeds of its predecessor. Ann's practically self-annihilating sense of duty earns her little esteem from her family. Hugh blames her outright for becoming invisible; Randall accuses her of being "as messy and flabby and open as a bloody dogrose"; Miranda refers to her as "an anonymous faceless figure" and "a shapeless directionless mass, full of guilt and confused attachments, still hopelessly married." Ann's adherence to the morals of her parents and of her religion leads her, ironically, to the point at which she hopelessly realizes that she has sacrificed a warm, reversible human relationship to a brittle abstraction.

She erroneously expects to achieve a new personality to aid her in the choice between marrying Felix Meecham or abiding by her vows to Randall. She comes to realize, however, that her concept of rectitude, which she cannot name or really understand, concerns only herself. Randall, having legislated for himself, is beyond her influence, and Miranda has acted independently. Guilt continues to haunt Ann, but now for selfishly indulging a private duty at the expense of another person. Randall thinks rightly of Ann as "the incarnate spirit of the Negative," without will or form. Later, after learning that duty has distorted and annihilated her personality, Ann calls herself "the spirit that says no"; "I am always saying no, said Ann to herself, all my strength has gone into saying no. I have no strength left for the positive." A negative response to life does, in fact, inform practically all of her acts in the novel, but she cannot alter her conduct. She declines Mildred's invitation to Seton Blaise, Randall's request for a divorce, the Swanns' invitation to join them for a vacation, Felix's offer to drive her to Greece, and, most significantly, Felix's love. Doubt and guilt have choked self-realization and moral clarity, virtues attainable only through interaction with another; although she cannot logically understand the impulse to conventional decorum that governs her conduct so severely, she performs no act more daring and adventuresome than brooding unhappily on her own inanition:

Ann had never really had the conception of doing what she

wanted. The idea of doing what she ought, early and deeply implanted in her soul, and sedulously ever since cultivated, had by now almost removed from her the possibility, even as something *prima facie,* of a pure self-regarding movement of will. . . . There was, in her open, formless life, some dreadful lack of vigour, some lack of any hard surface to grasp or to brace oneself against. . . . She had not got a new personality. But the old one was certainly cracked.

Mill's objection to Christianity was its inordinate concern with negativism; the virtue of resisting temptation, said Mill, overlooks a vast glorious world of events and people. Iris Murdoch's characterization of Ann reveals that modern man needs more ethical tenets than those supplied by Scripture. Ann cannot act in keeping with her desires; on the other hand, the characters who do follow their selfish impulses prove themselves to be no more self-absorbed than Ann. As it turns out, her stultifying fidelity to Christian decorum and the selfishness of Miranda, Lindsay, Randall, and Hugh are similar.

An Unofficial Rose is Iris Murdoch's invitation to moralists to work out bracing, invigorating ontologies that will comprise the reality of multiple points of view and be elastic enough to suit man's changing needs. The most conventionally dutiful person in the novel is also the most unhappy and causes unhappiness in those close to her; as colorless and equivocal as Ann is, she makes deep impressions on the hearts of Douglas Swann, Felix, and Randall. Ann can claim no decisively taken acts; her negativism allows her to survive only on a marginal human scale. Conversely, the machinations of Emma Sands, Mildred Finch, and probably Miranda, as well, also amount to little more than marginal survival, in the last analysis. Utterly different kinds of values and personal conduct, then, yield a curiously identical result.

The final meaning of *An Unofficial Rose,* symbolized by the sea journey in the last chapter, is the existential dictum that the being and the becoming, as continuing events, have far more importance than any achieved result. In exalting the struggle over definitive accomplishment, however, Iris Murdoch includes a veiled plea for the establishment of a metaphysic that will enrich and glorify our transphenomenal status. To Iris Murdoch, life should involve more than mere survival. Aside from Mildred and Hugh, who wait until their sixties to face the challenge of freedom, all of the other characters in the novel are menaced by stale routine or downright violence. The promise of excitement and novelty at Rome and Notting Hill Gate proves to be as deadening as the regimen at Grayhallock under Ann's tutelary spirit.

Iris Murdoch continues to study the question of transient values in her next novel. The character who prefigures the thematic link between *An Unofficial Rose* and *The Unicorn* is Ann Peronett. But whereas she is insipid, frail, and foolish, Hannah Crean-Smith, who is even more passive and pliable on the surface than Ann, suggests ambiguities that indicate an enlargement of moral commitment. Perseverance in the unexistential form of creative renunciation occupies the thematic center of *The Unicorn*. The philosophical and artistic continuum joining Martin Lynch-Gibbon, Ann Peronett, and Hannah Crean-Smith attests to a growing concern with both paradox, the heart of religious experience, and experimental forms of self-realization. As we shall see, *The Unicorn* represents an important development in Iris Murdoch's progress both as a moralist and as a student of the different sorts of human experience that constitute social reality.

Notes to Chapter Eight

1. Robert Liddell, *A Treatise on the Novel* (London, 1947), 43.

2. Kermode, 66.

3. Forster, 90.

4. F. O. Matthiessen, *Henry James: The Major Phase* (New York, 1963), xiv.

5. Robert Taubman, "L'Année Dernière at Dungeness," *New Statesman,* 63 (8 June 1962), 836.

6. Frederick P. W. McDowell, " 'The Devious Involutions of Human Character and Emotions': Reflections on Some Recent British Novels," *Wisconsin Studies in Contemporary Literature,* 4 (Autumn, 1963), 353.

7. Grene, 72.

8. Robert Nye, "Ending the World," *John O'London's,* 7 (5 July 1962), 9.

9. Taubman, 836.

10. McDowell, 352.

11. O'Sullivan, 35.

12. Ronald Bryden, "Living Dolls," *The Spectator* (8 June 1962), 756.

13. Taubman, 836.

Nine

THE UNICORN

PERCEPTION AS MORAL VISION

I RIS MURDOCH brings the literature of situations to a
new focus in *The Unicorn*. Social relationships in the novel have
such far-reaching moral implications that discussion of character as
a thing-in-itself is practically meaningless. More than in any of her
other works, the people in *The Unicorn* acquire substance and identity
through their personal relations. Infusing the novel's complex web
of surprises, mistakes, and oversights is the principle that one's
choices, and even one's failure to choose, affect other people. The
verbal and thematic similarities[1] shared by *An Unofficial Rose* and
The Unicorn—the stylized social matrix as a function of two large
estates, the unusual age difference between siblings, and the failure
of male characters to sustain rewarding emotional attachments—suggest that Iris Murdoch had not exhausted her subject matter in the
earlier novel. But although her treatment in *An Unofficial Rose* was
comic, her intention in *The Unicorn* is tragic and more discernibly
metaphysical. The hollow disembodied voices that begin *The Unicorn*
convey the remoteness, frustration, and inaccessibility that characterize
Marian Taylor's entire sojourn at Gaze Castle and environs:

> "How far away is it?"
> "Fifteen miles."
> "Is there a bus?"
> "There is not."
> "Is there a taxi or a car I can hire in the village?"

183

"There is not."

"Then how am I to get there?"

"You might hire a horse hereabouts," someone suggested after a silence.

"I can't ride a horse," she said in exasperation, "and in any case there's my luggage."

Far different from the high color of *An Unofficial Rose,* conveyed by Hugh's Tintoretto, the rich foods and wines consumed by the characters, and the plump verdure surrounding Grayhallock and Seton Blaise, is the lank spareness *The Unicorn* introduces as its dominant mood in the opening chapter. The ancient ravaged land, the swiftly eddying sea, and the premonitory bog—which, unlike the Dungeness swamp in *An Unofficial Rose,* functions thematically—foreshadow a grimness that Iris Murdoch retains and exploits dramatically in later scenes. The themes of shifting personal loyalties and self-deprivation, which were treated within the thematic frame of sexuality in *A Severed Head* and *An Unofficial Rose,* aspire to the dimension of tragedy in *The Unicorn.* The basic human ingredients are the same, as well as her moral attitude. *The Unicorn* differs from its two immediate predecessors both in the degree and quality of personal engagement exemplified by the characters and in the tragic reverberations of their commitments.

Perhaps the most profitable method of approaching *The Unicorn* is to cite literary antecedents. Reviewers have been impressed by the alleged influence of *Wuthering Heights* upon the book; no doubt the sizable tract of land dividing Heathcliff and the Heights from Catherine Earnshaw and Thrushcross Grange, together with the poetic realization of setting in both novels, have prompted the search for narrative similarities. A more important point of comparison has been the treatment of the theme of love in both works. Yet here the critics have gone wrong. Emily Brontë depicts fierce passions suffocated within social conventions, but the term *passions* cannot explain the feelings of the lovers in *The Unicorn*; whatever diluted emotion they feel vaporizes at the first real challenge from the outside world. Nor does Iris Murdoch inherit her predecessor's mysticism; if Hannah Crean-Smith, Effingham Cooper, and Max Le Jour prefer symbolic rather than direct encounters with others, it is because they lack the energy and sense of realism to pursue the substance instead of the illusion of life.

Mme. de Lafayette's *La Princesse de Clèves* and Valéry's *Le Cimitière Marin*, both of which Hannah and Marian read together, probably augur the mood of Gaze Castle and the Greytown-Blackport locale more pointedly than Emily Brontë's novel. Valéry's enrapt absorption in immobility and death forecasts the self-annihilating stasis sought by the residents of Gaze and Riders:

> *Ici venu, l'avenir est paresse.*
> *L'insecte net gratte la sécheresse;*
> *Tout est brûlé, défait, recu dans l'air*
> *A je ne sais quelle sévère essence . . .*
> *La vie est vaste, étant ivre d'absence,*
> *Et l'amertume est douce, et l'esprit clair. . . .*
>
> *Maigre immortalité noire et dorée,*
> *Consolatrice affreusement laurée,*
> *Qui de la mort fais un sein maternel,*
> *Le beau mesonge et la pieuse ruse!*
> *Qui ne connaît, et qui ne les refuse,*
> *Ce crâne vide et ce rire éternel!*

More central to the moral climate of *The Unicorn* is *La Princesse de Clèves*: in *La Princesse,* the heroine renounces love with the Duke of Nemours to preserve the sanity of a husband she does not love and whom she married only to satisfy her mother's wishes. Even after the Prince dies she persists in her renunciation, arguing that her relationship with the Duke must not flourish at the expense of her husband's misfortune. The questions that Mme. de Lafayette seems to be asking have far-reaching social and moral import: Does the Princess transcend her station by the purity of her motives? Or does she sacrifice a real duty (her mutual love with the Duke) to one that is both abstract and arbitrary? Finally, both Mme. de Lafayette and Iris Murdoch seem to be wondering if social convention, and even a refined understanding of social convention, may be no more than bloated escapism.

Social convention of any sort generally implies consent, or at least acquiescence. Hannah Crean-Smith and her retainer friends have voluntarily forfeited both vocational and social advantages for a nonsecular goal. The violence and, perhaps, the tragedy that life at Gaze ultimately begets springs from the ease with which the characters drift into an unnatural regimen. As with Mme. de Lafayette, Iris Murdoch's dark social satire has significant philosophical undertones:

Marian Taylor, the university graduate who journeys to Gaze to be Hannah's tutor-companion, reacts to her new situation with the same bewilderment as the reader. Yet Marian, with the others, soon becomes involved in guilt and evil.

Dismissing for the moment the question of her responsibility, we may nonetheless observe that life at Gaze is so flaccid and evanescent that the inhabitants of the estate are defenseless against violence and injustice. First, duties pertaining to business and housekeeping are not specific: We are told that Denis Nolan is the clerk and book-keeper for the estate, yet Denis spends most of his time and effort superintending the wild life around the Castle; although Jamesie Evercreech is employed by Hannah as her chauffeur, either Denis or Gerald Scottow seems to do most of the driving; Violet, Jamesie's much older sister, appears to have been hired as a housekeeper or housekeeper-companion to Hannah, but, oddly, she provides Hannah scant personal comfort and most of the household chores are per-formed by the non-English-speaking Negro maids. Marian's ritual of after-dinner whiskey and leisurely walks with Hannah, although nourished by and reducible to violence, produces a deceptive mood of tedium and staleness. Unrelated values like time, space, and current events count negligibly at Gaze; jet airplanes create the illusion that New York and Riders, the nearby home of the Le Jour family, are equidistant from Gaze, even though the exact location of the Castle is never divulged. There is no electricity at Gaze, and none of the inhabitants ever seem to read a newspaper; even the bookcases have presumably been locked for years prior to Marian's arrival.

Social interaction in this pseudofairy-tale world is, therefore, never normal; the self-elected isolation of Gaze from the pragmatic secular world has severed the Castle from its sources of morality and social freedom. Gerald Scottow and Jamesie Evercreech conduct a sado-masochistic homosexual relationship; Marian Taylor discovers herself always whispering furtively whenever she addresses Denis Nolan; Violet Evercreech and Gerald frequently make surprising, melodra-matic entrances from behind and above Marian, usually eliciting a somewhat shocked, defensive response from her. Hannah, in addition, seems to have quasi-feudal relationships with both Denis and Gerald. Qualifiers like *pseudo* or *quasi* must, in fact, be called upon in any discussion of the moral climate of Gaze. Values there are either jealously hidden, producing, as suggested, an invisible tension, or amorphous and indeterminate.

As was demonstrated in *A Severed Head,* life needs form and structure in order to ensure personal dignity. Iris Murdoch scorns the trend in both existentialism and modern linguistic analysis to "theorize away" moral concerns and transcendent values. Freedom and truth are both functions of consciousness; the failure to perceive this reality in a context of social responsibility eventuates in one's finding oneself trapped within a pattern. We have seen the blighting determinism of recurring acts and relations in *The Bell* and in the patterns of diagrammatic sexuality in *A Severed Head.* Hannah Crean-Smith in *The Unicorn* justifies the legend about her dying as soon as she leaves her garden by encasing herself within the rigid determinism at Gaze. Again, the failure, or refusal, to choose is a surrender of personal freedom and dignity to an arbitrary code that can engulf other persons. The relapse into patterned determinism after Marian Taylor and Effingham Cooper fail to rescue Hannah is expressed in just these terms. Although Alice Le Jour had driven to Gaze by herself and Gerald had arrived in the Land-Rover with Jamesie, the characters regroup in formalized pairs for their return to the Castle:

> Gerald said, "Hannah."
> She moved towards him like a sleep walker, and as she almost stumbled he moved to give her his arm, and led her to the Land Rover. . . .
> "Effie." Alice opened the passenger door of the Austin.
> Effingham looked vaguely across at her. . . . Then he frowned, shook his head almost absently, and went across to the car. He got in and the door banged. . . .
> Marian began to pick her way back to the gravel. Her shoes were covered with black soil.
> Jamesie was still standing where he had been left, and as Marian looked at him he seemed to be glowing with some sort of secret pleasure. . . . He slowly turned his head towards her and smiled. "Marian!"

Iris Murdoch is not experimenting in *The Unicorn* with an Oriental quietism based upon endurance and patient suffering. Hannah and the characters grouped around her are captives of the indeterminacy their antihumanistic vision has begotten. Denis Nolan is correct when he calls Gaze a prison. The difficulty arises when one tries to identify the jailer or jailers and the jailed. Peter Crean-Smith, seven years before, had confined his young wife Hannah to Gaze Castle for committing adultery and for trying to murder him. This situation is complicated by Hannah's belief in God, by Peter's homosexuality, and by the fact that husband and wife are first cousins; Peter, furthermore, has recruited his poor cousins (the Evercreeches) and his former partner in homosexual bouts (Gerald Scottow) to preside over Hannah in his absence. Hannah admits that her situation is worse for the others than for herself, and her satellites do experience a good deal of shame and suffering. Cyrena Norman Pondrom calls them both worshippers and jailers of Hannah,[2] a paradox that achieves reality through the natural dialectic that power engenders.

In her most overtly Platonic novel, Iris Murdoch employs terms like "the Good" and "Truth"; *The Unicorn* can be labeled a study of the search for absolutes like goodness and truth in a relative, contingent world. The major obstacle dividing the characters from transcendent reality is their inverted vision. As do Plato's mortals, they mistake the shadow for the concrete actuality. Iris Murdoch extols elsewhere Simone Weil's concept of "attention" as "the idea of a just and loving gaze directed upon an individual reality."[3] The people in *The Unicorn* invest the unseen and the unknown with fascinating possibilities that have no equivalent in the material world: Effie falls in love with Hannah before meeting her; Hannah makes Max Le Jour, the aged scholar whom she has never seen, her heir; Marian spins fantasies to herself about Gaze Castle that are never realized. The canker at the core, in Iris Murdoch's judgment, is that people tend to color the sensory world as well as the world of the spirit with their own emotions and expectations. The result is not only a distortion of reality but a willful sealing off of our sole access to reality. We shall see in the central episode of the novel, Effingham Cooper's discovery that he is about to be sucked into the bog, a dramatization of the novelist's governing concept that truth and substance dwell incontrovertibly in the region external to the perceiver and that the individual himself must cultivate this mode of civilized awareness.

Mrs. Pondrom observes that the setting of the novel, Gaze Castle, refers to "gazing and uninvolved watching."[4] The lack of other-directed involvement at Gaze does prevent Hannah's retainers from understanding her emotional state or assessing their own. Iris Murdoch demonstrates her affinity to the Marcel-Buber-Jaspers school of existentialism by reducing a good deal of the inner unrest at Gaze to the characters' failure to participate in solid reality. Hannah merely symbolizes for the others the Christian experience of guilt and pain; she is never seen, as it were, from the inside as an authentic suffering being. The others impose their romantic sensibilities upon her and attempt to subsist on their ungrounded illusions. Hannah's actual psychic state can hardly resemble the absolutism they impose upon it. As a passively suffering mortal who is expiating an unverified crime, she does, however, invite appropriation by others. There *is* something compellingly beautiful about her confinement, but, as Max Le Jour indicates, she must be responded to as a person rather than as a justification of one's private concept of beauty or guilt. Gaze Castle, to repeat Mrs. Pondrom's point, suggests this kind of romantic contemplation at the expense of direct participation. Hannah's openness to the interference of others is a question we shall discuss later; the issue at hand is that none of the others view her with the loving attention to diagnose her plight with any depth or sincerity. The unreal and the illusory yield a mortality both spurious and fragile.

Although Peter Crean-Smith, as a figure lurking in the unspecified background of the action, contributes vividly to the moral climate of Gaze, the prospect of his actual presence destroys the arbitrary conventions that govern the behavior of Hannah and the others. The ensuing chaos attests to the folly of constructing social values around a romanticized personalism: Hannah kills Gerald and dies shortly thereafter herself; Pip Le Jour, her former lover, commits suicide; Denis Nolan murders Peter. Furthermore, Effingham Cooper ends his long association with the Le Jour family, and torrential rains inundate the bog and then flood the countryside, incongruously scattering dead fish on the neighboring hills. Even the organization of the novel reflects the widespread destruction engendered by the fatuous social morality of the Gaze-Riders contingent. The point of view shifts in the first six parts of the novel between Marian Taylor and Effingham Cooper at the end of each part; in the seventh and final part, however, the point of view alters with each chapter.

As their religious conscience, Hannah invites the resentment of the others for occupying so much of their minds. Yet when the incubus of her resigned suffering is removed, their lives become charged with new purpose. As soon as Gerald announces his plan to take her away from Gaze, they feel free. Although neither attachment flourishes, Alice Le Jour and Effingham and Marian Taylor and Denis Nolan see each other in a fresh exciting way. After she and Denis make love by the salmon pool, Marian feels emotionally fulfilled and gratified: "Her encounter with Denis, for all its surprisingness and oddness, had so much of the feeling of coming into real life." Without question, Hannah deters the formation of more direct human relationships. Jamesie Evercreech is wrong when he declares, after the news breaks that Peter has canceled his trip, that life at Gaze may now recover its former equilibrium. Hannah's servant-jailers feel too elated by the prospect of her departure from Gaze to welcome her decision to remain. Since Hannah stands as the direction toward which all of the emotional and spiritual energy in the novel flows, the other characters relinquish their freedom to their romantic conception of her. She is the ambiguous legendary unicorn of the novel's title and, therefore, the test of her associates' purity and innocence.

Mrs. Pondrom's observation that *The Unicorn* explores religious experience[5] refers directly to Hannah. Both as an object of the other characters' needs and as a suffering individual in her own right, Hannah evokes religious sentiments. But, as James Wait in Conrad's *The Nigger of the "Narcissus,"* she becomes a demoralizing force. Her meekness, fragility, and endurance seem to make her, in this respect, a travesty of Mischa Fox, whose neurosis in *The Flight from the Enchanter* tended to reduce other characters to depersonalized mental constructs. The following assessments of Hannah express the feminine mystique and, simultaneously, the frightening ambiguity she evokes:

> Hannah's central role in the novel is indicated by the images associated with her. She is the enchanted princess, the sleeping beauty, whose awakening to the reality of her situation spells not happiness but catastrophe. She is to be identified with the wounded bat which Denis brings in to her early in the novel and which later dies. About her exists a golden atmosphere, a saintly halo; she is "golden-eyed," her face capable of sudden and strong illumination, and for Effingham she becomes "a great placid golden idol" at the center of his existence. About her is the air of legend, a "medieval" aspect, a pre-Raphaelite opulence, and an atmosphere of fatality. According to local lore, she will die if she comes out of the garden at Gaze, and the prophecy is later fulfilled.

*   *   *

She is described as a "scapegoat," "our image of the significance of suffering," "a legendary creature, a beautiful unicorn," "an ordinary guilty person," "a sort of enchantress, a Circe," "a false God," "whore and murdress," [*sic*] and "Virgin mother." Her seclusion is depicted as capture, voluntary, imprisonment, the legendary situation of a sleeping beauty, and Christian or classical expiation of guilt. What, after all, is the truth about Hannah?[6]

A clue to Hannah's personality resides in her name: the two parts of her surname suggest both elegance and banality; her first name, as that of Nan Mor in *The Sandcastle*, is a palindrome, implying that she is locked within her own delimiting morality. This idea gains in force when we recall the numerous mirrors in her room and her total inadaptability to the world beyond that imagined reality both she and her worshipper-jailers have fabricated.

Although she ventures into the storm at the end of Chapter XXXI, the opening words of the next chapter ("Take her inside.") convey the futility of her first act of freedom. Her self-immolation has deprived her of functioning both creatively and with regard to the creativity of others. When she learns that her husband has changed his mind about coming back to Gaze, Hannah vows to inaugurate a new social order based upon her spiritual energy. The kinetic force of suffering and power, Iris Murdoch believes, is remarkably potent: by installing Gerald Scottow as her tormenter and scourge, a role previously occupied by her husband *in absentia,* Hannah objectifies her suffering. But her murder of Gerald reveals that as soon as she ceases contemplating her experience and enters into it emotionally, destruction is inevitable.

Iris Murdoch, then, is a good deal more outspoken about the shortcomings of religious experience in *The Unicorn* than she was in *The Bell*. Hannah serves as her dramatized refutation of the ontological argument that the belief in, or the desire for, an entity endows that entity with the property of existence. Speaking of her own religious beliefs, Hannah says, "In a way you can't love something that isn't there. I think if you really love, then something *is* there." The inescapability of the indifferent material world destroys this fiction. The reality of the external world, Iris Murdoch insists, cannot be neglected or subordinated to an arbitrarily postulated idea. Falseness and unreality, in fact, beget further deception. As time progresses, life at Gaze grows more remote from the reality it must eventually answer to. Iris Murdoch has observed that subjective reactions to an actual experience often falsify the experience. When Hannah tries to convert the collective thought-process permeating Gaze into concrete action, she is immediately destroyed.

Aside from adducing the fallacy of the ontological argument, Iris Murdoch uses Wittgensteinian reasoning to attack the life of the spirit. Man is contingent, material, and explicable by his social relations; religion ultimately refers to a region that is unbounded, impalpable, and governed by absolute moral criteria. The attempt to define a historical social entity by a nonhistorical, asocial code entails a distortion. Instead of being free, the individual is trapped within an arbitrary mechanistic network. Hannah Crean-Smith allows herself to become a mental object of her associates, who construct images of her in accord with existentialism's passion for paradox and romantic isolation. And Hannah herself instigates this pattern by her uncritical acceptance of her punishment. None of the characters witness her crime, but Hannah's pushing Peter over the cliff seven years earlier matters less than her claiming the act and responding to it as a privately elected experience.

Allen has called Iris Murdoch the leading symbolic novelist of the postwar period.[7] Arguing by analogy and by the inferences implied in McDowell's critique of the novel, we can posit Hannah herself as the author's allegorized refutation of religious devotion. This interpretation explains Hannah's ambiguity, the great emotional force with which the others respond to her, and the great psychological burden she is forced to bear:

> Philosophically and symbolically, the novel focuses upon Hannah Crean-Smith, who is seen only through other people's eyes and who gains what vitality she possesses (even if she feels this) from the preoccupation of others with her personality and situation.[8]

This grim criticism of religion, underscored by the novel's crabbed, sparse texture, revolves around the failure of everyone, including Hannah, to align their subjective values with the contingency and spontaneity of the empirical world. In her essay "The Idea of Perfection," Iris Murdoch defines freedom as "a function of the progressive attempt to see an object clearly" and, therefore, as an activity that is "essentially something progressive, something infinitely perfectible."[9] The discipline she recommends throughout her fiction is the cultivation of a loving and just objectivity. She differs from writers like Amis, Wain, and Kerouac by emphasizing the selfless, other-directed concept of objective truth rather than the self-centered concept of sincerity. Introspection only upsets one's sense of proportion and reality. Instead of directing his awareness to the concrete presence of material objects and other people, the introvert shapes and colors reality in line with his own values and perceptions. When carried to its destructive conclusion, this kind of activity sacrifices sensory evidence to neurosis and solipsism. On the other hand, the progressive enterprise of focusing one's moral vision upon the empirical world promises rich encounters with an order of being that is not derived, but a solid context free of categories or classification. By acquiescing in the inert role of the to-be-perceived, Hannah has become the embodiment of the others' guilt and suffering. They come to depend upon her passivity to justify their moral principles and spiritual needs. It is here that the unicorn symbol becomes central to the novel's philosophical undergirding, for Hannah's alleged crime and her response to it coalesce remarkably with the familiar Christian concept of sin and redemption.

Seconding Pliny, Bulfinch interprets the mythical unicorn as an animal characterized by ferocity and by the high value it bestows upon purity and innocence. Only a virgin, we are told, can capture the beast. According to legend, after the unicorn fell asleep with his head in the virgin's lap, she betrayed him by summoning a band of hunters.[10] Other accounts associate the unicorn with a broad symbolic panorama, including the qualities of strength, ferocity, swiftness, and feminine chastity.[11] The radical indeterminacy of Hannah's situation at Gaze and the polarization of innocence to guilt develops her affinity with the unicorn myth. Max Le Jour states that the unicorn is the image of Christ, but he reminds us that Hannah is simply a guilty person. It is never decided whether Hannah is a pure being who unconsciously causes others pain. Iris Murdoch, in fact, follows existentialist doctrine by discrediting the salience of immediate motives. The points of view surrounding any event are too numerous and variable for a single individual to create a static situation. The social-religious order at Gaze is the bitter product of common accord. Hannah, then, dramatizes with chilling accuracy the obverse side of the novelist's belief that identity is gained only by submerging the self in immediate experience. Hannah's immobility and her rare moments of emotional imbalance invite the others to project their own ideas of guilt and pain upon her. Thus, she comes to represent a multiple embodiment of their innermost lives, which explains why everyone is so resentful and at the same time so protective toward her. The power she gains, both socially and psychologically, is enormous but grotesquely out of phase with what seems to be the truth of her personal state.

As did St. Paul, Iris Murdoch dwells upon the concrete significance of religious experience as it is manifested in actual human lives. Man, as an unresolved, progressive psychic entity, behaves unnaturally when he subscribes to a morality that is static and derived; he needs free encounters with others like him in order to discover his selfhood. Marian Taylor judges correctly when, upon leaving Gaze, she states that none of the Gaze-Riders group understood each other. Hannah and the others cannot progress morally and refine their perceptions of reality within a social order so desperately involute. "Riders," the name for the Le Jour estate, suggests a more athletic participation in life than Gaze offers. Yet, in that Alice and Pip leave their jobs to witness the end of Hannah's seven-year ordeal, they, too, surrender freedom to fantasy.

As has been stated above, Iris Murdoch's minimal definition of man is that he is a social creature. Accordingly, the attainment of selfhood through social interaction presupposes extremely powerful fields of force between people. Unable to induce a flow of kinetic energy fed by other-directed perception, the Gaze-Riders cortege establish a continuum of suffering based on their collective notions about sin and guilt. Hannah, as the pivotal point, acts as a distribution point for the suffering. In other words, the person who has disavowed both forceful personal encounters and shapely self-legislating acts assumes the queenly and even saintly position of ultimate responsibility. The theoretical explanation for the resulting disorder is supplied by Max Le Jour's remarks about the Greek concept of Ate, which refers to the contagion of suffering. Max Le Jour argues that power reproduces itself to the degree at which its absence constitutes a form of itself. Goodness, however, shares no affinities with power, either as powerless submission or vigorous self-assertion. Hannah may be guilty of transferring her affliction to others, but she is not entirely culpable. For if she sows guilt, the others should not have placed her in a position in which she is most conscious of her emotional extremity as the moral backdrop for their acts.

The passage that Max Le Jour chants from Aeschylus underscores

Iris Murdoch's belief that suffering and knowledge are naturally interconnected:

> Zeus, who leads men into the ways of understanding, has established the rule that we must learn by suffering. As sad care, with memories of pain, comes dropping upon the heart in sleep, so even against our will does wisdom come upon us.

At Gaze, however, the suffering fails to give birth to any kind of usable knowledge. Denis Nolan and Pip Le Jour both think that Hannah's ambiguous vigil will end with her husband's death. But the power and suffering begotten at Gaze install Gerald Scottow in Peter's place when Peter changes his plans about flying from New York. Although the reader is never privileged to observe the interviews that take place between Hannah and Gerald, incremental repetition conveys the idea of his newly established ascendancy:

> Marian wondered vaguely what would happen when Hannah was gone and they were all left behind. . . . They would stay there till Peter Crean-Smith arrived, and he would whip them into the stables and change them into swine.
>
>   *   *   *
>
> It's odd, she thought, there is no one to appeal to any more, not even Peter. . . . Pip had gone. . . . Effingham had deserted to the world of ordinary life and reason. She and Denis were ruined servants. . . . Now they could only wait for Gerald to come down and whip them to the stables and turn them into swine.

Gerald, in addition, seems to be altogether refreshed by the transfer of power from Peter to himself: "He looked larger, browner, healthier than ever before. His big well-shaven face glowed, ruddy with power." But power, which grows out of the apprehension of another person as something to be arbitrarily annexed, can only promote violence and suffering. As soon as Hannah's smouldering resentment kindles into retaliation, she murders Gerald, who may have recently become her lover as well as her spiritual mentor in suffering.

The novel contains its own refutation of the cycle of power and suffering engendered at Gaze. The fourth part, in which Effingham Cooper is trapped in the bog, is the book's symbolic and philosophical nucleus. The premonition of death awakens Effingham to his own insignificance and the plenitude of that which is not himself. Freedom, then, once again, demands our reversing the existential practice of exalting the alienated self. As Effingham intuits his death, the surviving world trembles with being. Effie's subsequent failure to profit morally from the self-denying transfer of feeling he experiences in the bog does not diminish the force of Iris Murdoch's ethical message. To emphasize the cogency of her idea, she again employs stylistic repetition. Max Le Jour, speaking of power, had referred to Ate as "the *almost automatic* transfer of suffering from one being to another." (Italics are mine.) What seems to be at stake, in everyday human terms, is the perpetuation of either misery or love. The social adjuncts of Effingham's act of self-naughting or "nothinging" promises a freedom and liberality directly opposed to the destructive fantasy world of Gaze:

> What was left was everything else, all that was not himself, that object which he had never before seen and upon which he now gazed with the passion of a lover. . . . He looked, and knew . . . that with the death of the self the world becomes quite automatically the object of a perfect love. He clung on to the words "quite automatically" and murmured them to himself as a charm.

This episode dramatizes perhaps more clearly than any other in Iris Murdoch's work her opposition to the radical individualism promulgated by Sartre's theory of the for-itself (*l'être pour-soi*) and the in-itself (*l'être en-soi*). To popularize the cleavage, the for-itself intuits its own existence by engaging in an operation of naughting; it claims existence by describing itself as that which is not inert and opaque, the nonreflective to-be-known. Roquentin, in *Nausea,* is horrified at the bloated abundance of being-in-itself. But where the Sartrean self recoils from the viscous (*la viscosité*),[12] Iris Murdoch's perceiver can proclaim his creativity and spontaneity without sacrificing the coordinate status of the material world. The way to freedom is not by conquering and owning, but by entering sympathetically into life. Dissolution of selfhood permits the mind to embrace the untheoretical, self-justifying reality of other people and things. Iris Murdoch's judgments, like Sartre's, are based on the concreteness of sensory objects. But by showing the objects of sense as things that are thought as well as seen, heard, or felt, she is able to posit a rich, harmonious world—a world, furthermore, that derives too much of its meaning from willed self-effacement to be discredited as romantic escapism.

The romantic passion for symbolism, organic synthesis, necessity, and the perfection of man actuates the spiritual fervor of the characters in *The Unicorn*. Iris Murdoch reveals the influence of Henry James and of Elizabeth Bowen in her treatment of both character and dramatic motivation. As with Maisie, Milly Theale, and Portia Quayne, nobody in the novel is interested in Hannah Crean-Smith for herself. The Abbess in *The Bell* had said that most of the mistakes we make are mistakes in loving and that our duty is to refine love by moving perpetually forward in the region of emotional commitment. To be human is to be uncreated and unresolved; nobody in *The Unicorn* is receptive enough to Hannah as an independent reality to domesticate her. The character least culpable, perhaps, is Marian Taylor, the outsider who reacts to the enormities at Gaze with the same pragmatic-humanistic indignation as the reader. As does Georgie Hands of *A Severed Head*, Marian needs love desperately and has probably cultivated her flair for teaching to make others dependent upon her. An only child of modest Midlands shopkeepers and a recipient of a university scholarship, she is socially backward. Her first impressions of Alice Le Jour and Gerald Scottow indicate a livelier response to social class than to persons as ends in themselves. At twenty-nine, Marian is very much like Jake Donaghue, Rosa Keepe, Dora Greenfield, and Felix Meecham in that she oscillates between loneliness and emotional involvements without achieving anything like security or happiness.

Her moral confusion (she is even excited by the Lesbian advances of Violet Evercreech) undermines her pragmatic secularity, which, ironically, becomes the quality that prevents her from "seeing" Hannah. Marian's failure to swim in the chilly, moiling sea in Chapter III forecasts her later inability to immerse herself in Hannah's immediate needs and values. What cannot be readily decided is whether the impurity of Marian's love kills the unicorn. After she murders Gerald Scottow, Hannah prefers escaping into the storm to awaiting the judgment of her husband, who has been away for seven years. Marian, by setting Hannah free, drives the reader to search for obscure motives of love, hate, or wisdom.

The last part of the novel bristles with moral ambiguities like this. Pip Le Jour, Hannah's former lover, comes to take her away when he learns of Peter's expected visit. Rebuffed, Pip leaves behind him the rifle she later uses to murder Gerald Scottow. It is doubtful that Pip, a dedicated outdoorsman, would forget his rifle, even under emotional strain. Moreover, he carried the weapon from Riders to Gaze in heavy rains, and he would certainly have had no use for it in the field, if, in fact, he came from the field and not from Riders directly. This rather labored motive-seeking is hardly decisive, but it at least makes respectable the belief that Pip left his rifle in Hannah's room deliberately and that he himself sent the cable announcing Peter's return to Gaze. Yet, even if we grant these concessions, we still cannot decide whether Pip acted in compliance with an old agreement or out of resentment. His subsequent suicide can be evidence for either possibility.

Equally baffling is the conduct of Gerald and Violet Evercreech. By attempting to take Hannah away, does Gerald manifest a finer sympathy than the others, who are content to let her continue paying ambiguous obeisance to Peter's shadow? Or is Gerald pandering to Hannah's masochism by assuming the role of her tormenter? It is even suggested that Peter never planned to come to Gaze at all. Gerald informs the others about his return, and nobody ever asks to see the cable. Yet even if he sent the cable himself or if no cable ever existed, how then do we explain Gerald's conduct? Accordingly, Violet Evercreech, the poor, aging relative of a wealthy young woman, is strongly actuated by money in her association with Hannah. She calls Hannah "Whore and murderess!" and "a perfect bitch!" but insists that she loves her, a claim Marian Taylor supports. Violet betrays early in the novel her interest in money, and she hastily destroys various letters and documents after Gerald's death. Yet she does not accept Gaze when it is offered her by Alice Le Jour, and her advice that the others leave Gaze to avoid bloodshed and suffering may have sprung from a sincere other-regarding impulse.

The ambiguities, ironies, and paradoxes at the end of *The Unicorn* defy easy explanation. Perhaps the reason for their presence is to describe how intimately and unknowingly we can become involved in suffering. There are, however, elements in plotting and incident that do reflect Iris Murdoch's moral position. One inescapable tendency is her sustained disenchantment with men; although several of the male characters excel professionally or morally, they do not perform uniformly well. Effingham Cooper, a highly placed civil servant, enjoys the love of three women—Alice Le Jour, Marian Taylor, and Elizabeth, a co-worker who sends him letters at Riders. Yet his Freudian bias prompts him to favor a sporadic quasi-feudalistic romance with Hannah. And even as a devotee of Hannah, he fails to acquit himself: he muddles his mission of rescuing her and seems always to be drunk, sleeping, or away from Gaze when she needs him. His vision of the world's shimmering fullness soon disappears; although his experience in the bog and his associations with Marian, Hannah, and Alice prepare him for a compassionate awareness of others, he leaves Gaze and Riders more isolated than he was before his visit. He has severed his long-standing friendship with the Le Jour family, and the terrible calamities he has witnessed count for him only as an awkward interlude to be chatted about as a way of passing time.

Unlike Effingham, Max Le Jour *has* cultivated the other-regarding impulses that could grant him freedom and humane knowledge. Armed with the formal theoretical background to help Hannah, he nonetheless keeps her at a distance to maintain his routine of study and writing. Ironically, the authority on Plato is as guilty as the others of mistaking illusion for reality. Similarly to Shakespeare's Henry IV, he never takes the spiritual pilgrimage he has looked forward to in his maturity; Effingham is right when he indicts his former tutor for being a prisoner of his books, his old age, and his failing health. The theoretical moralist and the studious disciple of the philosopher most profoundly concerned with the Good, the True, and the Beautiful never applies his wisdom to a concrete situation.

Balancing Max Le Jour's vast formal learning is the intuitive knowledge of Denis Nolan. Both men frequently admit their ignorance, a tendency that, more often than not, indicates intelligence as well as honesty. Called an "untouched puritan" by Marian Taylor, Denis is like Lawrence's Mellors and Lewis (*St. Mawr*) in that he has a keen appreciation of personal sanctity, especially in regard to the physical self. He loves wildlife, sings, plays the piano, reads French, and audits the accounts of Gaze. His benevolence and topographical knowledge enable him to rescue Effingham from the bog. Yet in spite of his devotion to Hannah and his basic purity, Denis too enters the vortex of violence that destroys the physical and human landscape of Gaze and Riders. Hannah evinces her imperfection symbolically by failing to cross the flooded valley; the saintlike Denis (at thirty-three, he is a fallen Christ-Robin Hood figure, having been seduced by Maid Marian) manages to cross the bog to save

Effingham, and he survives the storm that kills Hannah. But he drives back to Gaze only to report his having murdered Peter Crean-Smith at the Devil's Causeway. The last two survivors of the flood and the carnage, Denis and Marian, escape inheriting Hannah's vigil only by virtue of their fallibility and the violence they create.

The destruction and the moral isolation registered in *The Unicorn* grow out of the unnaturalness of the conditions engendered at Gaze and Riders. The search for abstract Goodness, in the person of a spiritually cleansed and regenerated Hannah, has created a deterministic continuum that collapses under its own weight. Ironically, it is the Christian impulse that launches the characters' quests for absolute terminal values. The Good depends upon choice and will but transcends them;[13] as imperfect beings, we can approach the Good only in gradual stages. As G. E. Moore states in *Principia Ethica,* Goodness is not an existing quantity but the function of a relation. The people in *The Unicorn* try to appropriate and exhaust the Good by one magnetic gesture of the will, that is, by projecting their spiritual needs upon a self-stylization of Hannah. The collective religious conscience of Gaze and Riders, then, is nonsharable. Contrary to liberal Protestantism, Iris Murdoch sees the life of the spirit as hidden, antisocial, and vulnerable to the excesses of surrealism. She uses our underived spontaneity and the abrasiveness of a creative social framework to refute dramatically the ontological argument of Anselm, Descartes, and Leibniz. The mind may arbitrarily posit the real existence of its own contents, but existence is not derivable from a mental operation. Only the world of facts and interacting mortals can ratify the concrete actuality of a value or goal. Thus Hannah (the God-figure), Gerald (the priest-lover), Marian (the confidante or confessor), Denis (the tarnished saint), and Max Le Jour (the idealist in search of transcendent values) are all responsible for the bloodshed and waste experienced at Gaze. By creating a situation that has no validity in the material world, they enact the destructive consequences of wishing a situation into existence—regardless of their lofty motives.

The spiritual life, the mainspring of religious experience, does not derive its being through a disinterested urge to resemble or to describe the familiar world of sense objects; it is colored by inner need and volition. Tragedy inheres in resisting this arbitrary kind of synthesis. Pascal said that the reed in the field is stronger than the wind that snaps it, because it is conscious. To struggle against change, pain, and indifference is to triumph spiritually. By intuiting our personal insignificance amid impermanence and sorrow, we learn to overcome temporary desires. This other-directed awareness, in addition, imparts a nobility to our efforts; Iris Murdoch is unlike the Beat writers in America in that the refusal to prostrate oneself before time and death in the spirit of Oriental primitivism constitutes for her the tragic vision.

Notes to Chapter Nine

1. Most of the stylistic similarities occur in dialogue. The first quotation in each of the following pairs is taken from *An Unofficial Rose*:

Hugh poured out. "Now don't put me off this time, Emma. Don't treat me as if I scarcely existed. Talk to me properly. I deserve some real speech."

*

"Look, Pip, let's sit down, shall we, while you have your pipe. There are a lot of things I want you to tell me and which I think I ought to know. . . ."

"Come on, Pip," said Effingham. "I deserve it."

*   *   *

"Well, what do you want, roughly?"

"Roughly, everything."

*

"What was it you wanted me to tell you, Effie?"

"Everything, roughly."

*   *   *

"Why did you come to Fanny's funeral?" said Hugh.

"A final act of brutality."

"Rubbish."

*

"Mrs. Crean-Smith doesn't want to be, as you put it, rescued. She's all right as she is . . . and we must respect what she has chosen."

"Rubbish," said Miss Taylor.

2. Cyrena Norman Pondrom, "Iris Murdoch: *The Unicorn*," *Critique*, 6 (Winter, 1963), 177-78.

3. Murdoch, "The Idea of Perfection," 371.

4. Pondrom, 180.

5. *Ibid.,* 178.

6. McDowell, 357; Pondrom, 178.

7. Allen, 282.

8. McDowell, 356.

9. Murdoch, "The Idea of Perfection," 361.

10. [Thomas Bulfinch,] *Bulfinch's Mythology* (New York, n. d.), 251-52.

11. Hangen, 260.

12. Sartre, *Being and Nothingness,* 605-6.

13. Murdoch, "The Idea of Perfection," 344.

Ten

THE ITALIAN GIRL

A Weary Homecoming

T HE ITALIAN GIRL adds little to the development of
Iris Murdoch's thought. The events and characters in her latest work
create a fictional milieu too incredible to signify, morally or artistically.
A brief summary of this crowded book will show Iris Murdoch
possessed of more data than she can command. Edmund Narraway,
a London wood engraver of about forty-five, returns to his family
home in the North of England for the first time in six years to attend
his mother's funeral. Narraway discovers that Otto and Isabel, his
brother and sister-in-law, have been conducting love affairs with Elsa
and David Levkin, the exiled son and daughter of a persecuted
Russian Jew. Otto's apprentice in the craft of stonemasonry, David,
has also been the lover of his master's teen-age daughter Flora. The
domestic arrangement is sheer fantasy: while Otto sleeps with Elsa,
her brother David alternates making love to Isabel and Flora. His
Slavic-Judaic mystique has not merely enraptured mother and daughter; it has also made both women pregnant.

When Edmund accidentally unmasks the complicated love pattern,
Otto cannot stand the shame of public disclosure; he orders the
Russians away. But at a point when a captivating moral issue
promises to evolve naturally from action and character, Elsa returns
spectacularly and burns to death. Sobered by this violent incident,
the survivors resume their lives with new vision and moral penetration.
(David, echoing Eliot's Thomas à Becket, says to Edmund late in the

novel, "It is better to do the wrong thing for the right reason than
to do the right thing for the wrong reason.") Isabel returns to her
father in Scotland, where she will bear David's child; David goes
back to Russia to pursue truth within the context of his racial origins;
Flora, having had an abortion, remains at the family estate to look
after her father; Edmund learns that, to confront his identity
directly, he must acknowledge his love for Maggie, the Italian girl
who has served the Narraway family as housekeeper and governess
for thirty years. On the last page Maggie and Edmund prepare to
drive to Rome, where they will presumably marry.

Like Martin Lynch-Gibbon of *A Severed Head,* Edmund is a
Knight of Infinite Humiliation, inclined to prostrate himself before
what he understands to be the female image. His indecisiveness has
made him a sexual and vocational nonentity, and, as that of his
predecessor, his struggle for personal integrity entails a descriptive,
historical inquiry into his mana-complex.

The symbolism of Edmund's surname explains his narrow existence
and his need to exorcise folly (*Narr*). His progress in human understanding, although discernible, is extremely slight and comes only as
the product of great suffering—Elsa's death by fire, Isabel and Otto's
unhappy marriage, and his own lifetime of suppressed emotions. But
his ability to escape the shadow of his mother's dark influence,
conveyed symbolically by her dread of fire and her insistence on
lighting the house with low-powered electric light bulbs, attests to the
resilience and renewability of the human spirit. Iris Murdoch uses
boxwood, a material for engravers' blocks, to show that Edmund's
homecoming will effect an organic change in his personality, altering
his standing as a man as well as his professional career:

> The best way of curing a crack in boxwood is to leave the block
> in a cool damp place for twenty-four hours or so; usually the
> patient makes a miraculous recovery from quite a severe split. I
> examined with satisfaction the blocks which I had just retrieved
> from the cellar. They had healed well. Those who do not work
> with such material, such thingy, aspects of nature, may not quite
> imagine or credit the way in which a piece of unformed stuff can
> seem pregnant, inspiring. . . . There is the lovely difference between
> boxwood and pear wood, the male and female of the wood-
> engraver's world. But there is also the strong individual difference
> between one piece of boxwood and another. Each one is full of a
> different picture.

The cool damp place in the first sentence of the quotation is the lake where Flora tells Edmund about her pregnancy and evokes in him the selfless, other-directed response that forms the mainspring of Iris Murdoch's social morality. In the early part of the novel, Edmund describes people as subjects for painting—Flora as a theme for Manet and Lydia, his dead mother, as a Grünewald St. Anthony. This mode of perception changes, however, after he grows conscious of persons as distinct, self-justifying entities. His forced proximity to Otto brings out in Edmund a capacity for both physical appetite and human relations in general that he never knew he possessed. Isabel's mention of several traits he and Otto share and the epithet *Rhino,* which is applied to both brothers, point out that years of self-suppression have not blunted Edmund's ability to create a balanced intimate relationship. He finally emerges as an actor in the arena of life.

The theme of man's ability to re-create his personality after a crisis is generalized in the novel and is underscored by the homecoming motif. At the end, all of the characters freely choose their futures, and they are all invigorated by the robustness of their self-legislating acts. Going to Scotland and Russia, Isabel and David opt for the North, where they can interpret their muddled lives within the cold lucidity of race and heredity. The decision of Otto and Flora to remain at the Northumbrian estate reflects their need to discover being within the continuum of the family. Edmund, contrarily, takes Maggie south in order to cultivate the warm, loving human relationship he needs to complete himself as a man. Each character knows that the search for identity is a radically individual problem, and each faces the problem bravely. That they all yield to a private or ancestral obsession is no sign of weakness. As Nietzsche's doctrine of self-overcoming insists, human progress is a synthetic accumulation rather than an abrupt break with the past. The knowledge that one is not given a new personality in critical moments constitutes a creative act. Prior to accepting the fullness of life around him, the individual must accept his own contingency in all of its ramifications.

Although the motivations for the self-disclosures at the end are clear, the skimpy narrative structure of *The Italian Girl* robs them of significance. Edmund, we are reminded, is said to resemble his brother. The idea never gains credibility because Otto has no discernible identity. He is by far the most eloquent speaker in the novel, and his remarks about transcending suffering to discover truth reflect an incisive moral vision. On the other hand, he is mercenary, weak-willed, and cowardly enough to attack his wife with a chisel. Physically, moreover, he is one of the most repulsive characters in modern literature:

> Most of the room was occupied by the divan on which my brother was sprawled. . . . A half-empty whisky bottle was standing upright in one of Otto's shoes. Otto, uncovered by the surge of the blankets, was wearing two very dirty round-necked vests rolled up in tubes about his chest and a pair of equally reprehensible long woollen pants pulled well down upon his hips. His thick soft waist was revealed, covered with a straggle of dark curly hairs, and below it the bare white protuberance of his stomach and the black cup of his navel, seemingly full of earth. His bull-head was thrown back and his face seemed a crumpled mass of fleshy lines, his moist shapeless mouth ajar and gurgling. He seemed more like the debris of a human being than like a man.

Anyone can certainly combine inconsistencies in his personality and even in his scale of moral values. Iris Murdoch's failure to develop Otto's character in depth, however, makes the fusion unconvincing. There is no solid middle ground to Otto's personality; he is either offensively gross or sublimely eloquent, never simply a person. And because he emerges only as a congeries, he cannot stand either as a character in his own right or as an accurate reflector of Edmund's personality.

Perhaps the most serious flaw in *The Italian Girl* is its lack of dramatic execution. The difficult moral questions that provoke Iris Murdoch suggest that the long, shifting-point-of-view novel is her natural artistic milieu. To develop a liberal, humane point of reference for the ironies and subtly interweaving motives that constitute social reality, a novelist needs artistic scope. *The Italian Girl,* related in only two hundred and fourteen pages of large print and wide margins, does not provide the latitude and mobility essential to a cogent rendering of man's moral ambiguity.

Although Maggie Magistretti is the Italian girl in the title, her character is also dimly conceived. In her case, however, the author's failure is philosophical as well as novelistic or dramatic. We are told in the first chapter that to employ an Italian nurse has always been a Narraway family tradition; Maggie, or Maria, is the last in a series of Giulias, Gemmas, Vittorias, and Carlas who have served the Narraways since the nineteenth century. Commenting upon this peculiar family tradition, Edmund views Maggie as a collective ingredient of his mana-fixation: "The past had become, in a manner, traditional, so that I always had, as it were, two mothers, my own mother and the Italian Girl." By using Maggie to rout the blighting influence of his mother, Edmund accomplishes more than just an exchange of mother images. His eating of the apple in the last chapter squares with his free choice of Maggie as a love partner. Even though the projected trip to Rome and Maggie's last name suggest that Edmund at this point can have only a self-abasing, perhaps masochistic, understanding with a woman, he has at least discovered a context for sexual union.

Where Lydia, Edmund's mother, imposed only limits and conditions, Maggie is will-less; she has for years given of herself unconditionally to the Narraways and to the Italian families in the nearby village. Edmund's direct naming of her ("I said 'Maria.'") reveals that he has already objectified her as a private individual rather than the swarthy mana-archetype, the Medusa or the wrathful deity who cannot be faced or named directly. Throughout the action, Maggie is unpretentious and invisible in her goodness; she cheerfully loans Flora the money for her abortion, and she does not enforce her claim on the family estate after Lydia wills it to her. This self-negating aspect of goodness may be sound philosophy, but it does not always create exciting fiction. Maggie is a minor character. Her appearances are few and brief, and she fails to instigate any decisive action until the closing chapters. Iris Murdoch has not proved, in her portrait of Maggie, that goodness can be a shapely, energetic force in social morality.

By denying us access to Maggie's mind, the author forfeits the opportunity to predicate a morally tenable position between gross debauchery and nonparticipation. Her frequent use of melodramatic contrivances cheapens any statement she had intended to make concerning the ethical requirements of selfhood. Although the work abounds in dramatic interplay, chance entrances during crucial interviews, the unabashed staging of Elsa's death, the chases, the fights, and the two startling pregnancies are more artifice than a short novel can bear. *The Unicorn* had included jagged, mangled incidents (the entire situation at Gaze Castle was wasteful and painfully ludicrous to begin with), but with the positive aim of describing the dislocation of cause and effect in both human motives and social relationships. The deaths at the end proved that real devastation can grow out of absurd human predicaments. But where incident and character did interpenetrate in *The Unicorn* in a network of mutually illuminating moral questions, contrivance runs wild in *The Italian Girl*. Practically every scene includes farcical or melo-dramatic elements; they are, in fact, so closely enmeshed into the structure that without them there would have been no execution of plot. Any novel that takes raw sensationalism as its motive principle cannot be regarded as serious literature. *The Italian Girl's* lack of dramatic plausibility renders it the author's weakest novel.

We have observed that a Murdoch novel often resembles the one that immediately preceded it. The play version of *A Severed Head*, first produced in Bristol in May, 1963,[1] accounts perhaps for Ed-mund's similarity to Martin Lynch-Gibbon and for the three-part division of *The Italian Girl*. At this stage in her career, Iris Murdoch's creativity seems threatened by her apparent lack of self-awareness. *The Italian Girl* was imperfectly conceived in the image of *A Severed Head* and, despite its substructure of sound moral doctrine, never stimulated the author's best efforts. The strain of concentrated effort that produced four novels, a play, and a long philosophical article ("The Idea of Perfection") within four years is evident in *The Italian Girl*. This tired, blotched, careless work indicates clearly that, for the sake of her artistic growth, Iris Murdoch must now refresh her imagination and creative energy—most probably by enjoying a sustained rest from the demands of prose fiction. Instead of develop-ing her commanding theme, *The Italian Girl* merely restates it in a confused, diluted way.

Note to Chapter Ten

1. Iris Murdoch and J. B. Priestley, *A Severed Head: A Play in Three Acts* (London, 1964), 7.

Eleven

CONCLUSION

Iris Murdoch merits the label *philosophical novelist* not only because her fiction expresses a discernible attitude toward human conduct, but also because her driving principle is a descriptive inquiry into moral values as they occur in daily human life. Myth and philosophy, she believes, are not secondary interests: we live in them all the time and must perpetually clarify and reconstruct them to illuminate our changing predicament. Her world is rich and ebullient. The role of the perceiving self as an active moral agent prevents the surrounding social frame from chilling into lifeless materialism. At the same time, the reality that the perceiver confers upon external objects and selves safeguards the solidity of individual substances and staves off the dead hand of solipsism. She understands that all efforts to make life comprehensible require theories and ideas; as Hume and Wittgenstein insist, raw experience is something that merely occurs, containing in itself no positive values. Yet traditional metaphysics, by frequently overlooking the distinction between *is* and *ought,* is not close enough to finite experience to convey the reality of individuals. She preserves the dignity and substance of the phenomenal world by "theorizing away," to use her expression, all theory, including the existential antitheoretical method of describing reality.

She qualifies, then, practically in spite of herself, as a theoretical moralist. To eschew all theory would grant the individual two alternatives, both unsatisfactory: either to assert his personal sov-

209

ereignty in a meaningless, valueless world by desperately projecting his will upon it or to pledge a Kantian allegiance to the law for the reason's sake. Neither response accounts for the evidence furnished by sensory and psychic experience. Descartes said that the perceiving self intuits his existence by introspection. By directing the act of perception outward rather than inward, Iris Murdoch is able to bestow this same degree of selfhood upon the subject *and* to populate the world with active substances. But sensory objects are not only seen, heard, or touched; they are also reflected upon. Their concreteness and our civilized response to them constitute the basic premises of her theoretical program. Quietism and moral anarchy are not feasible because the individual is driven to act in keeping with the status he extends to others after they make themselves known to him.

Ironically, this depersonalization process does not guarantee universal happiness or rational order, nor is it designed to. The prima facie establishment of happiness and rationality as goals implies that the human focus is the correct standpoint from which to study the objective world. But Iris Murdoch sees no reason for subscribing to a human-centered interpretation of reality; her novels bristle with events that defy both rational explanation and human volition. By asking us to attune ourselves to the unpredictable and the unwilled, she retains the vital continuity between the self and the empirical world. Man's responsibility is to align his fragmentary, inchoate sensibilities with the intractable, discontinuous world he inhabits. The superimposition of one kind of eccentricity or disorder upon another must be enacted without any items or aids except the individual's understanding of himself as a social being. Even without trying to own, control, or pre-empt the world external to him, as the Sartrean self does, the perceiver faces the unnerving challenge of the unexpected. The very difficult task that Iris Murdoch enjoins is the selfless apprehension of external reality as a phenomenon that exists independent of ourselves. Her picture of the world is not comforting and reassuring, nor is it meant to be. She is interested only in describing the world and the individual's reactions to it accurately and honestly. One's phenomenological being *is* the way he reacts to specified reality. Each person is a congeries of affinities, potentialities, and psychic directions. Only by projecting the self against the rough surface of life does the individual acquire identity.

When transferred to a social context, this aggressive, forward-moving ontology has countless possibilities, many of them shocking. The conferral of equal status upon others discovers the individual adrift in a world of people *to* whom he is responsible, *by* whom he is definable, and *about* whom he can learn very little. The writer's insistence upon flexible human values places her in the tradition of social comedy, a movement that flourished in British fiction in the nineteenth century. When we recall that this remarkable literary achievement was unaccompanied by tragic depth, Iris Murdoch's boldness and originality strike us with authority. What incites pity and terror in her novels is the recognition that, without a supervening preserver, the line between comedy and tragedy becomes less fixed and less arbitrary. The province of comedy has generally been confined to the daily comings and goings of characters drawn from the middle strata of society. Her novels attempt to show that all morality originates in our daily movements and that each of us is vulnerable to injustice and falsity, consciously or otherwise. The noble, elevated soul is a stale fiction, for society is commandeered nowadays by people like Mischa Fox and Palmer Anderson. Iris Murdoch has stripped tragedy of its heroic grandeur, but for the creative purpose of redefining and universalizing it. She departs from the mood of the 1950's, which is associated, in varying accents, with writers like Camus, Kerouac, and Wain. Her view of modern man denies the idea that he is a confused, perhaps good-natured searcher for meaning in a meaningless universe. Modern man, according to her, houses potential meaning and value within himself. His greatest social and political challenge is the exercise of consciousness through specific decisions that affirm and dignify the reality of other persons.

The various teacher-pupil relationships in Iris Murdoch's fiction are another facet of the same principle, the richness and the transience of social reality. She exploits relentlessly Nietzsche's remark that a pupil does not reward his teacher by remaining a pupil forever. The Lusiewicz brothers, in *The Flight from the Enchanter,* narrate to Rosa Keepe their seduction of their teacher in Poland and her subsequent suicide, which foreshadows roughly Rosa's own experience with them. Jimmy Carde, Mor's student, holds an obscure but powerful advantage over Mor by being his son's best friend and chief influence. The homosexual love of Michael Meade for Nick Fawley is transformed at the end of *The Bell* when Nick prevents his

sister's entry into Imber Convent and kills himself to free Michael for
Catherine's heterosexual love. Hannah Crean-Smith and Marian
Taylor, Effingham Cooper and Max Le Jour, and Marian and
Effingham (*The Unicorn*) also establish teacher-pupil relationships
that are violently reversed by the unpredictable flow of life. Man
creates his own values in specific contexts of action; Iris Murdoch's
moral goal is not only to show the instability of reality, but also to
demonstrate that each social situation is so densely particular that it
generates its own perceptions and values.

Although any judgment about Iris Murdoch's contribution to
British fiction can be only tentatively valid, her eight published novels
do establish a direction and a moral focus. Remaining within the
logical and descriptive limits of a contingent world, she constantly
underscores the importance of free choice. Her continuous engagement with the problem of how-to-be makes her a novelist of morals
rather than one of manners or ideas. By rejecting the world of
profit and loss and material possessions as a possible source of public
values, she has sought to define and establish a transcendent morality.
And even though she has also repudiated conventional religion as a
way of interpreting man's estate, her novels aspire toward a religious
apprehension of reality. Both Christianity and her secular humanism
regard man as an ambiguous collection of affinities capable of perceiving supersensible values; she likewise concurs with the orthodox
Christian practice of emphasizing social justice and the uniqueness of
the individual. But although her ontology and Christian orthodoxy
both describe man as a conscious, self-responsible agent, she does
not interpret human conduct by supernatural sanctions. Without
explicitly gainsaying the validity of divine values, she concentrates on
observable reality. What is known to be true through the deliverances
of sense experience assumes priority in her thought over what may
be true; before man can approach God, he must first achieve a
mature, balanced understanding of God's creatures, that is, other
people. Instead of imposing a set of timeless spiritual truths upon
the empirical world, she accepts man as she finds him—a conscious
being who must solve the problem of how-to-be within the arena of
time, space, and material objects. *The Bell* and *The Italian Girl*
both describe the importance of acting in accord with the moral
consequences of one's freely elected acts. To sacrifice an insistently
present social context to an unascertainable realm is to undermine

the immediate in favor of an abstract mental construct. Moral action entails the refusal to subordinate other persons to a set of private prejudices, regardless of one's motives. By interpreting human conduct according to a theological plan, one violates the essential character of social experience as a vital organism within which people act as coordinate entities rather than as phases of an idea.

Although she regards religious idealism as a form of willed solipsism, Iris Murdoch is nonetheless a religious novelist. Her unrehearsed awareness of social reality leads her to an unqualified participation in the lives of other people. This act of community affirms and renews itself in practice as a total acceptance of the equality of other points of view. By building all her values around the concreteness of individuals, her moral philosophy assumes religious stature: only a reverent attitude, translatable as a vote of the highest confidence for the validity of other modes of being, allows a person to participate actively in the lives that surround him. Any act of faith requires a surrender of the self. By intuiting and partaking of concrete reality around him, the individual acknowledges the quivering, abounding richness of finite substances. The refusal to allow one's private concepts to screen immediate experience grants incisive interpenetration with other selves. Any metaphysic rising from this energetic, disciplined understanding of social reality will observe the sanctity of the individual; the ensuing social values will not derive from a set of abstract categories but will develop naturally from specific contexts of social interaction in which people see the problems of others as vividly as their own. This moral attitude may be labeled religious because of its selflessness, its perfectibility, and its recognition of the need for human values that transcend expediency and determinism. Iris Murdoch's reverent attention to immediate experience ensures that any conclusions she reaches will proceed organically from real situations rather than from a given interpretation of inherited values.

As has been suggested, she has not absorbed the life of the spirit within her metaphysical system. Her novels record only the interweaving patterns of motives and accidents established by social interaction. By remaining within the boundaries of finite reality, she remains faithful to her own philosophical tenets and to the traditional function of the novel as a time art that studies social reality. The novel's first significant developments occurred alongside the rise of empiricism in English philosophy. Berkeley insisted upon the particularity of existing substances; Hume disavowed the probitive force of all laws of reason, labeling them merely associative; Locke's "principle of individuation" refers to particular existence at a definite point on the spatiotemporal graph. Iris Murdoch's emphasis upon specific situations reflects her endorsement of both the empirical method and the rhetorical conventions of prose fiction. The particularity of time and place, conveyed by fidelity to sensory details, is well scaled to her view of life as an historical process and to her view of the novelist as one who describes rather than explains.

Her social criticism, then, gains weight by virtue of her authenticity of presentation. But in spite of the ease with which she adjusts her moral philosophy to novelistic conventions, we cannot read her fiction as an extended philosophical tract. Artistic form affects the expression of ideas in a way that formal philosophy does not. Her constant variations in setting, narrative pace, character types, and point of view suggest that she is trying to get closer to a complete statement of her theme. But it does not appear that her experiments in narrative structure have modified her basic attitude. What has undergone change as we move from one novel to the next is the perspective from which she observes social reality. Jake Donaghue's lonely excursions through London and Paris, Mischa Fox's enormous social power, the dreary private and professional life of Bill Mor, the intersecting love interests in *An Unofficial Rose,* and the surrealistic use of landscape in *The Unicorn* convey the need for creative values at different levels of experience. Mischa Fox's social power, which seems to permeate all of London society, and Hannah Crean-Smith's spiritual magnetism are aspects of the same fallacy, that of substituting a convenient mental construct for the deliverances of direct experience. The inability of Bill Mor, Michael Meade, Martin Lynch-Gibbon, and Edmund Narraway to balance conflicting impulses reflects Iris Murdoch's sustained belief that choice, as a conscious act, is the practical basis of all morality. She dramatizes the difficulty of making a creative decision that acknowledges the creativity of others through the theme of personal communication: Nina the dressmaker, Felix Meecham, and Marian Taylor understand that they must surrender to an emotional relationship, but in each case their love-object fails to accept them. Any emotional liaison involving Bill Mor, Catherine Fawley, or Martin Lynch-Gibbon will

be doomed unless they learn to accept and understand their past
lives. Iris Murdoch's variations in literary form have served to
broaden and deepen her abiding concern: the need to develop a
mature sense of other people within the framework of social experience. Her fidelity to certain cultural and aesthetic conventions of
the novel—the uniqueness of character, the particularity of time and
setting, the authenticated presentation of daily experience—allows her
to experiment in literary form while maintaining a uniform attitude
toward the question of the individual's life in society.

BIBLIOGRAPHY

I. Works by Iris Murdoch

"Against Dryness: A Polemical Sketch." *Encounter,* 16 (January, 1961), 16-20.

The Bell. London and New York, 1958.

"The Existentialist Hero." *The Listener,* 43 (23 March 1950), 523-24.

The Flight from the Enchanter. London and New York, 1956.

"Hegel in Modern Dress." *The New Statesman and Nation,* 53 (25 May 1957), 675.

"A House of Theory," in Norman Mackenzie, ed., *Conviction* (London, 1958), 218-33; reprinted in *Partisan Review,* 26 (Winter, 1959), 17-31.

"The Idea of Perfection." *The Yale Review,* 53 (March, 1964), 342-80.

The Italian Girl. London and New York, 1964.

"Knowing the Void." *Spectator* (2 November 1956), 613-14.

"Mass, Might and Myth." *Spectator* (7 September 1962), 337-38.

"Metaphysics and Ethics," in D. F. Pears, ed., *The Nature of Metaphysics* (London, 1957), 99-123.

"Nostalgia for the Particular." *Proceedings of the Aristotelian Society,* 52 (London, 1952), 243-60.

"The Novelist as Metaphysician." *The Listener,* 43 (16 March 1950), 473, 476.

The Sandcastle. London and New York, 1957.

Sartre: Romantic Rationalist. New Haven, 1953.

A Severed Head. London and New York, 1961.

"The Sublime and the Beautiful Revisited." *The Yale Review,* 49 (December, 1959), 247-71.

"The Sublime and the Good." *Chicago Review,* 13 (Autumn, 1959), 42-55.

"T. S. Eliot As a Moralist," in Neville Braybrooke, ed., *T. S. Eliot: A Symposium for His Seventieth Birthday* (New York, 1958), 152-60.

Under the Net. London and New York, 1954.

216

The Unicorn. London and New York, 1963.

An Unofficial Rose. London and New York, 1962.

"Vision and Choice in Morality." *Aristotelian Society: Dreams and Self-Knowledge*, Supplementary Volume 30 (London, 1956), 32-58.

II. COLLABORATION

Murdoch, Iris, and J. B. Priestley, *A Severed Head: A Play in Three Acts*. London, 1964.

III. SECONDARY SOURCES

Ahlin, Lars, "Den berusade baten." *Bonniers Litterära Magasin,* 30 (April, 1961), 280-86.

Allen, Walter, *The Modern Novel in Britain and the United States*. New York, 1964.

Allsop, Kenneth, *The Angry Decade: A Survey of the Cultural Revolt of the Nineteen-Fifties*. London, 1958.

Ayer, Alfred Jules, *Language, Truth and Logic*. New York, n. d.

Balakian, Nona, "The Flight from Innocence: England's Newest Literary Generation." *Books Abroad,* 33 (Summer, 1959), 261-70.

Barnes, Hazel E., *Humanistic Existentialism: The Literature of Possibility*. Lincoln, Nebraska, 1959.

Barrows, John, "Living Writers—7: Iris Murdoch." *John O'London's,* 4 (4 May 1961), 498.

Bradbury, Malcolm, "Iris Murdoch's *Under the Net.*" *The Critical Quarterly,* 4 (Spring, 1962), 47-54.

Brown, E. K., *Rhythm in the Novel*. Toronto, 1950.

Bryden, Ronald, "Living Dolls." *The Spectator* (8 June 1962), 755-56.

Camus, Albert, *The Myth of Sisyphus and Other Essays,* trans. by Justin O'Brien, New York, 1955.

Charlesworth, Maxwell John, *Philosophy and Linguistic Analysis*. Pittsburgh, 1959.

Clayre, Alasdair, "Common Cause: A Garden in the Clearing." *TLS,* 7 August 1959, xxx-xxxi.

Collins, James, *The Existentialists: A Critical Study*. Chicago, 1952.

Felheim, Marvin, "Symbolic Characterization in the Novels of Iris Murdoch." *Texas Studies in Literature and Language,* 2 (Summer, 1960), 189-97.

Forster, E. M., *Aspects of the Novel*. New York, n. d.

Fraser, G. S., "Iris Murdoch: The Solidity of the Normal." *International Literary Annual,* John Wain, ed., II (London, 1959), 37-54.

――――――, *The Modern Writer and His World*. Baltimore, 1964.

Gindin, James, *Postwar British Fiction: New Accents and Attitudes*. Berkeley and Los Angeles, 1962.

Goldberg, Gerald Jay, "The Search for the Artist in Some Recent British Fiction." *SAQ,* 62 (Summer, 1963), 387-401.

Grene, Marjorie, *Introduction to Existentialism*. Chicago, 1960.

Gustafson, Lars, "Ord för drömmar beslut." *Bonniers Litterära Magasin,* 30 (April, 1961), 286-88.

Hall, James, *The Tragic Comedians: Seven Modern British Novelists.* Bloomington, Indiana, 1963.

Hoffmann, Frederick J., "Iris Murdoch: The Reality of Persons." *Critique,* 7 (Spring, 1964), 48-57.

Hope, Francis, "The Novels of Iris Murdoch." *The London Magazine,* 1 (August, 1961), 84-87.

Jacobson, Dan, "Farce, Totem and Taboo." *New Statesman,* 61 (16 June 1961), 956-57.

Josephson, Eric and Mary, eds., *Man Alone: Alienation in Modern Society.* New York, 1962.

Jung, Carl G[ustav]., *The Integration of the Personality,* trans. by Stanley M. Dell. New York, 1939.

————, *The Structure and Dynamics of the Psyche,* trans. by R. F. C. Hull. New York, 1960.

————, *Two Essays on Analytical Psychology,* trans. by R. F. C. Hull. New York, 1956.

Kaelin, Eugene F., *An Existentialist Aesthetic: the Theories of Sartre and Merleau-Ponty.* Madison, Wisconsin, 1962.

Kalb, Bernard, "Three Comers." *Saturday Review,* 37 (7 May 1955), 22.

Karl, Frederick R., *The Contemporary English Novel.* New York, 1962.

Kaufmann, R. J., "The Progress of Iris Murdoch." *The Nation,* 188 (21 March 1959), 255-56.

Kaufmann, Walter A., ed., *Existentialism from Dostoevsky to Sartre.* New York, 1956.

Kermode, Frank, "The House of Fiction: Interviews with Seven English Novelists." *Partisan Review,* 30 (Spring, 1963), 61-82.

Lanoire, Maurice, *Les lorgnettes du roman anglais.* Paris, 1959, 234-39.

Ljungquist, Walter, "Med anledning av Iris Murdoch's 'Mot Torrheten.'" *Bonniers Litterära Magasin,* 30 (April, 1961), 289.

McCarthy, Mary, "Characters in Fiction." *Partisan Review,* 28 (March–April, 1961), 171-91.

McDowell, Frederick P. W., "'The Devious Involutions of Human Character and Emotions': Reflections on Some Recent British Novels." *Wisconsin Studies in Contemporary Literature,* 4 (Autumn, 1963), 339-66, esp. 352-59.

Maes-Jelinek, Hena, "A House for Free Characters: The Novels of Iris Murdoch." *Revue des langues vivantes,* 29 (1963), 45-69.

Marcel, Gabriel, *Homo Viator: Introduction to a Metaphysic of Hope,* trans. by Emma Craufurd. Chicago, 1951.

Mehta, Ved, *Fly and the Fly-Bottle: Encounters with British Intellectuals.* Boston, 1963.

Meidner, O[lga]. M[cDonald]., "The Progress of Iris Murdoch." *English Studies in Africa,* 4 (March, 1961), 17-38.

————, "Reviewer's Bane: A Study of Iris Murdoch's *The Flight from the*

Enchanter." *Essays in Criticism,* 11 (1961), 435-47.

Mercier, Vivien, "Arrival of the Anti-Novel." *The Commonweal,* 30 (8 May 1959), 149-51.

Micha, René, "Les Romans à machines d'Iris Murdoch." *Critique* [Paris], 16 (April, 1960), 291-301.

Moore, G. E., *Philosophical Papers.* New York, 1962.

Nye, Robert, "Ending the World." *John O'London's,* 7 (5 July 1962), 9.

O'Connor, William Van, *The New University Wits and the End of Modernism.* Carbondale, Illinois, 1963.

O'Sullivan, Kevin, "Iris Murdoch and the Image of Liberal Man." *The Yale Literary Magazine,* 131 (December, 1962), 27-36.

Pearson, Gabriel, "Iris Murdoch and the Romantic Novel." *New Left Review* (January–April, 1962), 137-45.

Pondrom, Cyrena Norman, "Iris Murdoch: *The Unicorn.*" *Critique,* 6 (Winter, 1963), 177-80.

Queneau, Raymond, "A World of Fantasy," trans. by David Pryce-Jones. *Time and Tide,* 42 (6 July 1961), 1119.

Quinton, Anthony, and others, "The New Novelists: an Enquiry." *The London Magazine,* 5 (November, 1958), 13-31.

Raymond, John, "The Unclassifiable Image." *New Statesman,* 56 (15 November 1958), 697-98.

Russell, Bertrand, *Logic and Knowledge: Essays 1901–1950,* Robert Charles Marsh, ed. London, 1956.

————, *Mysticism and Logic.* Garden City, New York, 1957.

Ryle, Gilbert, *The Concept of Mind.* New York, 1962.

Sartre, Jean-Paul, *Being and Nothingness,* trans. by Hazel E. Barnes. New York, 1956.

————, "Forgers of Myth: the Young Playwrights of France." *Theatre Arts,* 30 (June, 1946), 324-35.

————, *Nausea,* trans. by Lloyd Alexander. Norfolk, Connecticut, 1959.

————, *What Is Literature?* trans. by Bernard Frechtman. London, 1950.

Scholes, Robert, ed., *Approaches to the Novel: Materials for a Poetics.* San Francisco, 1961.

Schrickx, W., "Recente Englese Roman Kunst: Iris Murdoch." *Vlaamse Gids,* 46 (August, 1962), 516-32.

Souvage, Jacques, "Symbol as Narrative Device: An Interpretation of Iris Murdoch's *The Bell.*" *English Studies,* 43 (April, 1962), 81-96.

————, "Theme and Structure in Iris Murdoch's *The Flight from the Enchanter.*" *Spieghel Historiael van de Bond van Gentste Germanisten,* 3 (1960-61), 73-88.

————, "The Unresolved Tension: An Interpretation of Iris Murdoch's *Under the Net.*" *Revue des longues vivantes,* 26 (1960), 420-30.

Taubman, Robert, "L'Année Dernière at Dungeness." *New Statesman,* 63 (8 June 1962), 836.

Tracy, Honor, "Misgivings about Miss Murdoch." *The New Republic,* 151 (10 October 1964), 21-22.

Trilling, Lionel, "On the Modern Element in Literature." *Partisan Review,* 28 (January–February, 1961), 9-35.

Trotzig, Birgitta, "Den moderna romanen." *Bonniers Litterära Magasin,* 30 (May-June, 1961), 369-70.

Urmson, J. O., *Philosophical Analysis: Its Development Between the Two World Wars.* Oxford, 1956.

Wall, Stephen, "The Bell in *The Bell.*" *Essays in Criticism,* 13 (July, 1963), 265-73.

Watt, Ian, *The Rise of the Novel: Studies in Defoe, Richardson, and Fielding.* Los Angeles and Berkeley, 1959, 9-34.

West, Paul, *The Modern Novel.* London, 1963.

Whiteside, George, "The Novels of Iris Murdoch." *Critique,* 7 (Spring, 1964), 27-47.

Wittgenstein, Ludwig, *Philosophical Investigations,* trans. by G. E. M. Anscombe. Oxford, 1963.

_____, *Tractatus logico-philsophicus,* with an introduction by Bertrand Russell. London, 1955.